OUTDOORS SAN DIEGO

HIKING, BIKING
&
CAMPING

by

Tom Leech & Jack Farnan

A Premier Publishing Book
San Diego, California

OUTDOORS SAN DIEGO
HIKING, BIKING & CAMPING

DISCLAIMER
Every attempt has been made to provide correct information on the destinations listed. However, the Publisher does not guarantee the accuracy of the information. At press time, the information in this book was current; however some information may be subject to change.

Editors:	Susan Humason, Tom Leech, Jack Farnan, Stacey Bugsch
Map Creation:	Dana Southwood
Photo Scanning:	Stacey Bugsch
Layout:	Chris Buscher
Cover Design:	Chris Buscher & Susan Humason
Cover Photo:	Tom Leech (Daley Ranch)
Interior Photos:	Tom Leech & Susan Humason

ISBN: 1-928905-04-8

PUBLISHER: **Premier Publishing**
Mailing Address:
15721 Bernardo Heights Parkway, Suite B- Box 17
San Diego, California 92128

Tel: 858-922-7692
Fax: 858-586-7389
Email: dayoutings@earthlink.net

Printed in the United States of America

PREFACE

We extend our appreciation to the many people who, over the years, have made extraordinary efforts so that we today can have all the parks, preserves, open spaces and trails that add so much to the joys of living in San Diego. To the advocates, planners, political leaders, trail builders, rangers, preserve managers, educators, organizations, lecturers, donators, trail companions, fellow authors...we thank you. Keep right on doing all those good things.

Thanks to the many trip leaders and docents for their guidance, and to old pals Everett and Ken for helping scout out the trails. And for the valuable aid so necessary in getting this work to a finished product, thanks to Susan Humason for editorial and publishing, San Diego Magazine Online (especially Jim Fitzpatrick, Tom Blair, Mike James, and Ron James for their support of the Outdoors Forum, in which much of this material originally appeared. And to partners Leslie and Sue for companionship and patience during the writing process.

Finally, dear reader, should you spot some error that has somehow snuck its way into our text, and wish to enlighten us, or offer commentary or suggestions, please convey that via email to outdoorssd@aol.com. And for continued tips about our ever-changing world, check with us at www.sandiegomag.com/forums/outdoors.

Tom Leech & Jack Farnan

ABOUT THE AUTHORS

Tom Leech is Outdoors Forum Editor for San Diego Magazine Online, where many of these outdoors tips have previouwly appeared. He authored the outdoors chapter for *The Best of San Diego* (RoseBud, 1982). Since arriving here over four decades ago from his home state of Indiana, he's been enjoying San Diego's many natural attractions. On most weekends, he will be found hiking with hardy trekkers from Walkabout, Sierra Club, Canyoneers and other outdoors groups.With family and friends, he's camped all around the country and the West, progressing from bare ground to tent to VW bus to RV. He belongs to many local and national outdoors organizations and is a former board member of The Nature Conservancy's Southern California Chapter. Wearing his weekday hat he is a nationally-known corporate speech coach and author of *How To Prepare, Stage & Deliver Winning Presentations*, 3rd Edition (AMACOM) and *Say It Like Shakespeare: the Bard's Tips for Successful Communication* (McGraw-Hill).

Jack Farnan is a San Diego Human Resources Executive who has been cycling for over 40 years and been exploring the roadways and off-road trails of San Diego County for over 20 years. The father of three children, many of his rides through the years have focused on family-friendly pathways that provided safe, enjoyable riding for children. As an avid triathlete, his training rides have also led him to some of San Diego's longer and more demanding rides. He is currently on the Board of Directors of a world renowned multi-sport corporation specializing in state-of-the-art equipment for cyclists and triathletes.

CONTENTS

✤✤ Denotes Special Places To Enjoy

Hiking...Urban North

Chapter 4 - HIKING...SAN DIEGO - INLAND 4-1

Hiking...Inland South

Hiking...Inland Central

Hiking...Inland North

Chapter 5 - HIKING...MTNS & BACKCOUNTRY 5-1

Hiking...Mountains & Backcountry South

Hiking...Mountains & Backcountry Central

Hiking...Mountains & Backcountry North

Chapter 6 - HIKING...DESERT REGION 6-1

Hiking...Desert South

Hiking...Desert Central

Hiking...Desert North

Chapter 7 - BIKING...COASTAL REGION 7-1

Biking...Coastal South

Biking...Coastal North

Chapter 8 - BIKING...URBAN SAN DIEGO 8-1

Chapter 9 - BIKING...SAN DIEGO INLAND 9-1

Chapter 10 - BIKING...MTNS & BACKCOUNTRY...10-1

INTRODUCTION

One touch of nature makes the whole world kin.
Wm. Shakespeare, Troilus & Cressida

San Diego is one of only a few places in the world where you can begin your day with a dip in the surf, head to the mountains for a trek among the oaks and pines, have lunch in a desert palm canyon, scoot across the border for a margarita at cocktail hour, and wrap up the day around a bonfire at a beach party.

Because of San Diego's mixture of many climatic and geographic conditions, a diversity of outdoor scenic and recreational opportunities await residents and visitors. First, there's the beach. The Pacific Ocean and the adjoining bays create the setting for the outdoor activities and scenes most closely associated with San Diego. Sailing, surfing, beach volleyball, waterskiing, sport fishing— these are shown on nearly every travel poster to illustrate the attractions of the sea. Here is the annual gathering of thousands for the World Championship Over-The-Line Tournament, an event with 50 years of tradition but hard to describe in a family publication. Parties around the fire rings and grunion hunting keep the beaches stirring at night.

Visitors often marvel at the lovely foliage in the parks and older neighborhoods. Where cultivation has occurred, San Diego is a horticultural paradise. Oaks, sycamores, eucalyptus, and palms surrounding grassy lawns present inviting places for picnicking, strolling, or romance. Bougainvillea, jacaranda, trumpet vines, and even good old ice plant splash the scene with pastels of many colors. Ah, thank heaven for irrigation.

Between the mountains and the sea can be found something for almost every taste — lakes, rivers, avocado-covered hills, wooded parks, and countryside covered with chaparral, standard foliage in this basically arid region.

The mountains are not the 12-14,000 foot mountains of the Sierra Nevada, but at 6,000 they are still real mountains, with evergreen forests, open meadows, wildflowers, streams, and enough deer and mountain lions to add flavor. There's even snow in winter for some major sledding.

Then there's the desert, threatening to the pioneers who had to cross it in covered wagons or on horseback, now a special source of solitude and beauty to those who have come to know and enjoy it. Some never develop an appreciation for the desert, but those who do speak of the pleasures of its annual wildflower displays, the canyons which lead along stream beds or dry washes to much-welcomed palm oases, the massive boulders for rock climbing, the colors and textures of the land. Some especially savor the sunsets, then evening stillness, broken sporadically with musical selections from coyotes communicating across the terrain.

An unplanned event occurred in late October 2003 which had major impact on many of the places covered in this book. That event was the fires that raced across much of our backcountry, covering over 300,000 acres, damaging 2500 homes, and causing 16 deaths. While the losses were severe, nature has shown its ability to recover. For now, many of the places won't look quite as we describe them and will be in various states of rehabilitation. But, with the spring a likely rich wildflowers display will provide the clearest sign of recovery throughout our San Diego outdoors scene. While not as severe as the most recent fire, previous ones at Iron Mountain, San Pasqual Valley, Elfin Forest, the Lagunas and more have come back well.

ENJOYING OUR
OUTDOOR WORLD

Such places as these play vital roles for rejuvenation, appreciation, and introspection. When the pressures of the office or market become excessive, when the hassles of traffic and bill-paying get ridiculous, an afternoon at the beach or in the park can do wonders. Thoreau went to Walden Pond to find out more about himself and his world. Our Native Americans went on "vision quests" for spiritual renewal or to acknowledge their links to nature. We can find our own Walden, make our own vision quests, or just have a fine time at the many outdoor recreation spots in our area.

Our purpose is to provide you with a variety of outdoors opportunities to enjoy. No matter what your fitness or experience level you'll find ways to start or expand your outdoors adventures:

- What's here: basic information about where to go in coast, parks, preserves, and open spaces, with quizzes to check your outdoors SDNQ (San Diego Nature Quotient).

- Where to hike, amble, cavort or poke around.

- Where to bike, from casual to heavy-duty rides.

- Where to camp, in public and private campgrounds.

- Lots of encouragement to get off the couch — away from the TV, PC and SUV — and outside, reaping the many benefits of nature for your physical and mental well-being.

- Special sections with tips for those who are mobility-limited, who want to ooh and aah at a scenic view, show the visiting relatives from back East why we live here or take a stroll with the pooch. Even some history is thrown in.

- Tips for helping you better prepare for a rewarding and safe outdoors experience-hiking, biking, camping.

- Resources, contacts and organizations to contact for more detailed information and ways to become an active supporter of a park or activity.

You will absolutely find this book useful for another important objective - creating a healthier you. Lots of articles and hard data shows a steady increase in overweight and obese people, even in health-conscious San Diego. Health researchers have clear evidence that exposure to nature makes us healthier, happier, and even smarter. Do these sound appealing?

Recommendations from the experts start out with two basics: exercise and diet. We don't offer much in the diet line, except for some suggestions for dining nicely as a reward for your exertions. However, we offer plenty of tips about exercise. Walking and biking are among the easiest and most enjoyable ways to get out there and move around. Change your pattern from sedentary to mobile, head for the many options in this book, and start checking your scale. You might see a slow but valuable reduction in excess poundage, improvements in fitness level and cholesterol reduction, and overall peace of mind.

Introduction

1 - 4

PARKS IN SAN DIEGO

MAJOR RESOURCE, MAJOR PRESSURE

We also have another - sneaky - purpose, of the persuasion category: to get you to become a hard-core, card-carrying, letter-writing, outdoors-voting member of "The (Unofficial) Fervent Friends of the San Diego Outdoors World", with the purpose of helping preserve this environment under the heavy onslaught from population expansion, growth pressures, traffic jams and shrinking parks and open space (just in case you haven't noticed).

"Great cities are known for their great parks, and one measure of any city's greatness is its ability to provide recreation, natural beauty and signature open spaces for its citizens." Given the nature of this book, we applaud that introduction to *The Excellent Park System*, by Peter Harnik (The Trust for Public Land 2003).

And how does San Diego City stack up vs. other "great cities?" In the category of medium-high densities, San Diego tops the list at 32 acres of parkland per 1000 people (surprisingly ahead of Portland, OR; at 24.5, then Cincinnati and Dallas). This is double the average for all cities in the poll. In a different category—park spending per resident— we score well-below cities such as Seattle, San Jose, Denver and Minneapolis, with each of these investing double over San Diego (FY 2001).

Within the city are several very large parks, such as Mission Bay, Balboa, Mission Trails and Los Penasquitos (jointly with SD County). This might skew the data from another question of how well are we doing with adequate and easily-accessible neighborhood parks. The TPL report notes that in Denver 9 out of 10 residents live within 6 blocks of a park; it's doubtful we can approach that figure. Janesville, Wisconsin's motto is "The City of Parks;" checking out the parks there is simple as they are so prevalent and pleasant.

Expanding this to the full county, we are blessed with some very large parks and open spaces, such as in the mountains and desert. The various cities have their own parks and trail systems. And starting several years ago, preservation emphasis picked up with the aggressive Multiple Species Conservation Program (MSCP), with a goal by SD County, SD City and Chula Vista of setting aside 172,000 acres. Many acquisitions have been made, with the 2003 report showing 57,000 acres of the County's portion (98,000) set aside

Another measure of the outdoors and recreational situation can be seen in the number of people per campsite. That's not an encouraging trend, with the ratio on a steady increase from 1300:1 (1940) to 4400:1 (1965) to 10,000:1 (1995).We obviously have not kept pace. It's worse along the coast as reservations there better be in about six months in advance during summer months.

Thus recent progress has occurred, yet other key statistics, such as population growth and traffic congestion, indicate we must continue to add to our park/ open space system, especially near the cities, to maintain a quality environment for flora, fauna and us people...And those kids of 2020 or 2050!

Layout Ahead...

In the following chapters you'll read about many San Diego special outdoor places, in sequence from the ocean to the desert, from south to north. You may already know many of these places. We've been visiting them for over four decades, yet continually find enjoyable areas that are new to us, discovering there is much more yet to be experienced in places we've been a dozen times before.

❖❖ Look for this symbol to identify the most special places to visit and enjoy. Also, you will find invaluable (1) a current Thomas Brothers map and (2) city or regional transportation maps.

We recognize that outdoor folks have a range of interests, desires and capabilities, so we've provided options to meet those varied levels.

 **For hikers**, you'll find a plethora of trails waiting for you from introductory short strolls to half- or full-day workouts, with tips about length or difficulty of hikes, what you'll see and when to go or not to go.

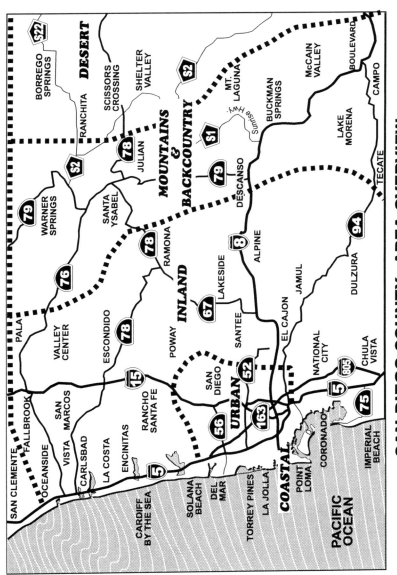

SAN DIEGO COUNTY...AREA OVERVIEW

Bicyclists will find a range of riding options fitting into three categories:

• **Cruisin'** — Typically less than 10 miles and usually have minimal to no automobile traffic. They are good rides for beginning cyclists, children or anyone interested in just "cruisin."

• **Energized** — Typically in the 15-20 mile range and many have some hills as well as automobile traffic.

• **Demanding** — Typically in the 25-50 mile range and may involve some challenging hills and narrow bike lanes. Riders should be well-conditioned and comfortable with riding in traffic.

While we have made strong efforts to ensure accuracy, the outdoors can be hazardous. When hiking, biking, camping or exploring, take extra efforts to be safe. The mountains and desert especially require careful planning.

Thus, now that you're well prepared with the right information, gear, companionship and spirit, we encourage you to get out there and enjoy San Diego for all it has to offer. It's waiting, just a short haul away.

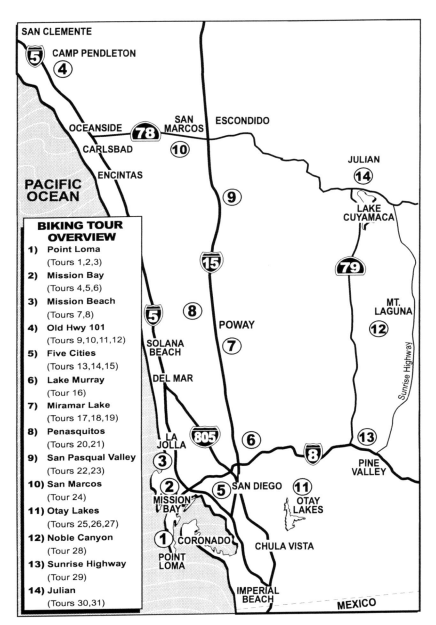

BIKING TOUR - OVERVIEW

CHAPTER 2

HIKING
COASTAL REGION

OVERVIEW

SOUTH

CENTRAL

NORTH

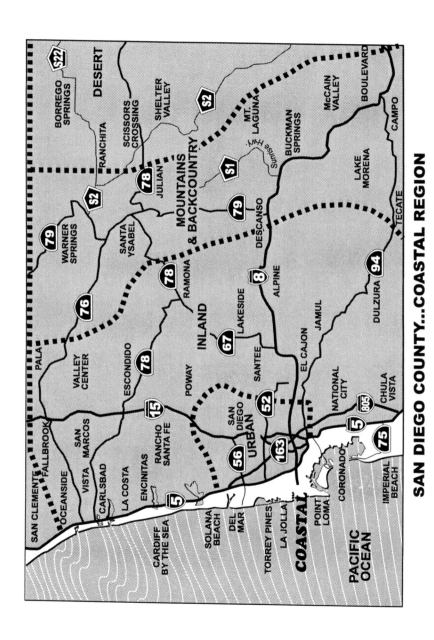

COASTAL REGION
HIKING OVERVIEW

I must go down to the sea again, for the call of the running tide
Is a wild call and a clear call that may not be denied.

John Masefield, Sea Fever

In this chapter we provide opportunities for enjoying the area most people, here and otherwise, associate with San Diego – the coast. Here we define it primarily as west of or next to I-5. The options are varied and plentiful, grouped into three areas: south, central and north. And we will examine three categories of visitation as follows:

Shoreline Strolls. "Invigorating" is the standard word people use who like to walk along the shores or overlooks of the Pacific Ocean. When close to the ocean - strolling, exploring, bird watching, clamming, or enjoying the sunset, people tend to look happy. We are blessed with miles of lovely beaches, fortunately almost all accessible for the public's enjoyment. That's a fact we often forget to appreciate - a visit to many east coast communities, with mostly private beaches, is a jolting reminder.

Coastal Wetlands. A characteristic of our coast is the large number of waterways - bays, lagoons, estuaries and rivers - that are beneficial to nature, create some breathing space among our densely populated communities, and provide pleasant spots for outdoors activities. Bird watchers especially frequent such areas. And we get plenty to watch. Counts at the Tijuana Estuary list 370 bird types seen there, 320 migrants. Whether you're an avid birder or barely know a young duck from an old coot, it's mighty pleasant mixing a fine stroll along the shore with seeing the variety of birds on display.

Coastal Parks. Another way to enjoy the coastal outdoors environment is by visiting the many parks located right by or near the ocean, bays and waterways. These include a national monument, state reserves and community parks.

Before getting on to the specifics, try your hand at our outdoors coastal region quiz. Look for the answers as your read on.

1. Prime visiting grounds are our coastal lagoons and estuaries.
What's the difference?

2. Gunpowder Point has some history behind the name.

> Where is it and what is it?

3. Is Shelter Island really an island?

4. What national monument is named after a Portuguese explorer?

5. Which beaches are famous for

> (a) dogs romping freely in the surf?

> (b) for bathers romping in the buff?

> (c) for the turf meeting the surf?

> (d) making the top 10 list of the country's best beaches?

6. Where can you spend the night in a comfortable hotel room above the ocean?

7. Why is the name "Guy Fleming" important to San Diego's nature heritage?

8. Where the heck is Torrey Pines Extension?

9. What well-known north county beach is linked to a religious leader?

10. There's a lovely lagoon just south of Carlsbad.

> (a) What is its name?

> (b) How do you spell it?

> (c) What does the name mean?

COASTAL REGION - SOUTH

1. Border Field State Park

The name is not kidding. From the parking lot, you can look right over to Plaza Monumental, the Tijuana Plaza de Toros, which comes alive on many Sunday afternoons at 4 p.m. You'll recall an old Herb Alpert classic song. The beach is right below the parking area, which gives you plenty of space to stroll (check the signs before going in the water here). A fence extending out into the water marks the border, and the Tijuana River empties into the Pacific just to the north. On the way in you'll see some marked areas for bird sightings.

How to get there: I-5 to Dairy Mart Road to Monument Road to the ocean. (Note it has been closed recently for maintenance. Call State Parks to check access.)

2. Tijuana Estuary

You may be pleasantly surprised when you visit the **Estuary Nature Center**, with its many exhibits and trail system leading out along ponds, gardens, streams and marshland (2500 acres in all). And you will be absolutely amazed when you discover this was an industrial dump only a couple of decades back. Also bet you didn't know the Tijuana River watershed starts in the Lagunas at Sheepshead Mountain (see what you can learn by popping in for visits down in the South Bay?)

The center opened ten years ago and received one of the cherished "Orchids" for design excellence in 1995. Enjoy the video, "The Timeless River" and the truly interesting exhibits. I found the bird wheel fascinating, showing which birds are here during each season. Did you know sanderling spend some time here during their migration from the Arctic to Chile's Tierra del Fuego, 18,000 miles round trip?

Step outside and you're in a 5-acre garden, with markers identifying what's here. For a longer hike and further into the estuary system, go a few blocks over to the trail off 5th Avenue. One of the trails goes past the Imperial Beach Naval Air Station fence. Another leads to the river and some good views of the ocean and the Los Coronados Islands.

In case you were wondering, a *lagoon* is separated from the ocean; ocean tides flow in and out of an *estuary*.

How to get there: Take I-5 south to Coronado Avenue west (becomes Imperial Avenue) and turn left at 3rd to the center (restrooms and parking here).

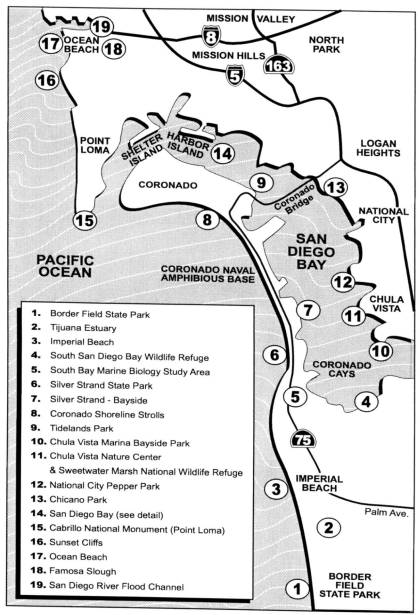

1. Border Field State Park
2. Tijuana Estuary
3. Imperial Beach
4. South San Diego Bay Wildlife Refuge
5. South Bay Marine Biology Study Area
6. Silver Strand State Park
7. Silver Strand - Bayside
8. Coronado Shoreline Strolls
9. Tidelands Park
10. Chula Vista Marina Bayside Park
11. Chula Vista Nature Center
 & Sweetwater Marsh National Wildlife Refuge
12. National City Pepper Park
13. Chicano Park
14. San Diego Bay (see detail)
15. Cabrillo National Monument (Point Loma)
16. Sunset Cliffs
17. Ocean Beach
18. Famosa Slough
19. San Diego River Flood Channel

COASTAL, SOUTH - HIKING

Hiking - Coastal Region

3. Imperial Beach (IB)

For beach strolling, start from the north end of Seacoast and walk out on the jetty, next to the YMCA Camp Surf and the large circular Navy Radio Facility, so obvious from the highway. A short walk south brings you to another jetty, always fun for getting right there with the waves and crabs. Continue a few blocks south to the pier (at Evergreen) and stroll out past many fisherfolk to the Tin Fish Restaurant at the end. On a sunny day this is southern California kickback at its finest, watching the surfers and soaring birds, enjoying refreshment, with often live music to entertain you.

Parking is generally easy in this area, on the streets (no meters!) and in off-street lots. Several shops and restaurants here. Keep walking south along the beach, down to the border if inclined. On the east side of Seacoast is the Tijuana Estuary Nature Preserve. Finally, after your variety of wanderings, take a coffee or snack respite at Café Thera, just south of the Palm Street jetty.

How to get there: I-5 to Palm Avenue, west, follow signs as Palm veers left, to Seacoast, pier is a few blocks to the left.

4. South San Diego Bay National Wildlife Refuge

Worth noting is that South San Diego Bay has been designated a "Globally Important Bird Area" by the American Bird Conservancy. With their notice to the SD Audubon Society, the Conservancy noted this area provides habitat for significant numbers of nesting gull-billed terns, surf scooters, caspian terns and western snowy plovers.

August 1999 marked the official opening of this extremely important project for the South Bay. It is a planned 3900-acre refuge, part of the big San Diego National Wildlife Refuge. Early in the acquisition and development stage, it will provide many opportunities for enjoying nature while preserving it. 2200 acres have been acquired as of the opening.

How to get there: See #7 Silver Strand.

5. South Bay Marine Biology Study Area

This reserve at the south end of the Silver Strand is managed by the City of San Diego Park & Recreation Department. You can stroll out along the bay here. Park off the highway.

How to get there: See #7 Silver Strand.

6. Silver Strand State Park (Coronado)

The Silver Strand is that strip of land that stretches south of Coronado to Imperial Beach. That strip is what keeps Coronado from being an island. Most people who visit Coronado make it as far south as the Hotel del, worth a visit anytime, and miss the Strand. Travelers from the south head north from Imperial Beach Drive or bike up the Silver Strand Highway (Route 75) to work or play in Coronado or to take the bridge or ferry across San Diego Bay (yes the ferry lives, catch it in San Diego at the foot of Broadway for an enjoyable ride).

This gem of a park spreads for 2.5 miles right along the Pacific Ocean. Most of the activity is day use, with ample parking, restrooms, and lots of sand. Surf, stroll, dig, flop as you choose. It's open year round; from Memorial Day to Labor Day park hours are 8 a.m. to 9 p.m. on Saturdays at 2 p.m. are activities for the Junior Rangers, with campfire programs for all in the evening. Restrooms, showers, ample parking, and broad beaches for loafing, surfing, strolling and watching the sunset. Spend the night in the campground, if your vehicle is self-contained and you get there first.

In addition to a stroll along the ocean, it's an easy trek from the park over to the bayside where you can rent a bike, walk the trails south of Loews Hotel or perhaps get a gondola ride, with singing oarsman.

How to get there: I-5 to Coronado Bridge to Orange Avenue. Left and onto the Strand Highway (75).

7. Silver Strand — Bayside (Coronado)

The Bayshore Bikeway is a paved strip, separated from the highway, from Imperial Beach to Coronado. This is better called a pathway, as bicyclists, walkers, joggers, skaters or wheelchairers can all take pleasure here. Take the whole stretch or bite off a section to fit specific tastes. The frequent local buses make access easy for all. The scenery is fine, with views of the bridge, Navy ships sailing or ashore, sailboats, inland mountains and the salt mounds at the southern end. Also along here are several sections set aside as reserves or parkland, providing great bird-watching, strolling, or swimming.

In Imperial Beach, the **Bikeway** starts at the north end of 13th Street (off the main drag, Palm Avenue). You can park here, next to the old railroad trestle, which once supported trains headed to the salt works. Eventually the bikeway may continue over to that area. You're looking at the section of the bay recently made part of the San Diego Wildlife Refuge

Still in Imperial Beach, another entry is at the north end of 7th, off Palm. The paved pathway is a good spot for bird-watching opportunities, but walking into the marshland is off limits.

Continuing north you'll see the marked signs and a small parking area for the **South Bay Marine Biology Study Area** (noted above), with a walking path.

Crown Cove area is just north of Loew's Coronado Resort (well worth checking out on your stroll) and the entrance to the state beach on the ocean side and north to the Navy housing section. Here are covered picnic tables, quiet waters, and perhaps a lifeguard.

Just north of the Cove is a preserve, with several footpaths and informational kiosks with restrooms, offering easy and enjoyable stroll, no dogs. Nearing completion is the **Southwestern College Marine Science Research Facility**. Limited parking is available at a small cul de sac right next to the Navy housing.

The section from Fiddler's Cove to Tulagi Road, the northern end of the bikeway, goes along a newly-created nature reserve and least tern preserve (which the Navy transformed from military use). Also labeled the **Bridge to Discovery**, this stretch has several turnouts for scenic views, rest and contemplation, native plants, perhaps wildflowers. Key to getting this section developed for natural and recreational use was the Silver Strand Beautification Project, boosted in 1993 with a $1 million grant. On the north end, Tulagi Road is at the **Naval Amphibious Base**.

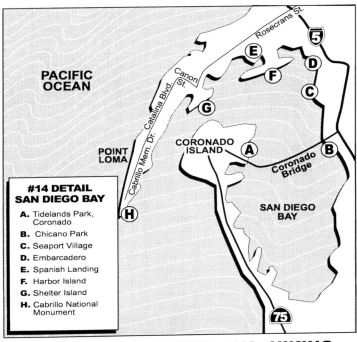

PACIFIC OCEAN

Rosecrans St.

Canon St.

Catalina Blvd.

Cabrillo Mem. Dr.

POINT LOMA

CORONADO ISLAND

Coronado Bridge

SAN DIEGO BAY

#14 DETAIL SAN DIEGO BAY

A. Tidelands Park, Coronado
B. Chicano Park
C. Seaport Village
D. Embarcadero
E. Spanish Landing
F. Harbor Island
G. Shelter Island
H. Cabrillo National Monument

COASTAL, SAN DIEGO BAY - HIKING

Hiking - Coastal Region

8. Coronado Shoreline Strolls

Most people tend to think of three things at mention of Coronado - **the Hotel del, the Navy and the Bridge**. Some mighty pleasant outdoors options there, and after a beach stroll stop in to browse awhile at **Bay Books** in the downtown Orange Avenue section.

South. From the Hotel del Coronado walk south onto the boardwalk for several blocks past the fancy condo complexes. Look out to the Coronado Islands, over to Pt. Loma, or flop onto the beach for awhile. You can also drive to this stretch of beach from Silver Strand Boulevard at either Ave Lunar or Ave de las Arenas, with some parking available. Further south is restricted, and backed up with uniformed Naval personnel.

North. From the Hotel del north, Ocean Boulevard backs up the long Coronado public beach to North Island Naval Station. This is our only beach to make the Top 10 U.S. beaches list by Travel Channel. The sidewalk goes right by a long rock (fence, hill, stack): to the west the ocean, to the east mansions galore. There is a restroom in the middle at the tall life guard tower. At the far north end, by **Sunset Park**, locate the plaque marking this as the site of the nation's First Military Flying School, founded by pioneer aviator Glenn Curtiss in 1911. At this end are trails in to a dog-allowed beach, which will be obvious from the many pooches strolling in and out.

How to get there: Take bridge to Coronado, left at Orange, turning right before Hotel del to Ocean.

9. Tidelands Park

This is that place where many people seem to always be having lots of fun right below as you arrive at Coronado on the bridge. Take the first right and swing into the parking lots past the large ball fields. Here is a stroll for the legs as well as the eyes as you take in downtown San Diego and all the maritime activity associated with the bay. Stroll left (north) on the wide walkway past the Marriott Hotel and definitely upscale residential complexes to the **Ferry Landing Marketplace** (taking the ferry from the Embarcadero at Broadway is a good way to get here). Walk to the right (south) directly under the bridge, past the golf course and over to Glorietta Boulevard. If wanting a long workout, walk along Glorietta to the Hotel del, up the beach along Ocean Boulevard and back over to Tidelands.

10. Chula Vista Marina Bayside Park

A popular spot for family outings, bayside strolls, dining, boat living and camping in style. There's an enjoyable paved trail along the bay for people and dogs. Our mutts ranked it high with lots of green grass to roll in, flowers to sniff, cool breezes, and a dog-friendly restaurant on its outdoors patio, **The Galley** at the Marina.

How to get there: I-5 to Marina Parkway, west to park.

11. Chula Vista Nature Center &
Sweetwater Marsh National Wildlife Refuge ❖❖

The **Refuge** is that open area to the west of I-5 at the north end of Chula Vista. Established in 1988 and managed by the U.S. Fish & Wildlife Service, its 316 acres provide a variety of natural habitat. The **Nature Center** provides educational support and access to the Refuge. This is a place to put on your must-visit list and one to definitely take the family to. It's set up for intriguing and fun exploration of nature. Take your binoculars so you can zero in on the many birds and sea life you'll pass near.

As you first arrive at the center, a tide pool will draw your attention. Also outside are markers noting the many coastal plants. (Would you believe a coastal jumping cholla?) A new clapper rail exhibit focuses attention on the most endangered species in the South Bay (and they will gladly receive more donations). Inside is a complete museum with many displays and hands-on exhibits. The center has an active educational program, with classes and hands-on workshops for kids of various ages.

From the **Nature Center** you can walk out along **Sweetwater Marsh** and **San Diego Bay** on several short trails making up the **Gunpowder Point Interpretive Trail System**. The trail markers provide information about the plant and animal life along here, making this a place for a leisurely, peaceful stroll.

Why is it called Gunpowder Point? A display in front of the center tells the story. During WWI, Hercules Powder Company operated the largest kelp processor on the West Coast here. Kelp was the key element in making cordite (a smokeless gunpowder), of which 45 million pounds were produced here for the British army. The tank farm for processing the kelp was the largest in the world.

How to get there: I-5 to the E Street exit. Drive into the parking lot for the Nature Center and pick up the shuttle here. Trolley to Bayfront E. Street and shuttle.

12. National City Pepper Park

This small park is right at Sweetwater River. It's well-used for launching boats heading out to ocean. It is a pleasant spot, a respite from the hectic freeway just a few blocks to the east. Across the river is the Sweetwater Wildlife Refuge so this is good for bird watching from several nicely-placed benches. Here are rest rooms, plenty of parking, playground, many picnic tables, and a bit of lawn. Everything here is modest size, including the fishing pier.

How to get there: I-5 to Marina Drive West, to Tidelands Avenue, south to park.

13. Chicano Park (San Diego City)

The most striking feature of this small park, located under the Coronado Bridge, is the colorful artwork. On the bridge structures are many large paintings, with a Mexican theme. The park came into existence as a result of community action, when citizens pushed for a park in this highly-industrialized area. The main activity is studying the Chicano culture or enjoying a picnic in the unusual surroundings. To take in more local flavor, stop in at nearby Chuey's Café, an institution for Mexican food. See (B) on page 2-9.

How to get there: I -5 to Crosby Street exit, left on Logan.

14. San Diego Bay ❖❖ (See detailed map on page 2-9)

The huge well-placed bay is why San Diego exists here in the first place, with early Portuguese explorer Juan Cabrillo arriving in 1542. The Navy and Marine Corps and marine industries are here because of the bay. Huge sportfishing and sailing fleets occupy the many marinas. Stretching for nearly 20 miles, the bay is home to a half-dozen cities. Here are some of its more scenic spots:

Seaport Village (C)/**The Embarcadero** (D). Walk out on the Broadway pier for a pelican's-eye view of the bay plus a few supercarriers. Catch the passenger ferry to **Coronado**. To the north the striking landmark is the **Star of India**, part of the **San Diego Maritime Museum**. You'll see art shows, fishermen repairing nets and lots of people loading and unloading from the tour boats and ocean liners. Stroll south from Broadway to experience a varied maritime world. A new arrival is the Midway carrier Naval museum. Stroll along the boardwalk in front of **Seaport Village** over to **Embarcadero Marina Park**, north and south. Fishing and picnicking are peaceful here almost under the shadow of the Coronado Bridge. For refreshment, try many places in the Village (a favorite Upstart Crow for books, coffee and author talks). Cross Market Street at the Kansas City BBQ, famous as, per the plaque, where "The Top Gun Sleazy Bar scene was filmed."

Spanish Landing (E)/**Harbor Island** (F). Along Harbor Drive near the airport is this small park which looks across to the colorful marinas and luxury hotels of Harbor Island, The park is grass-covered next to the rocks along the shore and is a pleasant setting for picnicking, bicycling, and fishing. The "island" is an artificially-created peninsula, made by dredging the bay. The views of the Coronado Bridge and the navy ships in the harbor or over at North Island are superb.

Shelter Island (G). For a place that once wasn't there, this palm-covered peninsula is a fine place to watch the bay action. This is fine anytime of the year for stress relief during lunch hour or after work. Take in the comings and goings in the bay, coach the fisherfolk on the piers, check out the airport, North Island, Pt. Loma's Naval activity, and, way off there on a clear day, the Coronado Islands. Along the way and at the west end are several interesting public art displays. All adds up to a good place to unwind.

How to get there: I-5 downtown to Second Avenue, right on Columbia to Market Street. Right to Seaport Village. To the Embarcadero; right on Ash Street to Harbor Drive. From the south on Interstate 5, take the Hawthorne turnoff and then go west to Harbor Drive. Reach Spanish Landing and Harbor Island by continuing north on Harbor Drive (or just follow directions to the airport). To Shelter Island, take I-8 to Rosecrans Street, continue west several miles to Shelter Island Drive and turn left.

15. Cabrillo National Monument (Point Loma) ❖❖

At the tip of Point Loma, the old lighthouse, built in 1854, and new Visitors' Center (with museum and gift shop) overlook San Diego Bay, Coronado, Mexico's Coronado Islands, and on a really clear day, perhaps Tahiti. A favorite of visitors and locals as the views are hard to beat. Many come to watch the whales as they head up and down the coast. The **Bayside Trail** leads right to the shore, and you can walk or drive down the ocean side to tide pools and the working lighthouse, moved here when the location up the hill was too often obscured by clouds and fog. See (H) on page 2-13.

How to get there: I-8 west to end, on to Nimitz Drive south, then off at Catalina up to Naval facilities, thru Fort Rosecrans National Cemetery to the end. Entrance fee. Phone: 619-557-5450.

16. Sunset Cliffs

The appealingly descriptive name, Sunset Cliffs, identifies a lovely stretch of shoreline between Ocean Beach and Point Loma. The road goes right next to the cliffs, presenting a terrific view of the immediate rocky shore and the distant Coronado Islands. Parking next to the road makes this a convenient stopping place. Be careful along the cliffs as frequently a careless stroller has discovered that first step over the edge is a long one.

Sunset Cliffs Natural Park is not huge except in setting and scenery. It is right at the ocean at the far end of Sunset Cliffs and below Pt. Loma Nazarene College. Here you can amble along several dirt trails and peruse pelicans, surfers and sunsets, even with man's best friend on a leash (before 9 a.m. or late afternoon). Perhaps even cheer for your favorite kid's team at the city's only ball field right at the ocean. If you come down from the college you can take your own tour of the grounds and historical buildings there. At low tides this is a good tide pool area. Combine this with a trip out to **Cabrillo National Monument**; or, walk along **Sunset Cliffs** over to **Ocean Beach**; or, for a hardy stroll through the **Pt. Loma** neighborhood, park down at **Shelter Island** and hike up to the college.

How to get there: To shore, I-8 west to Nimitz Drive, to Sunset Cliffs Boulevard and south. To Natural Park from the top, take Nimitz Drive south to Catalina right to Lomaland Drive, turning right into the college, then a short drive down to parking. From the bottom, take Sunset Cliffs Boulevard to the end at Ladera, left to Cornish, right into the small lot. Beach access is at Ladera.

17. Ocean Beach (OB)

OB South. Here's a fine area for some shoreline strolls, combined with a visit to one of our more interesting communities where you can still absorb the spirit of the '60s lifestyles. The pier at the end of Newport is the major OB landmark and a place to put on your visit-frequently list. Don't rush this as the many others out there won't either. Take it all in as you stroll along above the ocean, admiring the skills and patience of surfers and fisherfolk. Relax with a refreshment or a fish sandwich at the café half way out. Stroll south on the rocks.

OB North. Now refreshed, start from the pier and head north along the beach or sidewalk, ending up at the other major OB attraction – Dog Beach. The fun is right at the jetty where the tide comes and goes and the mutts romp on the sand, in the surf, or in the estuary.

How to get there: I-8 west to end, to Sunset Cliffs Boulevard. For OB Pier, stay on Sunset Cliffs Boulevard and right on Newport to the end. Park in the lot by the pier. For Dog Beach turn right at W. Pt. Loma Boulevard to end into parking lot.

18. Famosa Slough

Slightly east from OB in Loma Portal is this small but important 30-acre tidal wetland. Lots of people drive past it on W. Point Loma Boulevard, and don't even know it's there. Its value for hiking is small but for bird-watchers huge as it attracts lots of birds, both resident and migrating. Under management of San Diego Park & Recreation Department, and with diligent attention from the Friends of the Slough, it sits like an orphan cut off from the rest of Mission Bay of which it once was a part. With binoculars in hand, walk carefully in along a couple of small trails along the water on either side of the boulevard.

How to get there: I-8 west to West Mission Bay Drive/Midway, left, then right on West Point Loma Boulevard to Famosa.

19. San Diego River Flood Channel

This is the stretch west of I-5 where the San Diego River flows into the ocean. Good strolling and bird-watching on both sides. For the south side, park at Robb Field in Ocean Beach; walk east along the channel up to Pacific Coast Highway (entry here also) or west to Dog Beach. On the north side near Sea World, you're up on a bluff overlooking the river flats. Lots of good viewing, plus you can stroll about a mile out to the bay entrance.

How to get there: South side - I-8 west to end, left to Sunset Cliffs, to Pt. Loma Boulevard right, follow signs to Robb Field. North side - I-5 to Sea World exit, west. Park on frontage road along flood channel.

Jetties at Imperial Beach

COASTAL REGION - CENTRAL HIKING

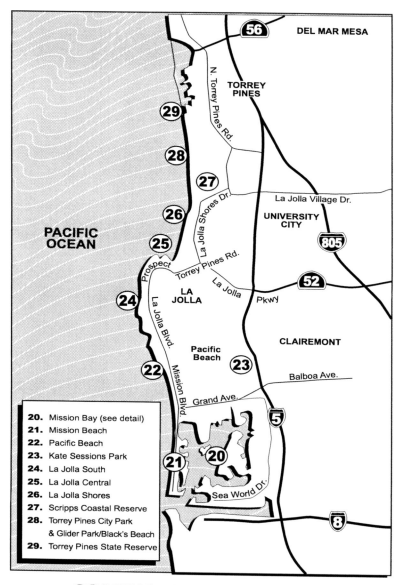

COASTAL, CENTRAL - HIKING

20. Mission Bay ✤✤

Created from a mostly shallow mud flat left by the San Diego River and developed over the past 5 decades, Mission Bay is the main center of recreational water activities in the region. Boats of all types and colors are seen, engaged in almost every nautical sport. Its nearly 30 miles of shoreline play host year-round to thousands of beach goers. Because of the multiplicity of uses and heavy demands, parts of the bay differ considerably in development and activities. Here are a few favorites;

Bay entrance. (A, B, C) Hospitality Point at the south end of **Quivira Basin** (location of summer concerts), and **Mission Point** at Mariners Basin, are fun for watching the traffic in and out of the bay. Both areas are landscaped and good for picnics, plus you can walk out on the jetties which form the bay entrance and the **San River Flood Channel**.

South Mission Bayside. (D) Have a party or ball game at Mariners Point, across from **Belmont Park** and the **Bahia**. Take a leisurely stroll along the bayside down to the park at the south end where you can watch the boats moving in and out of the bay. It's an easy walk over to the jetty at the ocean.

East Mission Bay Drive. (G) The eastern section of the bay along Interstate 5 is a popular area for families and heavily used by locals where you'll see walkers, joggers, sailors, water-skiers, bikers, skaters cavorting from De Anza Cove (J) south past the Hilton Hotel.

Fiesta Island. (H) This is a favorite for beach parties, fishing, biking and dog-walking. This big, mostly undeveloped island is generally uncrowded and one of the few shoreline areas where vehicles can be driven directly to the beach. The scout camp has been recently renovated. You can have a good walk by taking the road all the way around, passing **Sea World** a mere stone's throw across the water. A large area has been set aside for dog romps. ALERT: AVOID THIS AREA ENTIRELY CERTAIN WEEKENDS IN JULY, unless heading for the world-famed Over-The Line Tournament and a unique adult-oriented sporting experience.

Vacation Island. (K) The western half of the island is taken by the hotel, but all beaches are accessible to the public. Rent or just watch sailboats from a picnic table or while sipping a cool drink from the deck of the hotel restaurant. A popular activity is racing model boats on a small pond. The eastern part of the island is a popular fishing, kite, and game area and is where the racing powerboats are centered.

Crown Point. (L) On the eastern side of Crown Point, the south end of Pacific Beach (PB), is a landscaped area which is extremely popular and a favorite meeting place for groups. At the northern end is the **University of California Wildlife Preserve**. On the beach, cross under the Ingraham Street bridge to the beach along Riviera Drive. Walk along the new walkway all along the north side of **Sail Bay** (M) and continue on either side of Mission Beach.

How to get there: East bay/Fiesta Island: I-5 to either Clairemont Drive or Sea World Drive. Vacation Island and PB: I-8 west to Ingraham, north (or I-5 to Garnet west to Ingraham south. Hospitality Point and Mission Point, from Ingraham go west on West Mission Bay Drive. Turn left onto Quivira Way for Hospitality Point (go left past Marina Village to the end), and left onto Mission Boulevard for Mission Point (go to the end and turn left).

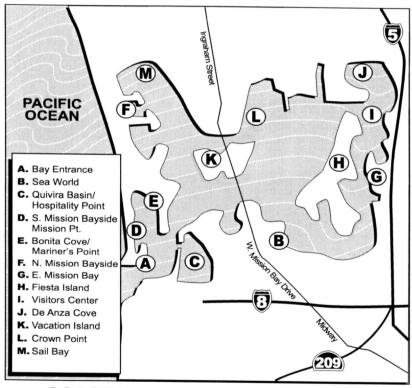

A. Bay Entrance
B. Sea World
C. Quivira Basin/
Hospitality Point
D. S. Mission Bayside
Mission Pt.
E. Bonita Cove/
Mariner's Point
F. N. Mission Bayside
G. E. Mission Bay
H. Fiesta Island
I. Visitors Center
J. De Anza Cove
K. Vacation Island
L. Crown Point
M. Sail Bay

COASTAL, MISSION BAY - HIKING

21. Mission Beach (MB)

Jetty. If you want to walk out and be surrounded by ocean without getting wet, one of the most enjoyable ways is to head out along the jetty which marks the end of South Mission Beach. This is actually not a very long hike, but as you'll be hopping from rock to rock and enjoying yourself along the way, plan for an hour or so. This is just plain fun, with boats of all breeds sailing along the waterway in and out of the bay. The waves will be crashing right beside you, the crabs scurrying for cover, the fisherfolk trying out their skills, the gulls soaring overhead, the surfers rolling around - the list goes on. Wear some sneakers with good grips and keep an eye or hand on the kids as this is a place where you can get into trouble.

Now should you be around here during the full moon, you may catch sight of the lovely woman who has long been rumored to dance on Mission Beach near the jetty...in the moonlight...in the nude. I've been looking for her during my over four decades here, without success. But the rumor never seems to die, so join the rest of us and pass it on.

How to get there: Go by bike if possible as parking is limited. Go early or later for best chances. Get to Mission or Pacific Beach, then take Mission Boulevard all the way south. Parking lot on the right, another off to the left. Then start walking west out along the jetty.

22. Pacific Beach (PB)

Boardwalk & Pier. You'll have plenty of company in this very popular strolling area. The boardwalk starts near the jetty and heads north to the pier plus a few blocks more. This is not exactly a quiet stroll, except perhaps around sunset. Here will be walkers, roller bladers, bicyclists all wandering at various paces up and down the boardwalk right by the beach. You'll find restaurants, coffee shops and small stores.

Definitely take a stroll out on **Crystal Pier** anytime you can use a bit of rejuvenation. Built originally in 1927, with occasional trimmings from high waves, it's a great place to watch birds, surfers and fisher folk. You can even spend the night here in a hotel room with your back deck over the waves. Right by the pier is one of those beach institutions, Kono's Café, where the locals gather for early breakfasts.

The shoreline north of Crystal Pier in Pacific Beach makes a pleasant stroll. The sidewalk follows an increasingly high bluff to a small grassy knoll, **Palisades Park**, at Law Street.

A few more blocks north takes you to **Tourmaline Surfing Park**. This active beach for board and wind surfing, plus a short stroll north takes you to the tide pool area where the cliffs of La Jolla begin.

How to get there: From the south, I-5 to Grand Avenue west to beach; from the north, I-5 to Garnet Avenue, west to beach. To Tourmaline Canyon, head north on Mission Boulevard to Tourmaline and west into parking lot. You can get directly to the tide pools via the stairs from Sea Ridge off La Jolla Boulevard.

23. Kate Sessions Park (PB)

With a grand overlook of Mission Bay and the ocean this is a pleasant spot for a picnic and strolls around the park or adjacent canyons.

How to get there: I-5 to Grand Ave west, to Lamont, right to the top.

24. La Jolla South ❖❖

Known as the Jewel City, La Jolla offers many options for getting right at the ocean.

Bird Rock. From La Jolla Boulevard, west on Camino de la Costa. Hard to get at the beach in this area except for the access, with parking, a few blocks along. Good place for swimming and snorkeling. Look across to the large rock covered with droppings, from heaven I guess. Continue north on the street observe the lifestyles of the rich (and maybe famous), leading to...

Windansea Beach. From La Jolla Boulevard, west on Nautilus. For my money, the most memorable beach scene of the whole county. Home of the legends: The Pump House Gang and Hot Curl (ask any old surfer or visit the Spot Restaurant on Prospect — that's Hot Curl greeting you at the door). Experience the wide scope of sensory experiences right here or for some strolling, head north along the beach. (Alternative is along the streets above). This is slightly challenging, with some rock-scrambling. Over the rocks you'll arrive at...

Marine Street Beach. One of the least crowded beaches in the area. Continue walking north over more rocks to...

25. La Jolla Central ❖❖

An extremely active area in general with locals and tourists. You can combine coastal scenery with shops, dining and cafes. Stop in at Warwick's Books, enjoy lunch with super view at George's, or sunset from La Valencia deck.

Coast Boulevard. This is a long grassy stretch above the rocky shoreline, popular for walkers, tide poolers, or sitters enjoying a picnic, swim and sunsets. Walk north past the Museum of Contemporary Art and along the rocky shoreline to where the crowds (and sometimes tour buses) are. You're now at **Children's Cove**, more recently the **Sea Lions' Cove** where you (and several hundred others with cameras at the ready) can observe 50 or so loafing, playing or swimming. Continue north to...

The Cove, Scripps Park and beyond. When I first hit San Diego 40 years back, the first truly stunning beach for me was the Cove, the second Windansea. **Ellen Browning Scripps Park** is probably our most visited coastal park. When people talk about the Cove, this is the park right beside it. Walk along the bluff right at the ocean by the park, past the Cove and continuing north. Now walking along the street, enjoy a lunch at the vintage and view-grabbing Brockton Villa restaurant or perhaps take a coffee and view break at the small café overlooking the ocean. Do take that multi-step journey right down to the caves where the breakers come crashing in. Back on top, by the shell shop, (if you're adventurous and definitely not vertigo-inclined) walk north on the trail. Now you'll be way up above the ocean, where your pals are families of gulls, pelicans and cormorants. And definitely watch your step up here. This leads out to Prospect Street and you can make your return hike through the shops and action along Prospect.

How to get there: I-5 to La Jolla Parkway (old Ardath Road) west, then left to Torrey Pines Road, right at Prospect and down on Cave Street to the park. Parking is often a problem, though there is a parking garage on Cave Street and several up in the shopping district above. Better to take a bike or bus.

26. La Jolla Shores

If you're into long-distance beach walking, here's a good starting place. You can start walking north from here and, at low tide, make it up to happy hour in Encinitas. Or if you're not that inclined, just join the many others who enjoy a stroll or trot along this lovely beach. At the southern end of the Shores is the Marine Room, a dining room and cocktail lounge always crowded at high tides (lots of fun watching the waves crash into, and once through, the large windows). A walkway just to the south side gives you access for exploring the rocky beach along the cliffs, at low, low tide.

Much of this area is the **Underwater Park Ecological Reserve**, meaning look but don't disturb. At the northern end is the Scripps Pier and above that you can enjoy a stroll through the world famous UCSD Scripps Institution of Oceanography with fine views from the hillsides.

From the pier north keep walking and you'll find lots of people enjoying the beach free-style, free of clothes, that is, at the also world famous Black's Beach;

then on to Torrey Pines State Beach and Del Mar.

How to get there: I-5 to La Jolla Parkway west, to Torrey Pines Road, left and quick right to La Jolla Shores Boulevard, left at Avenue de la Playa.

27. Scripps Coastal Reserve

This small gem is on a bluff near UCSD, with some of the most spectacular ocean views in the county. You can hike it in a half-hour, but this is a place where you'll want to stop often and smell the... everything. It's an ecologically-sensitive research area with many sections off limits. At the entry is information about the self-guided trail and the various plants and geological features. In spring, you're likely to see many flowers blooming (coast sunflowers, coast cholla, jimson weed - don't eat it), but here nature's primary wonders are the panoramic views of the ocean below and, if your vision is real good, Hawaii. To the south will be hang gliders, Scripps Pier and the Cove; to the north eroded sandstone cliffs and a whole bunch of folks trooping down the road to the legendary Black's Beach. (To pursue the political aspects of this well-known bit of beach turf, read "Black's Beach Bingo," San Diego Magazine, April 1978.) Where the bluffs meet the ocean is a fine spot to perch awhile and enjoy the incredible views, enjoyed every day by those living nearby in some of the city's most expensive homes.

How to get there: I-5 to La Jolla Village Drive west. Veer right onto Torrey Pines Road north. At La Jolla Shores Drive turn left, then right to La Jolla Farms Road. Entrance is on the left about 300 feet. Should you want to join those folks cavorting down on the beach, go another couple of blocks further north on La Jolla Farms to the marked walking road heading down to Black's Beach.

28. Torrey Pines City Park and Glider Park / Black's Beach

Visit here if you want to combine panoramic ocean views from high above the water with a veritable three-ring circus at the same time. On your way in you'll pass by the world-renowned Salk Institute. Drive in, park in the designated areas, wander around, have a snack, walk down (very carefully) to Black's Beach below.

Because the winds rise up so steadily from the ocean to these high bluffs, this is an ideal glider park. Depending on the season and the wind, many types of gliders may be soaring silently through the sky at the same time. The most spectacular are the hang gliders. You may see a half-dozen of these large, kite-like objects sitting near a small building. The pilots are waiting for the right wind conditions. When the wind is right, one of them will haul his rig over to the cliff edge and head off, soar back and forth along the cliff and land back on the top. With a weak wind, he may instead end up on the beach, with a long uphill walk. Small radio-controlled gliders often soar back and forth across the sky. In winter, fixed-wing gliders join the parade.

If you do make that trek from the top along the footpaths to the beach, walk with care. Frequently the evening news features someone who either got stuck part way down or up, or was injured from a fall. Stay on the heavily-traveled paths. Once there you'll be enjoying one of our most dramatic beaches, with the ocean ahead, the high cliffs behind. You can walk along the beach either way for a multi-sensory experience.

How to get there: I-5 north to Genesee Avenue west, left to Torrey Pines Road, right to the park.

29. Torrey Pines State Reserve ❖❖

Here's an inspirational setting on bluffs overlooking the Pacific Ocean. Only twenty minutes from downtown, it's one of our most frequently-visited parks, yet still many San Diegans are unaware of this gem just north of the jewel city, La Jolla. This was the first urban natural preserve in the country, created in 1899 and designated a **National Natural Landmark by the Department of Interior**. It takes its name from the rare pine that grows there, one of the few places that occurs.

In its 2000 acres, Torrey Pines offers a variety of hiking options to match any level of fitness, plus superb ocean views and beach adventure. A good place to begin a visit here is at the museum and park headquarters, where you also pay the nominal entrance fee. Exhibits inside and out make this worth your time before heading out.

Trails wind from here or other parts through chaparral, along the coastal bluffs and down to beach. Hikes range from 20-minute easy strolls to one-hour hikes down to ocean and back. On weekends leaders from the Torrey Pines Docents Society lead hikes, offering one of the best ways to get acquainted with what the park has to offer. You may also see gliders soaring back and forth along the bluffs.

Before you head out on a trail, pick up a map from headquarters. No, you won't find the old-timers favorite - **Fat Man's Misery** -as that was closed off to foot traffic years back. Some sample trails, from mild to more adventuresome:

Guy Fleming Trail starts as you arrive near the top of the road. It's a good trail for anyone, as it's easy, yet rich in natural rewards. From the parking area the trail winds through the pines out right along the ocean. You'll see a variety of plant life, including a variety of flowering ones, while gazing down onto the beach. The trail loops back to the parking lot, making this a genteel 20-30 minute amble. (Answering the Quiz, the trail is named after one of this area's most important nature advocates. He was District Superintendent of all Southern California state parks and the key player in getting this area preserved as a park for all of us.)

A set of trail options leads directly west from Park Headquarters parking lot (or its nearby restroom). The **Beach Trail** starts out as an easy, slightly downhill, winding trail out through chaparral. A short side trail lead up to the prominent jutting sandstone. The trail continues west; one option heads out to a bluff viewpoint. The other heads down along and through sandstone canyons to where it really gets fun with a final descent along a narrow ledge to **Flat Rock** and the beach. You'll find lug soles shoes come in handy, and hikers with vertigo will not enjoy this part. This is one of the most popular spots in the park, and lots of people will be gamboling on the beach or the rocks. This is the only place you can have a picnic in the park. Return the same way or make it a loop by walking up the beach and back up the park road (or wait for pickup by your designated driver). This is 1-2 hours round trip.

How to get there: I-5 to Carmel Valley Road west, turn left at Pacific Coast Highway to park entrance. You can park there at beach level, or continue up the hill to the lot near Park HQ. An alternative walk-in entrance is on Torrey Pines Road just north of the golf course, with some parking beside the road. The **South Fork Trail** *heads to the beach from here.*

COASTAL REGION - NORTH

A big advantage of this whole north section is that you can leave your car anywhere, and return by the #310 bus (North County Transit District) which runs frequently to stops near all the places mentioned (from Oceanside to University Town Center - UTC).

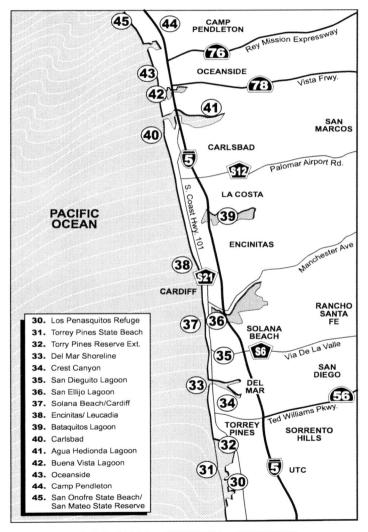

30. Los Penasquitos Refuge
31. Torrey Pines State Beach
32. Torry Pines Reserve Ext.
33. Del Mar Shoreline
34. Crest Canyon
35. San Dieguito Lagoon
36. San Ellijo Lagoon
37. Solana Beach/Cardiff
38. Encinitas/ Leucadia
39. Bataquitos Lagoon
40. Carlsbad
41. Agua Hedionda Lagoon
42. Buena Vista Lagoon
43. Oceanside
44. Camp Pendleton
45. San Onofre State Beach/ San Mateo State Reserve

COASTAL, NORTH - HIKING

Hiking - Coastal Region

30. Los Penasquitos Estuary

In Sorrento Valley, this is the westernmost end of Los Penasquitos Canyon Preserve, which follows Penasquitos Creek over from I-15.

How to get there: I-5 to Carmel Valley Road west. Park along the road and stroll along the estuary.

31. Torrey Pines State Beach

This is where Pacific Coast Highway dips down and goes right along the beach. Head south along the sand, pass or walk up into Torrey Pines State Reserve. You can make an interesting round trip hike past Black's Beach.

32. Torrey Pines Preserve Extension Area (Del Mar)

The extension area is far less visited than the main preserve. It also is a fine place for strolling and enjoying fabulous ocean vistas. The park offers four marked trails, from easy strolls to stiff workouts. You'll be walking among some of the rare pines, through some open chaparral-covered canyons and often wildflowers. In the late afternoons you beach to the Scripps Pier and return. North leads to Del Mar. East of the highway is **Los Penasquitos Estuary and Lagoon**, with a small family recreational area. You can stroll by the north side of the estuary along Carmel Valley Road.

How to get there: I-5 to Carmel Valley Road west. Parking just before Highway 101 or continue to Pacific Coast Highway (101) and left to parking along road or in lot at south end. You may see some hot air balloons and the colors of sunset. No dogs, no bikes here. Here are some options:

From the bottom, south entrance. Pick up a map and sometimes descriptions to match the markers along the trails. You have several choices from here. (a) Head straight in and head up to the Daughters of the American Revolution (DAR) area. (b) Veer off to the right onto the **Margaret Fleming Trail** and you'll head up toward Torrey Pines High. This is a variety of foliage, with numbers for the various types (that's where a descriptive list would come in handy). Lots of pines and shrubs here. You can loop back down on the **Gully Trail** to the **Mar Scenic Trail** and back to the start, or take the side trip up to the DAR area.

From the top, west side. Walk in a short ways, veer right to the **West Ridge Trail**. This winds through the pines to the DAR plaque, dedicated in 1971 as part of the U.S. Bicentennial. Not that you need a rest yet, but have a seat on the bench and enjoy the setting: pines, the sounds of the ocean, maybe a train whistle. Walk further along and out to the view point, overlooking the ocean, Torrey Pines Beach, San Dieguito Lagoon and the main preserve. For the easy hike, return the same way; for a loop, walk down the trail to the **Mar Scenic Trail** and back.

From the top, east side. (a) The easy option is to walk south along the trail through the trees to the end at 0.25 mile in. You'll have colorful eroded rock formations, expansive views to the east, and more superb views of the ocean and lagoon. (b) For more of a workout, walk in along the path that goes by the school ball fields. Stay on this and you'll start heading down some steps into marsh terrain, lots of bamboo, crossing a bridge to arrive at the main north-south trail (**Mar Scenic Trail**). Walk left to near the south entrance and pick up the **Margaret Fleming Trail** back up to the top. (Or reverse this, looking for the Fleming Trail, not marked except now with a saw horse).

How to get there: (Bottom) Take I-5 to Carmel Valley Road, west to Del Mar Scenic Parkway right. Drive left, to dead end.

(Top West) Take I-5 to Del Mar Heights Road, west to Mar Scenic Drive left, to dead end.

(Top East) From Del Mar Heights Road, west to Mercado, turning left or south, then left at Cordero. At Mira Montana, turn right, driving all the way in past the houses to the cul de sac and public parking lot.

33. Del Mar Shoreline

Walking from the state beach takes you into Del Mar. On the beach you'll have the ocean on the west (and plenty of surfers) and on the east Del Mar's cliffs plus Amtrak and the Coasters (sounds like a singing group). In the center of Del Mar is the small but thriving business district — don't miss Earth Song Books. A short block over is tiny **Seagrove Park**, embodying location, location, location. Seagrove is a popular site for weddings and sunsets, as it's on a bluff a short distance above the beach, which is easily accessible. Walk north along the beach and you arrive where "the turf meets the surf," at the Del Mar Race Track. Here you'll see people cavorting with their dogs where the lagoon meets the ocean.

Walk north and you're below the bluffs of Solana Beach.

How to get there: Seagrove Park: I-5 to Carmel Valley Road, north along Pacific Coast Highway to 15th Street and left to the park. North Del Mar: I-5 to Via de la Valle west to Pacific Coast Highway. Turn left and park on ocean side or side streets, paying required.

34. Crest Canyon Open Space Preserve (Del Mar)

A joint project of cities of Del Mar and San Diego, Crest Canyon is a short but scenic trail good for a brief getaway to nature in the midst of city life. Hiking from above, you'll head down a trail to **San Dieguito Lagoon**. It's a scenic peaceful stroll through mostly chaparral, a few pines, flowers in season, a couple of quail crossing swiftly. To either side are eroded canyon walls. After a fifteen minute hike you pick up a fine view of the lagoon and soon arrive at the end of the trail at Racetrack Drive. **Del Mar Racetrack** is the prominent structure across the lagoon. Here is marked the other trailhead to the canyon. Heading back up, try the smaller side trail to the east of the main trail. It will take you back to the starting place and you'll be closer to the foliage. This is a good hike for spending some time with young children who often lose interest in longer hikes. You can also take along the family hound, on a leash.

How to get there: I-5 to Del Mar Heights west. About 0.5 mile turn right at Durango Drive. Park anywhere along Durango or go to the end for the park sign and trail in to the canyon. Or you can enter from near the racetrack from Jimmy Durante Drive, turning east onto San Dieguito Drive. That becomes Racetrack Drive where you can park along the road by the Crest Canyon sign.

35. San Dieguito Lagoon

Located between Del Mar and Solana Beach, on either side of the Fairgrounds and racetrack. This is the westernmost end of the San Dieguito River Park, a major project stretching 55 miles from "Coast to Crest." Little access is available in this coastal region, though Crest Canyon Preserve ends up here and the popular dog beach is at the ocean end.

36. San Elijo Lagoon Ecological Reserve ❖❖

Combines pleasant aspects of interesting terrain, open vistas, plenty of birds, and several good hiking options This 1000-acre reserve is between Solana Beach and Cardiff and administered jointly by the County and State Fish & Game. On any weekend, many people will be here enjoying a pleasant stroll along the paths, while formations of geese soar by, and brightly-plumed ducks and black coots swim through the reeds.

West end, south side. I-5 north to Lomas Santa Fe Drive west. At Rios, turn right. Drive to the end and park. From the entrance, the trail left (west) takes you quickly down near the water where you can continue north along the lagoon and railroad tracks. The trail right (east) is a considerably different hike which stays well above the lagoon as it winds through a rich variety of foliage. This may be muddy in parts, but it's especially interesting.

West end, north side. To the west of I-5 on Manchester is a new informational building, with parking. A short marked trail runs right along the lagoon, and other trails go a short way eastward. The kiosks will inform you that over 300 different types of birds show up here, making 40% of all bird species in North America.

East end. I-5 to Lomas Santa Fe east. Immediately turn left onto Santa Helena (same as Marine View). Left at Santa Victoria and left at Santa Carina, to end. At the entrance you'll see a large sign, which says, among other things, you can take your dog along on these trails, on a leash and with poop sack at the ready please. Take the trail in to the large and obvious eucalyptus tree. Go east or west and you'll quickly be down along the shoreline among the fowl. To the west you'll walk by several large stands of beavertail cactus, which seem out of place amidst all the water-oriented foliage. Continue on toward the freeway. You'll be enjoying the expanse of lagoon below you, plus a view of several mountains way over to the east. A pleasant setting, with only eight lanes of freeway traffic noise just above you. The trail crosses under the highway and meets up with the west lagoon trail. You can hike over to the ocean or with two vehicles leave one at Rios and make this a less taxing one-way hike. Further east off Lomas Santa Fe, turn north on El Camino Real to the trail entrance near La Orilla. This takes you through a wooded and peaceful area over to the main trails noted above.

East end, north side. East on Manchester head toward the dominant golden-domed Greek Church. You'll see the an entry onto the dike over the lagoon. There is limited parking by the road or on weekends at nearby Mira Costa College.

37. Solana Beach/Cardiff Shoreline Strolls

Walking on the city streets is a bit frustrating as so many housing complexes are built along the bluff next to the ocean. The more pleasant walk is on the eastern side of Highway 101 through the Cedros Business District with cafes, stores and a lively flavor, day or night. From **Fletcher Cove Park** in midtown or **Tide Beach Park** further north, head down to the beach and walk either way. Take the north route to the interesting **"Table Top"** tide pools. **Cardiff State Beach** is between the two towns at the north end of San Elijo Lagoon. A pleasant stroll along Highway 101 and above the beach is on the walkway from here north to Encinitas.

How to get there: I-5 to Lomas Santa Fe, west to Fletcher Cove Park. To Tide Beach Park north to Sierra Avenue. To access the Table Top tide pool area, park in Cardiff State Beach and walk south along the beach.

38. Encinitas/Leucadia Shoreline Strolls

Walking north from Cardiff will take you to Swami's Beach, with a parking lot and restrooms. Right beside it is the exotic-looking Self Realization Fellowship, founded by Paramahansa Yogananda who authored the long-running book *Autobiography of a Yogi*. Guess where Swami's took its name. Away from the noisy highway and up the hill to the ocean is a lush garden open to the public. There are places to sit quietly, enjoy the scenery, or practice your T'ai Chi. Walking north from here is enjoyable as there are many access points down to the beach, plus interesting buildings and along the route. (Look for the two ships, actually residences, on the street.) At the north end of town is **Moonlight Beach**, a popular spot with many facilities and activities. This is another good starting place for exploring.

How to get there: To Moonlight Beach, take I-5 to Encinitas Boulevard, west to beach entrance or for parking above, take 3rd Street south. To Swami's, take Pacific Coast Highway south to just past the fellowship.

39. Bataquitos Lagoon Ecological Reserve

This is the large lagoon between Leucadia and Carlsbad. Major improvements in recent years have restored the lagoon to a more natural state. You can take a hike along the north side of the lagoon. From the parking lot, signs will direct you past the Lagoon Foundation's small office building and onto the trail. As this is tidal, you may be close to the water and the many shorebirds or maybe not. A series of information stanchions tell the story of the lagoon's natural features.

The first section is open trail, but soon you'll enter a stand of eucalyptus trees, and if it's a hot day you'll welcome some shade. As you continue east you'll walk close to the Aviara Golf Club. If your concept of hiking includes a cool margarita or even lunch while overlooking the bay, step through the gate, walk 50 feet and there's civilization, a fine restaurant and bar. Or keep on walking, with more shade and lots of flowers, past the golf course to where the trail enters from the easternmost parking lot. Someday the trail may continue further around the lagoon, but now it stops here. This hike is perhaps one hour and 1.5 miles round trip.

About that quiz question. The spelling is per current standard practice, but if you check in *San Diego County Place-Names*, the spelling is Batequito. And from author Lou Stein, "Scholars are not in agreement as to the explanation of this Spanish designation." He lists three options: the baptized ones, flat-bottomed boats, and small watering hole.

How to get there: I-5 north to Carlsbad and east on Poinsettia. Turn right at

Bataquitos Drive, go to Azure Cove, turn right (see the sign) and drive to the parking lot at the lagoon. Walk in past the Lagoon Foundation's office and continue along the path. Or enter from El Camino Real just north of the La Costa Resort onto Aviara Parkway. At Bataquitos Drive, turn left (south) toward the golf club. You'll see two parking lots with maps, information kiosks, and trails down to the lagoon.

40. Carlsbad Shoreline Stroll

This is an interesting town to explore on foot as it has several historical buildings, dating back to when this was a resort and spa, that are worth visiting. Pick up a brochure from the Chamber of Commerce, in the old train depot. For the ocean stroll, trek along **South Carlsbad** or **Carlsbad State Beaches**. Above the beach along Carlsbad Boulevard are always lots of walkers and joggers on the walkway from the Encino Power Plant at **Agua Hedionda Lagoon** north to the commercial district, ending at Pine Avenue. Along the way you can drop down to the beach at several access points, among them Tamarack Avenue (parking) or in town from Carlsbad Village Drive.

How to get there: I-5 to La Costa Boulevard, Poinsettia Lane or Cannon Road west to Carlsbad Boulevard. Some parking along Carlsbad Boulevard or lots north and south of campground.

41. Aqua Hedionda Lagoon (Carlsbad)

The primary public activity here is kayaking or canoeing, with rentals available from the Aquatic Center. Also you'll find some hiking and birding areas in the eastern lagoon, plus an active community park, with restrooms. At the eastern end is a 200-acre ecological reserve (riparian, salt marsh and coastal sage) under the aegis of California Fish & Game. In the works is a Discovery Center on the south side.

How to get there: I-5 to Tamarack east to Adams and right to the Aquatic Center; to east lagoon stay on Adams to Hoover, some access there, then right onto Park. Go left on Cove Drive to Bristol Cove to a small beach or continue on Park to some trails heading toward the lagoon.

42. Buena Vista Lagoon

Interstate 5 runs right through this 190-acre lagoon located between Oceanside and Carlsbad. A state ecological reserve, it's the only fresh water lagoon in the county. The reserve began with a gift of acreage to the Nature Conservancy which turned the land over to the state when it acquired the additional acreage and created the reserve.

This is a good area for bird watchers. The Buena Vista Audubon Society makes periodic educational field trips here and compiles an annual Christmas bird count; their yearly count is over two hundred species. Shore fishermen pull bass and catfish from the lagoon, but no boats or swimming are allowed. A weir between the lagoon and the ocean can be seen from the western end.

The **Audubon Society Nature Center** is on the northwest side of the lagoon. Here are nature displays, a book store, and meeting room for frequent programs. A short trail runs along the north side of the lagoon and picnic tables provide a good relaxing spot.

Lots of hungry shore birds congregate near **Hosp Grove Park** at the eastern end. Continue to Marion Road, turn left and left again down to a close-in bird-watching spot at the end of the frontage road.

How to get there: (Oceanside, west end) I-5 to Vista Way, west to Coast Boulevard, left to Nature Center. (Carlsbad) I-5 to Elm Avenue, west to Carlsbad Boulevard, right. (East end) I-5 to Las Flores Drive, west to Jefferson Street, right and along the south side of the lagoon.

43. Oceanside

You can get in plenty of strolling in this city right next to **Camp Pendleton**. It offers a long and wide beach (with many access points), a pier, harbor and several parking areas near the shoreline. The Amtrak/Coaster station is a short walk from the pier. Take this whole trek or any part of it, starting from the south part of the city. No dogs on beach.

Start near **Cassidy Street**. Walk on the beach or sidewalk along Pacific Street. A few blocks north and useful to know is tiny Buccaneer Park with rest rooms and a small parking lot.

Continue north to **Wisconsin Street** with entry to a parking lot. Walk either along the Strand near the beach or along Pacific, looking over beach houses. There is a park-like atmosphere along here with palm trees lining both sides of Pacific. Right by the beach are picnic tables, restrooms, McDonalds and the amphitheater (with summer concerts).

Walk out along the **Pier** (at Pier View Way, just north of Sea Gaze Drive). This is an active place with many strollers, fisherfolk and at the end Ruby's Diner, the only business on the pier. Ruby's is a 40's motif, with large windows, burgers, shakes and even a counter. You can dine inside or outside above the ocean.

Back on land, continue north until the road curves over the **San Luis Rey River**. You can walk right to the harbor outlet, with a large parking lot, snack spot, restrooms and camping (up to 5 days), with dump station. This is right across from the large Marina Inn. No dogs on beach, wood fires in rings are O.K. Walk back a short ways and you're just a block away from the Oceanside Harbor commercial area with restaurants and shops. Also a free lot under the railroad tracks to the east; for a long walk leave car here.

How to get there: I-5 north to Harbor exit. Drive along Harbor Drive south out to the beach and jetty.

44. Camp Pendleton (limited access)

When San Diegans think about the value of Camp Pendleton, we typically have three main thoughts: 1) it's an important military base; 2) it provides a scenic Amtrak or auto coastal journey; 3) thank heaven it's still there, to keep those spreading population hordes from the north at bay.

But few of us really get on to **Camp Pendleton** - we just go through it on the highway. Meanwhile each day thousands of Marines are going through it, by amphibious vehicle, helicopter, and afoot. This is the country's premiere (and world's largest) amphibious training base.

In 1942 the Marines bought Rancho Santa Margarita y Las Flores, a name it took way back as an old Mexican Land Grant. The U.S. government named it after Major General Joseph Pendleton, who had long advocated a Marine base in this area (and incidently became mayor of Coronado after his military service).

Pendleton is big at 125,000 acres with training facilities, community infrastructure, 17 miles of beaches, rolling hills, Santa Margarita Mountains and much open space. Of interest to outdoor devotees it is doing a lot to preserve the environment, with a policy of identifying, documenting and maintaining biological diversity. A number of locales have been restored to natural state. The Rancho Santa Margarita River runs through the southern edge, providing wildlife habitat, and its estuary is home to birds of many species.

Those with access credentials, can gain an appreciation of Pendleton's scope and value by taking the self-guided driving tour, starting from the main gate at Oceanside's northern edge. After receiving the required access permit, you can follow the tour signs and guidebook to take in many of the key attractions. I'll note only a few:

Lake O'Neill's 125 acres provides waterfowl habitat, several good picnic areas and a campground for military personnel. The large Naval hospital is nearby.

The Las Flores adobe dates back to 1865 and is a National Historic Land-mark. The adobe itself is in restoration and not open. The Orange County Boy Scouts lease land here and are constantly bringing in groups of young camp-ers. Nearby is a wildlife sanctuary.

The **Amphibian Vehicle Museum** is located near the main gate area, and will be of high interest to those who grew up with Marine WWII movies, as many of the vehicles on display were used in some of those battles.

For those who want to get really active, there are the **Mud Runs**. These are benefit foot races across the streams and hills of Pendleton that present some challenges not seen along any other race course in the county. For one run 3,000 runners — Marines and civilians, men, women, and some children - headed off from Lake O'Neill along a 10K course in specified groups, some with regular running garb, others in full boots and camouflage uniforms.

Spotlessly clean, sent off by cheering fans and families, they headed off into the wilds of Pendleton. They would cross two streams, tackle various ob-stacles, and finally head into the final stretch where the watchers were all assembled. This obstacle is where the Mud Runs get their name. All competi-tors now had to switch from being runners to crawlers as between them and the finish line was this swampy stretch, about 200 feet long and perhaps one foot deep, with wire strung across about one foot above the water, make that mud. Or glop. Just the stuff we all wanted to plop around in back when we were 5 years old.

45. San Onofre State Beach

North of Pendleton and next to San Clemente is this state beach, just north of the huge double-domed nuclear power facility. You can stroll along the beach for 3.5 miles or explore the nature trail over to **San Mateo State Reserve** (with major campground), where the creek meets the ocean, and **Trestles Beach**, well-known to surfers.

How to get there: I-5 north to Basilone Road, west to the beach.

Torry Pines
Beach & Bluffs

Hiking - Coastal Region

La Jolla Shores

Torrey Pines

La Jolla Cove

Imperial Beach Pier

Chicano Park

Black's Beach viewed from the Pier

Penasquitos Lagoon - East of Highway 101

Pacific Shoreline
at
Solana Beach

Tidepool Beach Park
in Solana Beach

Hiking - Coastal Region

Chula Vista Nature Interpretive Center

Chula Vista Nature Interpretive Center

San Elijo Lagoon

Tijuana Estuary

CHAPTER 3

HIKING
URBAN SAN DIEGO

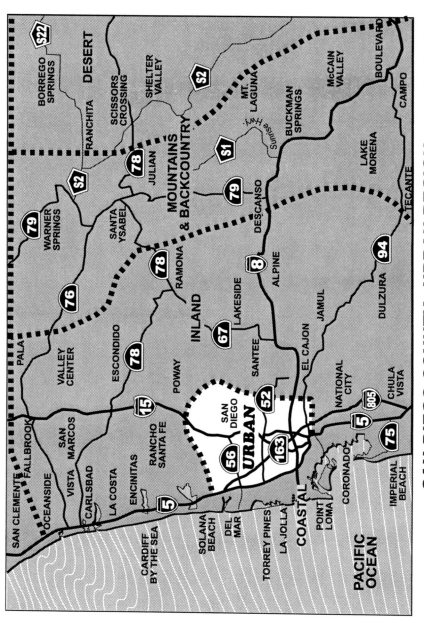

URBAN SAN DIEGO
HIKING OVERVIEW

"Great cities are known for their great parks, and one measure of any city's greatness is its ability to provide recreation, natural beauty and signature open spaces for its citizens."

Peter Harnik, The Excellent Park System

In this section we examine the many parks and canyons that provide havens of nature and recreation in the midst of the San Diego urban scene. This includes Balboa Park, Old Town, Presidio Park and our tri-canyon park system, plus opportunities along this segment of the San Diego River. Then we head further out, still within the city, to the outlying parks – Chollas, Shepard, Lake Miramar, and the big Kahunas, Mission Trails and Los Penasquitos.

First, here's a quiz about San Diego City's major urban parks.

1. Cowles Mountain is a prominent and busy landmark in Mission Trails Regional Park. How is it pronounced?

2. In what park can you visit the county's oldest residence (and even sit by a waterfall)?

3. What woman played a big role in Balboa Park's impressive horticulture and where's the park named after her?

4. Where can you walk across major city canyons on foot bridges?

5. In Old Town State Park sits a building which may have a ghost watching you. What is it?

6. How does one of our most popular San Diego parks owe its existence to a private citizen? And how does a legendary "white deer" tie in to that same park?

7. What is a tecolote and where's the canyon of that name?

8. What canyon is linked to San Diego's major earthquake fault?

9. Where are two parks built on reclaimed land?

10. A main entry into Mission Trails Park is Fr. Junipero Serra Trail. How do you pronounce his first name?

URBAN SAN DIEGO

1. Chollas Park

Here's a modest and popular park out in East San Diego, under the auspices of San Diego Park & Recreation Department. It shows what can be done when the will is strong, considering it's been developed from the old dump. Now you can walk around the lake under a canopy of eucalyptus, picnic, watch the geese squawking along the shore, or toss a line in and catch your dinner (that is, if you're 15 and under). Or invite the gang for an outdoors shindig, with BBQs, horseshoes or volleyball. One thing you can't do is swim.

The mostly level trail around the lake and over the dam is 0.8 mile and you'll find fitness types making a few laps around. On the north side are a couple of side trails up through the chaparral. Strollers and wheelchairs can maneuver here without too much hassle. And your pooch on leash is O.K. too.

You'll find two areas to park near the lake. The eastern entry is the main one, with good rest rooms, information booth, fishing piers. The western goes into **Gloria's Mesa**, named after Councilwoman Gloria Demers-McCool, a key player in getting this park developed. The dam is located at the south end as is a large pavilion for a group event.

There's more to come here, including a 9-hole golf course and playing fields. And let's hope, more walking trails.

How to get there: Take College Grove Drive between College Avenue and 54th.

2. Balboa Park ✤✤

This is the cultural and fun center of the city. On any Sunday the crowds abound on the Prado near the fountain, with jugglers, dancers, museums and small cafes. Lots of fun without spending a nickel should you choose to amble here and there. Make an early visit to the information center, just off the Plaza de Panama, with the striking statue of El Cid facing the Museum of Art.

My first visit to the park a few decades back was driving in from Park Boulevard on Laurel (you could do that then) and being enthralled by the Spanish-style architecture, the trees, and the lighting which gave it a Cervantes feeling.

The park is the magnet for locals and visitors, and cameras get a workout. You can see amazing contrasts in the foliage, from natural, chaparral hillsides in Florida Canyon to lots of trees and blooming plants, much of this courtesy of Kate Sessions, horticulturist a century ago who transformed this from semi-arid to the gem it now is. A beautiful park overlooking Mission Bay from Pacific Beach is named after her.

Weekdays are blissfully uncrowded; weekends will have lots of people and activities. Parking can be a problem, so take public transportation if possible or ride a bike. Plan to arrive early, e.g., before 1 p.m. or park either on the eastern side (Park Boulevard) or western (6th Avenue).

Here are museums for nearly every taste, some free on Tuesdays (check Sunday papers for which ones). Of special relevance to the outdoors world are the **Natural History Museum**, with on-going displays, special exhibits, and nature movies in their new section and the **Reuben Fleet Space Theater**, with IMAX movies bringing nature to life on the huge screen. For a distinctly different outdoors evening, take in a Starlight musical. And oh, yes, there's a zoo here, where you can stroll for fascinating hours.

The park has a long tradition of enjoyment of natural beauty. For example, for the 1935 Exposition, in **Zoro Gardens**, beside Reuben Fleet Space Theater, au natural was the wardrobe for a group of nature lovers. For some other explorations, try these:

Rose and Cactus Gardens. From the fountain area walk over the footbridge to the east side of Park Boulevard and you'll have the place mostly to yourself. Take your choice for poking around and enjoying – roses or cacti. You can make it educational as many of the plants are identified. The rose garden is colorful anytime; the cacti bloom April-June. Nearby is a latticed gazebo - a good place for contemplation.

Botanical Building. Right behind the reflection pool is this garden of greenery, with frequent seasonal changes.

Walk over to **Spanish Village** for a pleasant perusal of the architecture and artists' offerings. Toward the **San Diego Zoo** is the entrance to the pint-size railroad, and for some other old-time amusement near there is the full-sized carousel.

Almost hidden between the Mingei and Museum of Man is **Alcazar Garden**. Huge spreading trees, flowers, fountains and the breathtaking **California Tower** make this one of those special places. Walk over toward the **Organ Pavilion** across the wooden footbridge and take the steps down into **Palm Canyon**. The trees never cease to amaze as you wander down into the canyon (stop when you see the archery signs). You'll find a pathway leading up the other side to the **House of Pacific Relations**, with cottages of many countries.

Wander across the Laurel Street (Cabrillo) Bridge to the grassy stretch along 6th Avenue. Walk left for fine views of the Coronado Bridge, right among the trees where you'll see many people playing and picnicking.

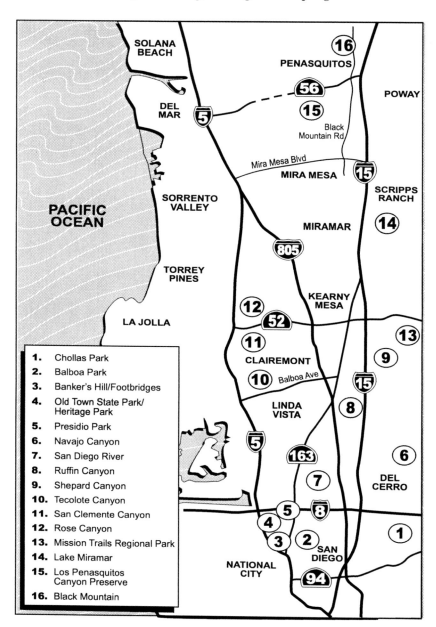

URBAN, SAN DIEGO - HIKING

1. Chollas Park
2. Balboa Park
3. Banker's Hill/Footbridges
4. Old Town State Park/ Heritage Park
5. Presidio Park
6. Navajo Canyon
7. San Diego River
8. Ruffin Canyon
9. Shepard Canyon
10. Tecolote Canyon
11. San Clemente Canyon
12. Rose Canyon
13. Mission Trails Regional Park
14. Lake Miramar
15. Los Penasquitos Canyon Preserve
16. Black Mountain

Just west of the bridge to the south is the much-visited dog-free area.

On the west side of Highway 163 is a trail that runs through the park's length. Pick it up by (a) walking down from dog-free area south of Laurel Street and under the bridge; (b) from north of Laurel and the lawn bowling courts; (c) across from the restrooms or (d) across from Upas street down a paved walkway to either the dirt trail or a pedestrian bridge across the highway. Popular with joggers, this trail goes up into Hillcrest onto Vermont Street.

On the eastern part of the park, **Florida Canyon** has several trails out through the chaparral, either from (a) the Park Boulevard side, (b) across the canyon near Texas Street and behind the Morley Field tennis courts, (c) Zoo Drive at Florida Street, or (d) way south at Florida Street and Pershing Drive.

From the **Morley Field** area walk along the grassy areas east of the pool, by Pershing Drive and 28th Street. This is an area of courses, for competitive Frisbee, bicycle racing course, and golf. Also beautiful homes in Burlingame.

Not part of the park but right at the north end is the **SD Historical Society's Marston House**. This is a 100 year old residence built for George Marston, first president of the society (you'll read more about him under Presidio Park). It's fully set-up as it was then, with place setting in the dining room as you see during the docent tours (Friday-Sunday). Stroll the placid gardens and down the stone-lined walkways through the trees to the bottom (by Highway 163). For tour info 619-2298-3142. Get there from Upas Street west from 6th Avenue.

3. Bankers' Hill/ Footbridges

Here's a hike (or several) that combines nature, history, a couple of fun foot-bridges, and potentially a good workout, and all right in the heart of the city. It's called the Bankers' Hill section, which puts it between the airport and Balboa Park. Here's a suggested itinerary, with a variety of options to fit your inclinations and energy.

If driving, park your car on Spruce Street, up by Balboa Park at 6th or any-where down to Front Street. Head south on 1st Street. At Palm walk over the bridge high above **Maple Canyon**. This gives you an impressive view of the bay and Point Loma as well as the canyon far below. Soon on your right will be the Self Realization Fellowship, with its memorable white structures. A related structure is the landmark at Encinitas South end, by Swami's Beach (see Coastal section)

Take a right on Maple. Walk to the end at Albatross. Here, easy to miss, locate the plaque, from **The Early Birds**, marking this as the place where Waldo Waterman made his first glider flight in July of 1909.

Retrace your steps back east on Maple to 6th Avenue. Go right one block, then left at Laurel and walk across the magnificent **Laurel Street Bridge**, with views in all directions, including the most dramatic structure in Balboa Park, the **Museum of Man**. Head back across the bridge to 6th, right and then left at Quince. You'll see a white footbridge straight ahead, built in 1905. Again fine views. Walk across the bridge (your kids may make this trip more than once), and at the west end turn right (you're on 3rd Street). About 100 feet along, you'll see a sign and trail heading down to **Maple Canyon**.

Walk down the trail, carefully in this section, through a thick pack of trees. (Or you can skip this option and stay on the street level.) This is dog-friendly, on leash. The trail levels off and heads down toward the bay. The environment totally changes as you stroll through the canyon, with an occasional stream, tall palm and Eucalyptus trees, prickly pear, likely blooming in spring, and a variety of shrubbery. The trail leads under that high 1st Street bridge you walked across before, with a very different perspective. It ends at Maple Street.

Here you have more options, such as a walk down to the **Embarcadero** for coffee on the outer deck where the harbor cruise boats embark. Otherwise to stick with the bridges, take a right on North Arroyo Street, then right on Dove, then a short jog left and again on Dove with a slight uphill walk to Spruce Street, noting some striking homes along the way. At Spruce Street, walk up on the north side under a canopy of greenery. At Brant you've arrived at the **Spruce Street Suspension Bridge**. This one sways as you walk across it, which may titillate some nerves.

This could end your trek, if you parked right here. Or you could walk over to Balboa Park, or reward your workout with a stroll south on 4th Street to Quince Street and up to 5th Street to Max's Deli or to Karen Krasne's Extraordinary Desserts. (FYI, parking by the bridge along 4th Street has no meters.)

These bridges date back to the early 1900s when local residents across the canyon wanted to ride the streetcars to town, but couldn't get over to pick them up. The solution? These bridges. May they long remain.

4. Old Town State Park/Heritage Park ❖❖

A popular locale for an amble through our early history - cemetery, casas, wagons - and Latin flavor - shops, restaurants, mariachis. **Old Town Park** is full of locals and tourists enjoying the ambience while dining or taking in the buildings, museums and shops oriented to the early days of San Diego. Often, such as on Cinco de Mayo (May 5) it will be especially crowded and the best way there on weekends is by bike or trolley, with a station right there.

A good starting place is the **Visitors' Center**, on the north side of the plaza. They can suggest a self-guided tour or a guided introductory tour departing from here daily. Otherwise get a map and pick out any of the historic places for a visit on your own – **Seeley Stables, Casa de Bandini** (once a hotel, now a colorful restaurant), **Casa de Estudillo, Mason Street School, Whaley House** (watch out for the ghosts), and more.

At the south end off San Diego Avenue, is the old **El Campo Cemetery**. You can stroll through here and learn a lot about the early days by reading the grave stones and related information. Locate the grave of Juan Mendoza for some juicy facts about Cave Couts, a key player in the mid 1800s, both in Old Town and up in Vista at Rancho Guajome. He crossed words with Mendoza, plugged him (some said murdered) and here lies Senor Mendoza.

Heritage Park, at the southeast end of Old Town, has many historic buildings that were moved here. It is a County Park, created in association with SOHO (Save Our Heritage Organization). Some buildings and shops will be open, plus a B&B for overnight stay or afternoon tea. Nearby is the **Mormon Battalion building**, with history of their trek west. For more about that group, head up the hill to...

5. Presidio Park ❖❖

Just above Old Town, among the charming old homes of Mission Hills, is this lovely park. From Old Town walk east past Casa de Bandini onto Mason Street to the dead end and onto the trail heading up. The white building so predominately seen from I-8 by Old Town, is one of the area's most recognizable landmarks. Many people think it's the original mission (wrong, that's out by the Stadium), or at least some mission, but it's actually **Junipero Serra Museum**. Lots of history has occurred here, and a major archaeological dig has been going on for years just west of the museum.

You can make a good day enjoying the many possibilities of this small park. Enjoy the museum, picnic on tables placed throughout the park or on the well-kept lawns, take in the views of Mission Bay and the ocean. Head over to the gazebo where a wedding may be going on. This pretty area is popular for family picnics and games. Nearby is the striking statue of Gustavo Diaz Ordaz, former president of Mexico.

And throughout, you and your family can absorb many important aspects of San Diego history. Walk over to the tall flagpole and bay overlook. This is a California Registered Historical Landmark. The plaques will explain that this was first fortified in 1838, became **Fort Dupont** in the 1846 war with Mexico, renamed as Fort Stockton in 1847 and abandoned the next year. The Mormon Battalion, 500 men and 80 women - battalions were different in those days – arrived here in January 1847. (For more about those times read *The Year of Decision, 1846* by Pulitzer Prize winner Bernard DeVoto).

After you've checked out the museum area, head eastward into the canyon via the trail beside the museum, from the gazebo area, or winding back from Taylor Street. The many palm trees and isolation from the other sections above make this a pleasant spot for a relaxing meander.

Continue east up the hill to another well-landscaped and lightly-visited park section, providing more good picnicking, views, and frequent solitude (ignoring the steady freeway hum). Here also you'll come upon the memorial to "The White Deer of Mission Hills." Look for a bench, three large rocks, and a concrete watering hole with imbedded animal tracks. Was there such a deer, or is that only legend?

So how did Presidio Park come into being? A leading businessman and civic stalwart named George Marston (old-timers will recall the evolution of Marston's-Broadway-Macy's) had a vision about what this barren hillside could actually be. He bought it, constructed the museum, and had all the lovely trees, lawns, and shrubs installed. In 1929 he gave it all to the city, choosing as dedication day July 16, the date Junipero Serra founded the first California mission in San Diego in 1769. You can visit Marston's home at 6th Avenue & Upas Street.

How to get there: (a) Take the Trolley to Old Town and walk over to Mason and up to the park near the flagpole. (b) From the west end of I-8, take the Taylor Street exit and right. The first turnoff left heads to the eastern, upper park section and parking lot. The second brings you to the canyon. The third takes you up Presidio Drive to the museum area.

6. Navajo Canyon/Adobe Falls

The city has many canyons which provide near access for a quick outdoors getaway right in the heart of the city. Out by the State College area is the **Navajo Canyon Open Space Park**, which goes from Waring Road down to Adobe Falls Road next to I-8. Start from either top or bottom and you can have a good workout, as it follows the creek as it heads down to the valley. You'll pass many palm and oak trees, likely see many rabbits, birds and squirrels, plus the occasional coyote, and in spring, might see water coursing through creating the falls and down into San Diego River. Lots of prickly pear and fields of daisies will bloom in May or June.

If you start at the top off Easton Court hike down on the dirt road behind the church. The first part is the steepest and it's not bad at all. In about fifteen minutes the main dirt road stays left and continues onto Adobe Falls Road.

Take the less-traveled right fork, dirt road plus trail and you're on the west side of the creek, ending up at Waring Road across from the tennis courts.

How to get there: From the top. I-8 to Waring Road, to red light at Edgridge, right and becomes Easton Avenue. Turn right into cul de sac and parking. The dirt road/trail is off the church parking lot. From the bottom. Best for parking is at Adobe Falls Road just east of Waring Road and the creek. Some parking on dirt off the road (across the street from the hotel).

7. San Diego River (Mission Valley)

Once upon a time the river was a major force in Mission Valley. Some will recall the occasional floods which filled roadways, parking areas, and buildings. With channeling and other control methods, combined with low rainfalls, we've not experienced much spreading water from the river. Plans are in progress for the San Diego River Park which could include Mission Trails, Santee, Lakeside and perhaps beyond.

In Mission Valley a walking path goes along both sides of the river. Here will be joggers, strollers and bird-watchers maneuvering by the heavy river foliage. The stress on natural habitat makes it rich for birds, but limits the river-perusing experience. Speaking of river experiences, many years back, following one of those heavy rains, a crony and I canoed from Qualcomm Stadium down to the flood channel, a memorable, if not repeated, paddle.

You have several options for getting onto the wide, paved walkway. As parking can be a problem here, you may want to hop the trolley. Get off at Hazard Center, walk over to the walkway from either west or east (Hazard Center Drive East) of the station, walk along the north side of the river up to Qualcomm Way, cross over to the other side, and back and you'll have had one healthy stroll. Or get off the trolley at Mission Valley station, stroll a few feet over to the walkway and have yourselves a good loop. For auto types, wheel into the parking lot just east of Hazard Center and start walking east. Wheelchair access from the lot. Walk past the informational kiosk and along the north side of the river to Rio del Este or Qualcomm Way, cross over and walk back on the south side for a loop back over to the lot. Observe the crossing signs as these are busy streets. And if you need some refreshment after your walk, you have your choice of about 2000 cafes right in this area. Dogs on leash O.K.

How to get there: (a) 163 to Friars Road east, to Mission Center Road right/ south, then left at Hazard Center Drive into parking lot. (b) Take Qualcomm Way to Rio San Diego (north side of river) west 2 blocks to Rio del Este, right on Station Village Lane for parking. On the river south side, turn from Qualcomm Way west to Caminito del la Reina (some street parking there).

From the west you can park west of Mission Center Road on Hazard Center Drive (north of river) or Camino del Reina (south of river with several public entries).

8. Ruffin Canyon

This is a lightly-hiked canyon leading down from Serra Mesa to Friars Road. The trails are obvious but in need of maintenance (the newly-formed Friends Of are working on it). Wear lug soles (and a walking stick will be helpful) as several places are on the rugged side. While a park sign is at the end of Ruffin Road, a better way down is roughly a block west from there. Locate a trail on the south side of Gramercy, east of Pasternack, with a sign at the east side of the barricade. This takes you down into an extensive palm grove and then to meet up with the trail from Ruffin Road. Hike down as much as you choose, through palm tree clusters, chaparral, and lots of wildflowers. A long stretch is on the rocks of the sometime stream bed, finally ending at a private development near Friars (with a tunnel undercrossing ahead).

How to get there: Friars Road to Mission Village Drive, up hill to Ruffin Road, turn in to left or continue on a short distance to the barrier, just before Pasternack Place. You can also get into the canyon from the end of Sandrock, on the trail past the mini-park. Another trail enters from Mobley Street with sometimes a locked gate. Other entries at end of (a) Shawn Avenue and (b) Chauncey Drive.

9. Shepard Canyon

Residents of Tierrasanta not only have ready access to the many pleasures of Mission Trails Park, they have this pocket canyon right in the midst of this bustling community. This once was the military's Camp Elliott and you may see some warning signs on some off-trail areas to be alert for possible unexploded ordnance.

Walk down into the canyon from various pathways and you're on a wide path through willow, pepper, and eucalyptus trees and in spring plenty of flowers. Perhaps some ducks by a small pond. Continue east among chaparral to Via Vallarta.

How to get there: Take Highway 52 east to Santo Road exit south. Access is east from Santo Road. Also off Antigua east of Santo; west of Santo at Amaro; from Vallarta.

10. Tecolote Canyon

The city's Tri-Canyon Park System adds up to about 2000 acres of open space right in the midst of the north city communities. They consist of **Tecolote, San Clemente** and **Rose Canyons**, all with a long history of Kumeyaay Indian activity.

Snaking for miles through Clairemont is this natural canyon, traversed by **Tecolote Creek** and home to lots of wildlife. The 915 acres (including golf course) in the canyon were saved from development largely through the efforts of a determined band of citizens. The name comes from the Indian name for the owls that call this home.

It's one long, mostly south-to-north canyon plus several finger canyons. With many trails leading into and through it, it provides a good getaway without leaving the city. This is mostly chaparral-covered hillside, with occasional groves of oaks and palms close to the creek. In spring you'll see daisies across the canyon floor and cacti in bloom; in winter toyon, with those bright red berries.

This is a popular locale for young explorers, many who live on or near the rim. Those who live in Clairemont, Linda Vista and Kearny Mesa can make their way into the canyon for a short getaway or a substantial trek, generally within a short stroll or five minute drive from home.

"Home base" for the canyon is from the south end on Tecolote Road east from I-5. Here is the **Nature Center**, a good starting place for information, parking, and an active recreational area. Be sure to pick up a map here. The center hosts various events and nature workshops for kids. You can start hiking in from here, and bite off as much as you choose. It's hard to get lost in Tecolote as it's all within the canyon. A short distance in you'll see the striking architecture of **University of San Diego** on the hill to your right. A side trail will take you right up there for a close look at some of the buildings and possibly some refreshment at the café, with outdoor tables looking out onto the canyon.

Still on the trail, walk along east of the 18-hole executive golf course and driving range. This is a good turnaround spot for about a 3-hour hike. Or continue up to the right where the trail comes out way over at Genesee. These give you a further workout and some interesting scenery along the way.

Coming from the north end, you'll head down from near Clairemont Mesa (take Genesee south two blocks to Bannock, right to Community Park). Park in lot or on street. Marked trail (#1 on the park map) starts behind the tennis court and grassy area. After about a mile a trail comes in from Genesee, with the main trail continuing for about 1 mile to Balboa. Return for a 3-mile trek.

To continue south is tricky as you either have to hike up and cross Balboa (use lights at Clairemont Drive) or work your way through the creek underpass. Continue following the creek with lots of oaks, palms and blooming shrubs. Finally you arrive at another busy thoroughfare, Mt. Acadia Boulevard, at the golf course entry. Turn around and you'll have done roughly a 6-mile hike. A major deficiency is failure to continue the main trail over or under Mt. Acacia Boulevard.

Following are some other places where you can head down into the canyon. Stick to the trails, as this is home to many patches of poison oak. Dogs on leash are O.K. on most trails, though some may indicate only early morning or late afternoon. These are generally from south to north.

East Side, Coming up Linda Vista Road (From Morena Boulevard)

For USD students. Walk down past football field and down past basketball arena, then down along power lines to end to entry sign to canyon.

Left at Via Las Cumbres (#8 on the park map). At Caminito del Cervato see sign and trail heading down (as they all do). Marked entry The trail splits about 200 feet in, with the left the usual route past the eucalyptus grove and to the main trail down to the Visitors' Center. The trail to the right is a good choice as well. Likely spreading daisies in spring.

Left on Tait, and right to Kelly Street and the Kelly Street Park (#7 on the park map), about 6600 block, parking only on the street. This is a small but pleasant park, with restrooms, picnic tables, and great view across the canyon. Catch the trail down across the park by the tall trees. A good walk in, meeting main trail near south end of golf course.

East Side, North Along Genesee (From Linda Vista Road)

Left on Osler (#6on the park map). Park by ball field on right. Walk past picnic tables to trail heading out through chaparral.

To Marlesta (#4 on the park map). Turn right and park on street near Mesa College stables (bet you didn't know Mesa had any). Parking is tough during the week as it's at a premium at Mesa. Walk across Genesee at light and to the left along this very busy road (be careful) down at the large sign. Quickly you'll see a major storm drain and stream, running rapidly after rain. The water makes this one of the greenest parts of the canyon, with huge palm trees, high shrubbery, poison oak (stay on wide main trail). Here, deep in the canyon it's quiet. Hike way in to the golf course and down to the nature center. No dogs, except early or late, on leash only.

To Boyd, west about six blocks, becomes Acworth. Park in lot (#5 on the park map). Trail heads out into open meadow, then down to meet the trail from Marlesta.

Continue north from Boyd/Acworth to Mt. Acadia to right. At Mt. Ararat, turn left and then right on Brundage. See sign behind Holmes Elementary School (#3). Hike down to meet the main south/north trail. (Alternative is take Balboa up to Mt. Everest, right, to Mt. Ararat right and right on Brundage.)

Further north to Chateau Drive. Parking on residential streets only. Start at sign and hike down to meet main trail.

West Side

From Balboa at Clairemont Drive. Park on Clairemont, walk east a short way along the south side of Balboa and see entry off to right just past small shopping mall. Goes down to pick up main trail to south. Or walk down on north side of Balboa to entry and walk north.

11. San Clemente Canyon

Paralleling Highway 52 between Clairemont and University City is this 467-acre San Diego City park. Because it's within a five-minute drive from either of those communities, and only slightly longer for others, this is a popular place for hiking, biking, picnicking and poking around. Along its trails you can enjoy a short amble or a hearty six mile loop hike. Take the kids for a picnic under the spreading sycamore trees and watch them have a ball climbing trees and cris-crossing the stream.

This is a good place to visit anytime of the year, but it's especially colorful in late fall. The sycamores display broad golden and gold-green leaves even later. Holly/toyon is in full bloom with clusters of red berries.

Start your visit at any of 3 developed areas, with parking lots, picnic tables and restrooms. Dogs on leash are O.K. From the Genesee entrance, hike 1.25 miles east to I-805, where the park ends and Miramar starts. You'll be hiking in heavily shaded areas, with benches from which to contemplate the surroundings (not necessarily in silence as Highway 52's traffic is within earshot). Or go west, cross under Genesee, and hike over to the Clairemont Mesa/Regents Road picnic areas and even further on to I-5. Along the way are trails into several side canyons and up into Clairemont or University City.

At this end is a kiosk with park information, including why it's properly called **Marian Bear Memorial Park**. Marian Bear was an active community leader and a key player in getting this park established, instead of the freeway originally planned to go right through where you'll be hiking. If you had met Marian about 25 years back, as I did, you might have been fooled by her gentle demeanor. She was, however, dedicated to her cause and tireless in her pursuit of it. And now we all get to enjoy Marian Bear Park (illustrating once more that one person can indeed make a difference).

At the start of the trail heading west from the picnic area are pamphlets (maybe) explaining the areas noted by trail markers. With low water flow, you can walk across the stream bed, past a large holly section, and cross the creek again. Soon a side trail down to the right leads along the creek and over to **Rose Creek**. If you want a real workout, hike up into **Rose Canyon** and loop back along Regents Road (or keep heading east and loop over at Genesee). Or walk south and you'll see where bikers make their way over to the paved bike path on the west side of I-5. The trail crosses back over Rose Creek to join up with the original trail. You can make a loop back along the trail on the south side of **San Clemente Creek**, with large live oak trees providing the shade on this side.

And as with that other river in Mission Valley, your guide holds the rare distinction of having actually canoed along San Clemente Creek. Again during a rare heavy rain stretch, Wes and I paddled (and frequently carried) his canoe down to Rose Creek. I don't recommend it.

How to get there: From Highway 52 turn off onto either Genesee (then right to entrance) or Regents Road/Clairemont Mesa Boulevard north (entrances east and west off road).

12. Rose Canyon

The third in the city's canyon trio is the one traversed by Rose Creek and the Santa Fe Railroad. The name has a certain other acclaim as it's our #1 earthquake fault (though we haven't had a serious quake in the last century or two). It separates University City from the UTC/Golden Triangle community and provides valuable undeveloped space for flora, fauna and us crowded urban dwellers. It's readily accessible for hikers, joggers and bikers and is joined by **San Clemente Canyon** before continuing to Mission Bay in Pacific Beach.

The most popular section starts from near University City High on Genesee. Hike in and you're in a lovely garden, developed by the La Jolla Golden Triangle Rotary Club. Here a short loop trail winds past markers describing the foliage. Continuing west, the trail is through a heavily wooded section (oaks, sycamores) and then mostly onto open terrain. This is a peaceful, rejuvenating retreat from the busy communities up on the hillsides. Several side trails provide excursions, and Amtrak and Coaster trains add some flavor.

At the western end, the creek turns south, with the trail on the east side and the paved bikeway over to the west. (That has a lot of two-wheel traffic from Santa Fe Street to Gilman along I-5.) At Highway 52 (here it gets noisy), you can (carefully) make your way along the edge of the concrete river channel, or even trot down and up to the bikeway. South of Highway 52 you can keep wandering with the creek or head east up onto San Clemente Canyon (hike in here up to Regents or Genesee and loop on over to Rose Canyon for a good day's workout).

Here are some other suggestions for getting into Rose Canyon (dogs on leash are O.K.): East end at University High. Highway 52 to Genesee north, cross Governor Drive to highschool. No parking on street, but on weekends park in highschool lot. Enter on north side of highschool, or cross street (carefully, very busy street) to the marked canyon entry. You can also find a trail down a bit north on Genesee and on west side.

South side. Just west of Governor Drive, turn north on Ratcliffe, then right on Condon and left on Tony Drive. This takes your right to the canyon edge with a short steep trail down to the main east-west trail.

South side, Regents Road. Highway 52 to Regents north to end. Lots of parking here. Hike down through thick chaparral to main trail.

Southwest corner. Roundabout entry. Governor Drive to west end, left on Stresemann, left on Bothe to end. Hike in a short distance to the west and meet the main trail just north of the concrete channel. Loop around to the north and come up the Regents Road trail for a good workout.

North side. Opposite the above Regents Road entry. I-5 to Nobel, east to Regents, south to end. (Observe the signs.)

13. Mission Trails Regional Park ❖❖

For San Diegans who want to experience a lot of the great outdoors, it's hard to beat the convenience of **Mission Trails**, one of the nation's premier urban parks. Most of us can get to some part of this sprawling 5800-acre park within a half hour drive. And once there, depending on your choice, and there are many, you can transfer your mind and body from the hectic freeway world to one of wide open meadows, bubbling streams, a lake, historic oak-covered gathering spots, and challenging peaks. Whew, all that with just a short drive!

If you haven't yet discovered the park's **Visitor Center**, you have a treat ahead. The center blends in beautifully with the surroundings so well it was honored with an Orchid in the annual Orchids and Onions Program. The center (open from 9 a.m.-5 p.m. every day) is a good place to make your first acquaintance with the park, with staff to make suggestions, nature displays inside and out, rotating art exhibits, a gift shop and the most inviting library in the county. The hands-on exhibits, with nature sounds and native American displays, will whet your exploring appetite. Get a map and some suggestions from the rangers or volunteers there. Ask about their guided introductory hikes, every Wednesday and weekends.

Or wander down the road to the developed area around the **Old Mission Dam** across the **San Diego River**. Much of the dam still remains, crafted by Kumeyaay Indians 180 years ago to provide water for the **Padres Mission de Alcala** 6 miles below. You'll see signs of the aqueduct they sent the water along in. Recently completed out near the old dam is a new viewing terrace and exhibits, including a hands-on model and an orientation map for this part of the park.

Just north of the dam is the first-rate **Kumeyaay Lake Campground**, set right next to the lake. So far the fishing report is so so, but the relaxation report is highly favorable. You can take a casual stroll along the trails around the lake, checking out the ducks as you peer through the trees. It's an easy walk over to the old dam or across a bridge and you're out there with the rest of the park at your disposal.

The eastern side of Mission Trails at **Lake Murray** and **Cowles Mountain** is among the most visited section and well-known to many. Cowles is the prominent peak east of Mission Gorge. The trails up are about as accessible as they get, which makes it popular with hikers and joggers of all types. If you don't mind traffic, this can give you a good workout with little hassle and you'll find some great views all around.

Cowles was once known as Black Mountain, which would have made it at least Black #3 in the County, so I'm glad it switched back to Cowles. That name came from rancher George Cowles, as noted in *San Diego County Place-Names*, by Lou Stein. He omits the pronunciation, however, so I have to rely on Bill White's flyer from Park Headquarters, which says it is pronounced "kohls." True, almost everyone calls it "cow-ulls," but there's the official story.

NOTE: Parts of Mission Trails, most notably between Highway 52, Mission Gorge and Tierrasanta, were severely damaged by the October 2003 fires.

How to get there: (a) Take Highway 52 east to Mast exit, under freeway, then right; at Mission Gorge go right or south. You'll quickly see the sign off to the right; this takes you to the campground and dam. To get to the Visitors Center, continue south on Mission Gorge Road for about 3 more miles to the southern end of Fr. Junipero (hoo-NIP-er-o) Serra Trail. Turn right into the center. (b) From I-8 take Mission Gorge Road north, 4 miles to Junipero Serra and turn left. (c) To Mast Boulevard entry, Highway 52 to the Mast exit, turn right into the dead end and parking. (d) To Cowles Mountain, turn east from Mission Gorge Road to Golfcrest. Parking, restrooms and main trail are at Navajo. (e) To Lake Murray, I-8 to Lake Murray Boulevard north exit. Left at Kiowa Drive to large parking area, restrooms, picnic tables. Other entries will be noted below.

Here are a few options in the easy stroll category:

From the Visitor Center ...The Oak Grove Loop Trail (off Junipero Serra Trail) is a 1 mile stroll out through a section where many oak trees are working their way into adulthood. It's a pleasant hike out toward the imposing steep rising hills. The **Visitor Center Loop** is a bit more challenging as it heads down and along the San Diego River. Pick up the trail just where the road heads up to the Visitor Center follow it east and south as it loops down to the river and back to the center (cross over a concrete weir into Suycott Wash for lots more exploring).Try the **Climbers Loop** for a hearty workout.

From the Old Mission Dam parking area or new campground... Kids love this area as a large part of the old dam is still in place, with many oaks surrounding it. The whole area is ideal for poking around. Walk over either of the footbridges and stroll along the river – look for the Native American grinding stones – and out into the meadow or onto **Oak Canyon**. Loop over the other bridge back to the parking area. You can get to the dam from Fr. Junipero Serra Trail.

Oak Canyon Trail...meanders up along a creek, flowing well in the spring. Lots of oaks and climbing rocks along here. Lug soles will help your footing better than tennis shoes. You can easily make this a good workout.

From the Mast Boulevard entrance off Highway 52... The entry is clearly marked with a kiosk. Head out along the trails into an open meadow, with the left fork leading over to the dam area, the right to **Oak Canyon** and **Fortuna Mountain**.

From Tierrasanta... At the eastern end of Clairemont Mesa Boulevard is a parking lot, with trails heading off onto a variety of trails. (Pick up a map here). For an enjoyable short hike, cross the footbridge and head off to the left. This is a steady uphill climb to the **Rim Trail**. Take the left trail at the stone building and water tank and loop around back to where you can pick up a different trail down. Follow the signs, though they could be clearer. In spring you'll see lots of prickly pear and other wildflowers in bloom. (Alternative trailhead is from east end of Clairemont Mesa Boulevard turn right on Rueda and follow signs to trail head at Calle de Vida and Colina Dorado. Parking along street.)

Lake Murray... Here you'll have plenty of company as this is one of the most popular hiking or jogging areas in the park. From gentle stroll to good workout. Besides the main parking area, here are 2 other easy access points:

(a) Continue on Golfcrest past Najavo to become Murray Park Drive to park entry; (b) Continue north on Lake Murray Drive, then left on Lakeshore Drive.

You say you're up for more of a workout? O.K., try these, with lug soles, sun screen, a hat and water:

Kway Paay... From the campground or dam area. Kway Paay awaits your zest with a heavy-duty challenge. It's only 1.3 miles up from the entrance near the campground, or less from the trail directly across from the dam, but your blood will be pumping on that last leg up. Once you get your breath back, you will have views of much of the County. An alternative is to cross the river onto **Oak Canyon** and up to **Fortuna Mountain**, another serious workout.

Fortuna Mountain... Have you ever wondered what Miramar Naval Air Station looks like from the pilot's viewpoint? Hike up Fortuna and you'll get a good idea. (Actually there are two Fortunas, with the higher the more-visited.) You'll take in most of the San Diego urban area from here, as well as the Cuyamaca range to the east. Three primary access points: (a) a hard 2-hour hike from the old dam off Mission Gorge Road; (b) from Mast Boulevard entry, (c) from Tierrasanta, for my money a more pleasant hiking experience. Start out from the end of Clairemont Mesa Boulevard.

Cowles Mountain...1592'. The main trail up at Navajo Road & Golfcrest is widely used, by fitness fans, groups of families and friends, and solo hikers. You can find a quick reward after only a 20 minute hike, with a good view of Lake Murray. Keep on trekking to the top (about 90 minutes) and you get the whole view package.

Pyles Peak... From Cowles you can pick up a second peak, and find yourself all alone on the trail, by continuing over to Pyles Peak (1379'). This is a pleasant add-on, plus you can do a loop or two-car trek by heading down from Pyles to Mission Gorge (trail ends/starts just north of Golfcrest).

Cowles the back way... On the other hand, if you want to have a peaceful hike up to the same peak, try any of 4 alternative trails up from the north and east side. (a) **Mesa Road**. Take Highway 52 east to Mission Gorge Road. Turn south (or right) and then left on Mesa Road. Just past Big Rock Park is a kiosk and trailhead. As you hike in from here moderately upward through the chaparral, you might meet a few other people while you enjoy the quiet and views of Cowles, Santee Lakes, Grossmont College and beyond. The hike is 2.5 miles from Mesa Road to the peak, where you'll see all those hordes who have come up the main way. (b) **Mesa Road also**. Continue past the first trail head to the end and find another kiosk and trail head. Hike in here and soon you'll meet Trail 1. (c) **Barker Way**. Locate this trail by driving east from Golfcrest on Navajo Road, turning left on Cowles Mountain Boulevard, left on Boulder Lake and right on Barker Way, where you'll see a clearly marked kiosk and trail head. Park on the street and walk in and up to where the previous trails come in. From that "T" the final assault on Cowles Mountain is another 0.9 miles. (Most of us can do this without oxygen.)

14. Lake Miramar

This is located past **Miramar Marine Corps Air Station** and in the Scripps Ranch/Mira Mesa area. Because of the proximity to several communities, it gets lots of traffic. This is a developed park with areas for picnicking. A 5-mile paved trail winds around the lake, making it a favorite for fitness buffs, roller bladers, and joggers, with the more casual walkers also finding this a pleasant getaway. Dogs on leash O.K.

How to get there: I-15 to Mira Mesa Boulevard, east to Scripps Ranch Boulevard, right; left onto Scripps Lake Drive; then to entry off Scripps Lake Drive on the left.

15. Los Penasquitos Canyon Preserve ❖❖

Another treasure in our midst is this 3700-acre park. Easily accessible, Penasquitos (for short) offers trails, wildflowers, history, trees galore, a creek, and, oh, yes, a waterfall. In this world of increasing congestion and vanishing open space, this is a place that brings forth the accolade "Thank God it's there," with a lot of help from a pack of determined community activists and far-sighted political leaders who managed to set the canyon aside as a county/city park instead of packing a few thousand houses there.

A good starting place is a visit to the historic adobe/ranch and museum. The **Rancho Santa Maria de los Penasquitos** is the county's oldest residence, built in 1823 on San Diego's first land grant. (The plaque identifies it as the Johnson-Taylor Adobe House, built in 1862; the historians came up with the 1823 information after the plaque was installed.) This is a living museum, with exhibits and gift shop, and the setting for many events. Docents, sometimes dressed in historic garb, will explain the history and natural aspects of the park. To get here walk over from the main lot or drive in from Black Mountain Road just north of the stables on Canyonside Park Driveway. The parking lot is all the way in past the recreational fields.

Just off the eastern parking lot is the **Elberta Fleming Trail**, inviting for a first visit or for those not ready for a six mile hike. This a short loop that provides an enjoyable educational experience as it winds through the woods and along the creek, with natural highlights described in the brochure you can pick up at the entrance. Fleming was a dedicated advocate and educator.

Penasquitos Canyon runs from I-5 eastward to I-15 (and beyond), from Sorrento Valley to Poway and between Mira Mesa and Del Mar.

From the western end of Penasquitos Canyon...

Take I-5 north to the Sorrento Valley Road turnoff exit. Turn left and a quick right onto Sorrento Valley Boulevard Cross the railroad tracks, and drive east past the commercial section to a parking lot on the right. From here you can hike south into **Lopez Canyon** or under the road into Penasquitos. The two were formerly directly linked before the road bisected them, another unfathomable decision. Lopez is well worth a trek, but we're focusing on the other option.

Having underpassed, you can now enjoy a hike through mostly open terrain along the south side of the creek, with a couple of crossovers. Dogs are allowed on leash and if picked up after. Horses may be joining you and bikers as well (on main trails only, not side trails.)

Three miles in you'll have little trouble locating the falls, a series of cataracts tumbling through boulders. (O.K. it's not Niagara Falls, but it's closer.) Walk down the stone steps and you're right there at a good spot to enjoy the rushing waters, let the outside world pass by, and contemplate the meaning of life. Head back the same way and you'll have hiked roughly six miles, taking about 2-3 hours.

You can return a different way, by crossing over the rocks to the north side, then walking back along that side of the creek. Or, if you're up for more of a workout, keep walking east along trails on either side of the creek to the eastern entrance. The full round trip will be twelve miles and take perhaps 4-5 hours.

From the eastern end, heading west of Penasquitos Canyon...

Take I-15 to Mercy Road, head west a mile right into the parking lot (crossing Black Mountain Road). You'll see stables just to the north where you can rent a horse for a ride in the canyon.

The main trail heads west through a heavily wooded section. Trail markers will keep you advised about distance until about 3 miles along you'll arrive at the falls. You can stick with the main dirt road or walk closer to the river on several smaller trails, where you'll hear the sounds of the river while walking under large oaks and sycamores.

You'll see several opportunities to cross over to the north side. One of those is 2.2 miles along, where you'll find a touch of history. **Carson's Crossing** refers to the time back in 1846 when Kit and a U. S. Army contingent licked their wounds after being put upon up in San Pasqual Valley by a determined band of Californios who were not thrilled about the army showing up on their turf. (More in Inland Section).

From the eastern end, north side of Penasquitos Canyon...

Drive a bit further along on Black Mountain Road, turning left or west on Park Village Drive. After 1.5 miles turn left at Camino Ruiz. Here's you'll see a park kiosk and trail heading down into the canyon.

Walk west about 1.5 miles and you'll be at the boulders and falls. Rather than stay on the unshaded dirt road, locate the smaller shaded trails nearer the creek. For a loop hike, cross the creek at the falls, and return on the south side. Return to the north side via either **Carson's Crossing or Penasquitos Creek Crossing** which places you near the parking lot. Take a short walk to the west and pick up the main trail up to the lot. (And if you need some nourishment about this time, enjoy a picnic in that pleasant neighborhood park.)

From the eastern end heading further east of Penasquitos Canyon...

This is a newly completed section on the City part of Los Penasquitos, and a continuation of the **Trans Country Trail System**. This also opens up interesting options. The basic hike starts at the trailhead entry across Black Canyon Road from the main parking lot. The dirt trail for hikers, bicyclists and equestrians heads east and slightly uphill in the canyon. To the north is the sycamore-lined creek, and the busy and muted Mercy Road to the south. The first part is open and on a warm day you'll welcome the oak shade at a side road crossing the stream. Then oak trees provide shade as you cross over three new wood footbridges. You'll pass a lone palm and some prickly pear along the way, with lots of flowers in the spring. Then you cross under the I-15 bridge and the old bridge, part of the bike trail. The trail comes out at a paved road.

To the left decorating the tall wall is the **"Rock of Aegis,"** a series of paintings inspired by Kumeyaay petroglyphs. Then you're at a special place, the memorial to Cara Knott (murdered near here a dozen years back), with a gazebo and a cluster of oak trees. Return from here and you'll have done about a 90 minute stroll.

You can continue east around the Penasquitos Pump Station and walk along a historic path eastward, paralleling Poway Road to Sabre Springs Road and Spring Brook. Or you can start at that end and walk as far west as you choose.

Another access to the **Trans County Trail** is from the Park 'n Ride just east of I-15 at Scripps Poway Parkway. Locate the paved bike road at the corner (right at I-15 entry). Walk down and take the right road (e.g. don't go over the bridge). Locate the trail head entry and head west. For modest hikers leave one car at Los Penasquitos Park parking lot.

16. Black Mountain (Poway/Penasquitos)

This is the Penasquitos one, not the Ramona one. If you've driven along I-15 in the Poway area, you may have wondered about that obvious peak just to the west. This Black Mountain has hiking trails leading up to a potpourri of views: far off the ocean and mountain ranges; nearby the 5-mile long Los Penasquitos Canyon; immediately before the hang gliders which soar back and forth a few hundred feet from your vantage point (on my last visit up there, 14 gliders were at nearly eye level).

How to get there: I-15 to Mercy Road west to Black Mountain Road, right. Pass Highway 56 and Carmel Mountain Road to near end of road; see sign toward dirt/asphalt road to right around the north side of the mountain. Pass the glider area to the parking lot, hike up via two main paths, one winding through the chaparral, the other straight up a dirt access road. Allow roughly 90 minutes to get up there (and about 10 minutes back down).

Balboa Park - Museum of Man

Hiking - Urban San Diego

Presidio Park- Serra Museum

Chollas Park

Rose Canyon

Mission Trails Park - Fortuna Mountain looking toward Miramar

Los Penasquitos Canyon Preserve...Penasquitos Creek

Lopez Canyon

Old Town State Historic Park

San Clemente Canyon

CHAPTER 4

HIKING
SAN DIEGO INLAND

OVERVIEW

SOUTH

CENTRAL

NORTH

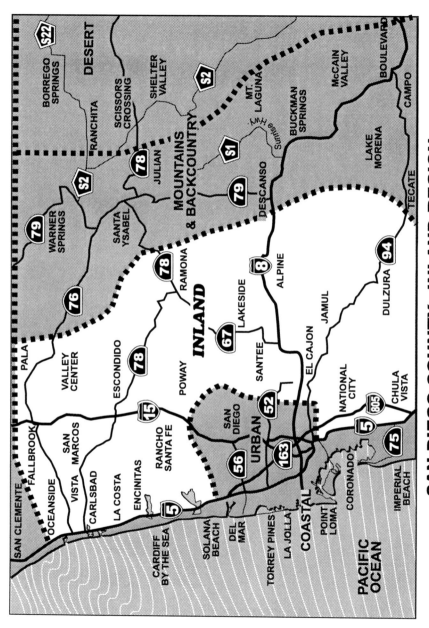

SAN DIEGO INLAND
HIKING OVERVIEW

To the body and mind which have been cramped by noxious work or company, nature is medicinal and restores their tone.

Ralph Waldo Emerson

Many scenic and recreational opportunities are located in the suburban communities and regions a short distance from center city. The diversity of the San Diego climate and geology makes for a wide variety of such settings: developed parks, local mountains and canyons, rugged hill country left mostly in its original state; even in this arid climate, rivers and reservoirs.

First try your hand at the Outdoors Quiz for the San Diego Inland region.

1. Where is Crest (as in San Diego County, not in toothpaste)?

   What new preserve is out there?

2. What dam is linked to the famous flood of 1916?

3. Daley Ranch is a fairly new park.

   (a) Which jurisdiction does it fall under?

   (b) Who was Daley?

4. Where is Elfin Forest? How did it get that name? What does it have to do with Mt. Israel and how did that get its name?

5. Mt. Gower – where is it, why's it called that, and what legendary sporting event occurred near there?

6. How do well-known names of history—Ramona, Bandini and Couts—relate to northern San Diego County?

7. Where is Mule Hill, how did it get its name, and what famed historical figures interacted here?

8. Why should the names Stelzer and Minshall be highly valued by San Diego outdoor enthusiasts?

9. Why is it called Mt. Woodson, and how does the name Archie Moore fit into a hike up the mountain?

10. Where the H____ is Hellhole Canyon and how did it get its name?

11. Why is it called Silverwood? And what's the absolutely best day to visit there?

Hiking - San Diego Inland

SAN DIEGO INLAND - SOUTH

1. Otay Valley Regional Park

This is a joint effort of the County of San Diego, San Diego City and Chula Vista to create a park extending from Otay Lakes to San Diego Bay. In addition to its value as a natural park and open space, the valley has some history. It was a natural site for native American communities. Father Juniper Serra set up his first camp here as he journeyed into now California to establish his missions, and cattle ranged on the California Ranchos here.

The eastern end of the Regional Park is **Otay Lakes County Park**. You can make an interesting day by heading out to this lake area. The park is heavily shaded, with plenty of good picnic spots overlooking the lake. You can stroll over to the dam and along trails downstream along Otay River. In spring with a heavy rainy season, the water surging over the dam is spectacular. This has high historical interest as this is where the predecessor dam broke in 1916 when **Hatfield the Rainmaker** plied his talents. Was it his efforts that brought the huge downpours? Who can say? This park has had some attempts at camping but presently this option is not available.

Back up the road is the **Arco Olympic Center**. This is one of only three such centers in the country and has sports facilities and residential areas for athletes honing their skills at such sports as soccer, rowing, and tennis. At the Visitor's Center will be films about the Olympics and the store sells related clothing and paraphernalia. Hosts lead jitney tours around the playing areas. A fun and informative visit.

From a departed hiking friend: "There's a nice path along the west side of **Lower Otay Lake Reservoir** accessible at many points and winding around the lake southward to the boat launch ramp. Beautiful colors on the lake and mountains in the late afternoon."

How to get there: I-805 to Telegraph Canyon Road east, becomes Otay Lakes Road, to Wueste, turn right; County Park is at the end.

2. Rice Canyon Open Space Preserve (Chula Vista)

This is a readily-accessible getaway in the midst of hustle. Hike into this peaceful, wide canyon and stroll whatever distance you choose, up to about a 4-mile round trip trek.

The well-marked eastern entry, across the road from Chula Vista's **Discovery Park** (restrooms here), has parking for autos and horse trailers. Check

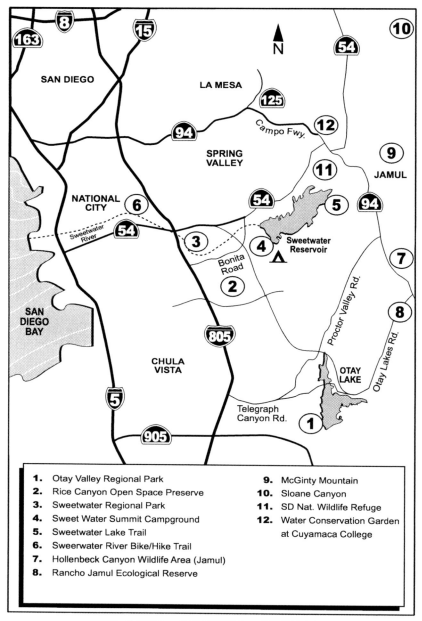

1. Otay Valley Regional Park
2. Rice Canyon Open Space Preserve
3. Sweetwater Regional Park
4. Sweet Water Summit Campground
5. Sweetwater Lake Trail
6. Sweerwater River Bike/Hike Trail
7. Hollenbeck Canyon Wildlife Area (Jamul)
8. Rancho Jamul Ecological Reserve

9. McGinty Mountain
10. Sloane Canyon
11. SD Nat. Wildlife Refuge
12. Water Conservation Garden at Cuyamaca College

INLAND, SOUTH - HIKING

the trail map on the kiosk and note the many trail options. Dogs O.K. on leash. Hike in and soon the roadway noise lessens, replaced by birds chirping. Lots of wildflowers on display in late spring. Maybe spot a coyote. Few trees along trail but an ocean breeze helps on a warm day. Take a side stroll over to the creek and unwind under the spreading willows.

About 2 miles along you'll arrive at Rancho Del Rey Parkway (it loops around). Cross over and continue to H Street (another parking area). Return back through the canyon or, for some variety, find the small foot path on the south side of H St. Behind Home Depot is a good trail back down into the canyon. Keep exploring and find your way back to the main entry.

How to get there: I-805 to H Street east. Turn left/north on Paseo Ranchero Road and a quick right on Rancho Del Rey Parkway. See preserve entry signs across from Discovery Park. Alternative is to park along H Street.

3. Sweetwater Regional Park

This starts just east of I-805 and extends eastward. Around the large golf course between Bonita and Sweetwater Roads are a series of trails, popular with hikers (dogs on leash O.K.) Pick it up any place along the path. Here are some options:

A. Start from the equestrian staging area just east I-805 and Plaza Bonita. Hike east to Conduit and loop over to the Sweetwater Road path, walking through the large Rohr Park. Continue back to the staging area and you'll have had about a 9-mile trek.

B. For a medium-long loop, start at Willow Street, walk up to either Central Avenue, Bonita Road (where it goes north, with trail under the bridge) or Conduit Road; cross over to the north side of the golf course and loop back, crossing the river just east of the Willow Street bridge.

C. For a pleasant but short walk, start at Otay Lakes Road, walk east to Bonita Road, cross under the bridge to the north side, walk west to Central Avenue, cross the river, then west to Otay Lakes Road.

How to get there: I-805 south to Bonita Road east. Western staging area is first street north, Plaza Bonita Road. Continue east on Bonita Road to pick up the other spots.

4. Sweetwater Summit Campground (Bonita)

Further east and on the south side of Sweetwater Reservoir is this first-rate county park for people and equestrian camping. Also here is a small picnic area, with tables, fire stands, lots of pines, a grassy playing field and view overlooking the lake. The campground is well-shaded, with complete restrooms. Trails, actually continuations of those around the golf course, lead here from Conduit Road, just to the west.

How to get there: I-805 south to Bonita Road east, becomes San Miguel Road. To Summit Meadow Road left.

5. Sweetwater Lake/Reservoir Trail
(Bonita-Rancho San Diego)

The County Park is the trailhead and equestrian staging area for access by riders, bikers and hikers (again with pooches on leash) to the Sweetwater (Lake/Reservoir) Trail. Pick up the eastward segment just inside the campground entry. Pass below the reservoir dike and then along the south side of the reservoir and eastward along the river. This is mostly open rolling terrain with views of the lake, with San Miguel Mountain dominant to the south. The trail continues for 4.5 miles to Highway 94, with the eastern part passing through the **San Diego National Wildlife Refuge**.

6. Sweetwater River Bike/Hike Trail (National City)

This is a wide paved path along the north side of the river, paralleling Highway 54 and continuing west to the boat launch ramp. It's popular for walkers, skaters and bikers. At first the traffic noise is obvious, then it gets slightly quieter. (This is not a walk in the woods.) It's not shaded but often there is a pleasant breeze coming off the ocean just ahead. Some sections have greenery and lots of birds.

How to get there: I-805 to Sweetwater Road East to Plaza Bonita Road right.

7. Hollenbeck Canyon Wildlife Area (Jamul)

Much is afoot in the Jamul area, with several agencies involved, including the San Diego Wildlife Refuge System (Federal), California Department of Fish & Game, the Multiple Species Conservation Program (County segment), and the Bureau of Land Management. The non-profit Jamul Trails Council actively supports improvements here.

The **Hollenbeck Canyon Wildlife Area** is a huge preserve on the east side of Highway 94, also known as the Daley Ranch Property (no connection to the Escondido Daley Ranch Preserve). Working with Lawrence & Barbara Daley, the County established this preserve in 2000, and was helped in large part by the Trust for Public Land. From the initial buy of 600 acres, the preserve is now at 3200 acres and managed by California Department of Fish & Game. With the **Jamul** and **Dulzura Creeks** running through here (on their way to Otay Lakes), this is an important project protecting critical habitat, including riparian, oak woodlands, marshes and grasslands.

From the **Honey Springs staging area**, for horse people and hikers, hike north along the wide path. A short stroll takes you to the **Dulzura Creek** with lots of oaks and sycamores (welcome on a hot day). The trail crosses the creek and then comes to a "T". Take your pick of which way to go; the right and shade to start, the left open.

For the right option, walk past the well-shaded and often dry creek for a good distance (perhaps a half-hour). The trail then heads off to the left and upward. This is pretty country, with rolling hills and valleys, with little shade except for the segments along the creek. Just as you leave the creek, a side trail off to the right takes you over to the creek again and then upward through a canyon. On the main trail, you can make a loop hike and come back on the other side of that "T" for a 6-mile workout. The highest peak in the area is 2,100 feet. Heavy-duty hikers can tie into the Daley Ranch Truck Trail.

For the left option, walk along the creek to a large water tank and big sycamores. The left fork heads over to Highway 94 and a locked gate. The right fork takes you on a dirt road northward beside a large drainage ditch. Soon you cross down and over the ditch, and to a wooded area along a creek. At the creek, the road heads west toward a large ranch complex (off limits). Take that about 200 feet along to another dirt road to the right across the often dry creek. Pass by some old corrals and continue on the dirt road eastward. You'll meet some other side trails but stay toward the right to complete the loop back to the "T" and over to the parking lot. This might be a better choice as you'll then end your hike in the shady area along the creek.

How to get there: Highway 94 (Campo Road) south through Jamul to Honey Springs Road (just before Otay Lakes Road). Turn left or east and quickly locate parking lot off to the left.

8. Rancho Jamul Ecological Reserve (Jamul)

Continuing the nature corridor to the west from Hollenbeck and Highway 94 is this major preserve along the **Dulzura Creek** and straddling both sides of Otay Lakes Road. As this is still undergoing environmental planning, this area is not yet accessible. Management is by California Fish & Game. More is yet to come here with a large segment of Proctor Valley targeted for preservation as well.

9. McGinty Mountain (Jamul)

A bit north from Hollenbeck is this preserve, established over 20 years ago with a 600-acre acquisition by The Nature Conservancy. Later land was acquired by The Environmental Trust with 360 acres set aside. Now managed by the U.S. Fish & Wildlife, it has no official trail system yet setup. However, the public can use existing trails.

From the small parking area, head in along the well-used trail through chaparral, then upward. Don't get too cocky– the peak you're hiking up is not yet McGinty. About 10 minutes along, and just before a gate (easy to miss), locate a trail off to the right. This is a series of switchbacks steadily going upward (watch out for the many rock erosion barriers). Take time to breathe while enjoying wide views of Mt. Miguel, Mt. Helix, Otay Mountain and on a clear day the ocean. This trail dead-ends at a dirt road. Take the left leg and soon you'll see the road continuing right up to the peak at 2304 feet. Allow about 3 hours round trip for the full journey.

As you hike up you can see another road further south. This is a shorter route up, but pretty plain hiking compared to the one just described.

How to get there: Take Highway 94 to Jamul. Turn left on Lyons Valley Road, then left on Jamul Road. Just past Mexican Canyon Road, 0.4 mile along, locate a small turnout on the right and a sign noting San Diego Wildlife Refuge. Three cars can fit into the turnout, and several others beside the road. The trail entry is off the right end of the turnout.

10. Sloane Canyon (Dehesa)

The **Sweetwater River** winds through this canyon, providing a scenic walk above the river and through a variety of natural habitat. Hike in on the dirt road which winds in nearly 3 miles, gaining 1000 feet in the process. A lovely hike with lots of wildflowers and birds. Recent acquisitions have added nearly 900 acres. Involved in preservation has been The Nature Conservancy and U.S. Fish & Wildlife Service. This area is managed by California Fish & Game. Upstream is the Loveland Reservoir. For a real change from the outdoors world, head over to nearby **Sycuan Indian Casino**.

How to get there: I-8 to Harbison Canyon Road, south, becomes Dehesa Road; at 6 miles from I-8, turn left onto Sloan Canyon Road (dirt), heads south 4 miles to end of road.

11. SD National Wildlife Refuge (Rancho San Diego)

The refuge area covers a lot of terrain from the east county down to the ocean refuges at San Diego Bay in Chula Vista and Imperial Beach. One eastern access point into the refuge is from Campo Road (Highway 94) in the Rancho San Diego area. Just off Highway 94 is a short road to the Water District. To the immediate left or south is a metal structure bridge, once the Campo Road bridge, now no longer in use. Walk across the bridge and you'll be in a rich area of woods and water-related habitat, from the Sweetwater River. You can spot the trail west along the north side of the river. Lots of foliage and birds. About 2 miles in is a footbridge; cross over and return along the south side of the river. Or just keep going west to the Sweetwater Reservoir.

How to get there: Highway 94 toward Jamul. Past Jamacha Road and large shopping complex, turn right onto Singer Road. Parking and footbridge to the left.

12. Water Conservation Garden at Cuyamaca College (Rancho San Diego)

This 4-acre garden features displays of water conservation, landscape planning and a living xeriscape demonstration. Admission is free. You can amble along several trails winding through the various habitats, displays and whimsical sculptures. Find a bench and let the peacefulness soak in or wander through the exhibits and add to your knowledge. If you're thinking about changing your backyard landscape, definitely visit here. The odds are good that someone can answer your questions or you can get really smart by attending one of their Saturday seminars. They have samples of various turf types and how much water they take; soil types and modifications; examples of trees, shrubs and cacti. Niceties such as very clean restrooms and a gift shop aren't bad either. The garden was selected by MWD (Metropolitan Water District) as one of 19 winners in their "Liquid Art" competition (out of over 100 entries). On weekends you might enjoy one of the concerts given here in this placid environment.

After you've adequately communed with the xeriscape world, take a short walk to the adjacent **Heritage of the Americas Museum**. This is mostly an indoors experience though they have two patios with plants identified. Drift slowly through the wings and enjoy the art, culture and history of the Americas. Open Tuesday-Saturday.

How to get there: Take Highway 94 to Highway 54 east (Jamacha Road); left on Cuyamaca College Drive; first right into parking lot.

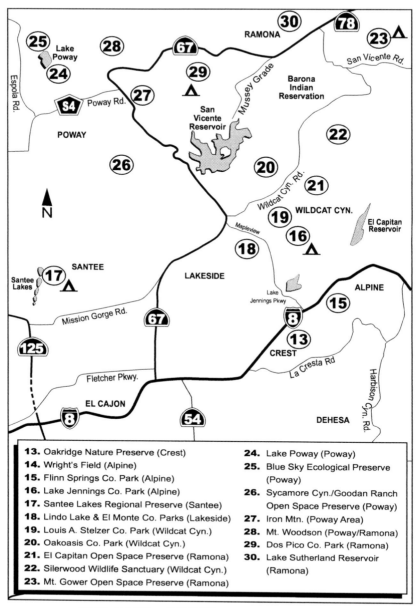

13. Oakridge Nature Preserve (Crest)
14. Wright's Field (Alpine)
15. Flinn Springs Co. Park (Alpine)
16. Lake Jennings Co. Park (Alpine)
17. Santee Lakes Regional Preserve (Santee)
18. Lindo Lake & El Monte Co. Parks (Lakeside)
19. Louis A. Stelzer Co. Park (Wildcat Cyn.)
20. Oakoasis Co. Park (Wildcat Cyn.)
21. El Capitan Open Space Preserve (Ramona)
22. Silerwood Wildlife Sanctuary (Wildcat Cyn.)
23. Mt. Gower Open Space Preserve (Ramona)

24. Lake Poway (Poway)
25. Blue Sky Ecological Preserve (Poway)
26. Sycamore Cyn./Goodan Ranch Open Space Preserve (Poway)
27. Iron Mtn. (Poway Area)
28. Mt. Woodson (Poway/Ramona)
29. Dos Pico Co. Park (Ramona)
30. Lake Sutherland Reservoir (Ramona)

INLAND, CENTRAL - HIKING

Hiking - San Diego Inland

SAN DIEGO INLAND - CENTRAL

13. Oakridge Nature Preserve (Crest)

The community of Crest spreads among the foothills between El Cajon and Alpine, just south of I-8. And that large undeveloped piece of land you see to your right as you drive east on I-8 is the new Oakridge Preserve (also known as Crestridge).

Oakridge is 2,600 acres of rolling hills, chaparral, some oaks, lots of boulders and a major addition to the County's natural open spaces. Combined with adjoining public land, it adds up to a total preserve of nearly 3,000 acres (for reference, about the same as Escondido's Daley Ranch). A variety of public and non-profit agencies were involved in saving this land from the bulldozers, as a development was imminent.

A key link in the County's Multiple Species Conservation Program, Oakridge is under the jurisdiction of the California Department of Fish & Game. Critical lead funding was provided by The Nature Conservancy. The nonprofit Back Country Land Trust was the key choreographer for making this project happen and has been designated by DFG as Land Manager. In that role they conduct surveys, restore habitat, maintain trails and provide educational programs.

NOTE: Oakridge was hit hard by the October 2003 fire, with many homes in Crest destroyed. These pre-fire descriptions will likely see some change during recovery.

The best way to get acquainted with Oakridge is to join one of the docent-led hikes along trails through chaparral and the extensive oak grove. This is the site of the original Oakridge Park, so-called by an earlier owner, Col. Fletcher. Going back further this was one of the original land grants, the El Cajon Ranchero.

On your own you can pick up trails from the entry point (noted below) and start in. As the preserve is nestled among hills, it's relatively easy to find your way back. You can make a modest hike or challenging one, up to the highest peak at 2,350 feet. (The low is about 600 so you can get a good workout here.) Lug boots and a hiking stick will prove valuable as you stroll through huge boulders and clamber across rock facings. From the peak you'll enjoy a 360 degrees splendid view of all the major landmarks — Mt. Helix, Lake Jennings, Viejas Mountain, Mt. Miguel, Tecate Peak, Cowles Mountain, plus an obvious earthquake fault.

This is home for wildlife - coyote, bobcat, fox, quail, and, oh yes, rattle-snakes. Here are Coastal Live and Engelmann Oaks, ceanothus, manzanita and a variety of chaparral. In the spring this area will be ablaze with color from many wildflowers. As more trails are developed, this will prove to be a valuable outdoors resource for many recreational uses — birdwatching, hiking, equestrian.

How to get there: Head out I-8 to the Greenfield/Crest exit at east El Cajon. Drive south to La Cresta Drive, left at the light. Head east 3 miles and turn left on Mountain View. Drive 1.1 mile to Horsemill, turn left and go to the end. The oak grove is a short distance to the left or you can follow a trail angling out to the right.

A second entrance is further along on Mountain View to Rios Road, turning left and driving to the end. From here walk past the gated entrance, and take the trail to the right and on up to the highest peak. From here you can also hike about 1.5 miles over to Flinn Springs County Park. (You can also hike in from the park, off old Highway 80 from Lake Jennings Park Road I-8 exit. From the furthest west parking lot, hike a short distance up the asphalt road and right onto the trail before the ball field.)

If you're coming from the east, turn off I-8 at Harbison Canyon Road. Follow the signs to Harbison. From the intersection with Arnold Way, drive 2.1 miles south to Frances Drive. Turn right, and onto Mountain View. Rios Road is 1.5 miles from Harbison.

14. Wright's Field (Alpine)

This is included as it's one of those important ongoing projects to preserve the last large undeveloped area in Alpine. And it has significant natural value and brings some history. The Back Country Land Trust, the non-profit group that had good success in getting Roberts Ranch into public ownership, is spearheading this effort. As of mid-2003, the area set aside is 230 acres, with a target of 500 acres. Keep alert for guided hikes here.

15. Flinn Springs County Park (Alpine)

This is a busy day use park with much picnic activity, including ball fields. Lots of trees here. For the hardy types, you can also hike over to the 3,000-acre **Oakridge Nature Park** which sits between Flinn Springs and the town of Crest. Just east of the park also is an interesting historical store and café, with products, books and memorabilia from the old days.

How to get there: I-8 to Lake Jennings Park Road and left onto Old Highway 80.

16. Lake Jennings County Park (Alpine)

Popular with fisherfolk, from boats or around the winding shoreline. Lots of woods and a nifty large campground high above the lake. Excellent views from up there. The road winds around the shore and you'll find the road plus occasional foot trails through the woods make this an appealing and close-in place to visit.

How to get there: I-8 east past El Cajon to Lake Jennings Park Road, north 1 mile.

17. Santee Lakes Regional Preserve (Santee)

Very accessible is this park created by the Padre Dam Municipal Water District with several lakes integrated with Sycamore Creek. One of the county's largest public campgrounds with over 150 spaces. Lots of picnic spots along the lake, well shaded, very relaxing. Birdwatching is a big activity here. Busy with fishing from boats or shore. Hike around the lakes for a loosener after your enjoyable picnic.

How to get there: (1) Highway 52 east to Mast exit north/east to Fanita Parkway to lake entrance.

18. Lindo Lake and El Monte County Parks (Lakeside)

Two popular county parks in Lakeside. **El Monte** is 98 acres, with several picnic areas (reservable for groups). **Lindo Lake** surrounds a small lake with lots of active water fowl (watch out for those geese).

How to get there: El Monte - I-8 to Lake Jennings Park Road, north 1.5 miles to El Monte Road, then 6 miles east. Lindo Lake - I-8 to Highway 67 north to Winter Gardens Boulevard. South to Woodside Avenue, becomes Lindo Lane.

19. Louis A. Stelzer County Park (Wildcat Canyon) ❖❖

Wildcat Canyon Road has become well-known to many as the route to the **Barona Indian Casino** and the most scenic way to get from Lakeside to Ramona. For those with a nature bent, however, the canyon is a hotbed of outdoors parks and hiking trails.

This is the first park you'll come to 1 mile along on the right. This is a 314-acre park dedicated in 1982, a gift from Mr. Stelzer. A native of Germany, he was a San Diego contractor and architect. He bought the land in the 1940s and called it Shadow Mountain Ranch. When he died at age 91 he had deeded the ranch to the County, dedicated to the children of San Diego for educational and recreational uses, and for all physical capabilities.

NOTE: Louis A. Stelzer County Park, along with other areas in Wildcat Canyon received considerable damage from the October 2003 fire.

The entrance is well-marked and inviting, with a large parking lot and ranger station. Access to the park is across **Wildcat Canyon Creek** along a wide path that is wheelchair usable, as are all the paths in this section. This part is a delightful picnic and play area, with wide-spreading oaks and sycamores, picnic tables, restrooms, a kids playground. A pleasant getaway from hectic civilization five minutes away.

For hikers the park offers several possibilities for about any level of fitness. For a genteel hike, take the **Riparian Trail** out along the creek and under the trees. This is an enjoyable dawdling stroll of 0.7 miles, with a picnic table at the end. Come back the same path or head across the creek and out into the chaparral to join the **Stelzer Trail**. One option is to take that back to the main picnic area for a 1.6 mile loop.

Or keep heading upward to a "T", with the right leg heading up along the power lines to **Kumeyaay Promontory**. This is a half-hour round trip providing 360-degree views of the surrounding hills, plus the Lakeside horse ranches. Back at the "T", the left leg goes up to **Stelzer Summit**. This quickly gets steep so wear lug soles and take water. The trail heads up through large boulders to the peak and more broad vistas. About one hour round trip. Note: dogs O.K., on leash in picnic area only.

Stelzer is especially oriented toward young people. The park sponsors many kid's oriented events, among them the Easter Bunny, Halloween costumes and Santa visits. Many youth groups take kids out for picnics, hikes and general fun. It's available for camping by recognized youth groups, with advance arrangements.

How to get there: I-8 to Highway 67 north. Pass Lakeside to Willow Road and turn right. About a mile in, turn left on Wildcat Canyon Road (follow the signs toward Barona Casino).

20. Oakoasis County Park (Wildcat Canyon) ❖❖

Keep heading out on Wildcat Canyon Road another 2.2 miles past Stelzer and you'll see signs for El Capitan on the right and Oakoasis on the left.

Oakoasis is a gift to the citizens of San Diego County from the Minshall family. It consists of 405 acres of woods, hills, hiking trails and views. Drive in a short way to a large parking lot. **Oakoasis was severely burned during**

the October 2003 fire. The access trail in is clearly marked. About 0.25 mile in the trail veers to the right through high shrubs, probably with ample blooming lilac ceanothus and red monkey flowers. You'll come upon a bench for rest and contemplation.

The trail then heads up a dirt road into the oaks area, and there are plenty of them. In their midst is a 1936 cabin which had just been restored and then severely damaged in the 2003 fire. Just beyond there the trail winds upward around the hill, with excellent views of San Vicente Reservoir. You have a couple of options - a trail to the left heading up for another lake view, to the right winding around the hill into an open meadow and back to the main trail (just keep going right and follow the trail signs).

A hike to the cabin area and first lake view is roughly 1.5 hours round trip; all around the mountain add another 45 minutes. Dogs on leashes and horses are O.K., but no bikes.

21. El Capitan Open Space Preserve (Wildcat Canyon)

For a real workout, park across the road from Oakoasis and take on El Capitan (also known as El Cajon Mountain). This is not exactly a fun hike - don't take the kids unless they're tough - but with expansive views, starting about a half-hour up and continuing for the next 2 hours to the ridge or 2 more out to the tip.

The county preserve contains 2,800 acres and the hike up is one of the most challenging in the County. That's why it's usually identified as a fitness hike. Altitude ranges from 600 feet up to 3,300 feet. The hike up the old dirt road is not thrilling as there's little foliage; however the views are memorable. The rest of the preserve contains dense chaparral, providing residence for raptors and related prey.

How to get there: Same as Oakoasis, out Wildcat Canyon Road 2.2 miles past Stelzer. At the parking area is a restroom (useful information for Oakoasis as well).

22. Silverwood Wildlife Sanctuary (Wildcat Canyon) ❖❖

Almost any season is good for a visit to this San Diego Audubon Society nature sanctuary out past Lakeside. Beginning with an 85-acre donation from Harry Woodward in 1966, it has grown to a 745-acre gem.

NOTE: Silverwood was severely damaged in the October 2003 fire, including all buildings destroyed.

This is a fine place to drop out from the freeway hassles and into a low stress place for bird watching, relaxing among nature, or hiking along 7 miles of trails. The preserve offers ample shade from many oaks during a hot day, a pleasant climate in the fall, and flowers galore on display in the spring. Oh yes, there are birds all year long, with different breeds on the scene as the seasons change.

From the parking lot a path leads 0.33 mile through the woods to the main visiting area. Benches under the spreading oaks allow relaxed viewing of birds carousing at nearby feeders and baths. On the current sighting list are about 145 different birds, including warblers, western bluebirds, three kinds of hummingbirds, plus raptors such as hawks, owls and vultures. On Sundays, with a resident guide, bird books and binoculars provided, this makes about as civilized an introduction to bird watching as you'll find.

And if you're not a birder, you might see some of the roughly 30 mammal types that call Silverwood home, especially ground squirrels, and maybe a grey fox (look close kids — there's one climbing a tree), skunk, bobcat or coyote.

For hikers, several trails head out into the chaparral (pick up a map at the parking lot). These offer mild exercise or sweat-generating climbs, especially as summer approaches. The most challenging is the 3-mile circuit trail, with plenty of up and down terrain. (The even tougher trail, up to a ridge along the largest granite dome in the County, is closed to protect mountain lion habitat.) You'll find some excellent views along the way and seasonal colors — red toyon berries, blue and white lilac, deep red manzanita. And you won't need a radio to hear music as birds are chirping everywhere. After the hike head back to the shaded oaks, a fine oasis for recovery and a picnic at the tables under the trees.

Silverwood is open to the public only on Sundays, from 9 a.m. to 4 p.m. with guided nature walks at 10 a.m and 1:30 p.m. Keep the dogs home. It's open at other times for groups, such as schools, scouts, nature, etc., making this one of the County's most valuable educational resources. Oh yes, the name comes from the color when the sun reflects on oak leaves. As this is a non-profit sanctuary, they will be delighted to receive your contributions.

How to get there: It's an easy place to miss. Many on their way to try their luck at the Barona Indian Casino have driven right past without a hint. From Willow Road turn onto Wildcat Canyon Road, look for the 4.5 mile road marker, slow down and then about 0.3 miles further, turn right at the marked Silverwood entry. (Or if you find yourself at Barona, turn around and go back about a mile.)

23. Mt. Gower Open Space Preserve (Ramona)

Many regular hikers often don't get out here, even though it's readily accessible and will certainly give anyone a workout. It's 6 miles SE of Ramona, a lovely drive out through San Vicente Country Estates, past the **International Equestrian Center**, on a pretty wooded avenue set among the rolling hills and equestrian trails.

NOTE: Mt. Gower was very close to where the October 2003 Cedar Fire began just east of San Diego Country Estates. Much of the open terrain was bured.

A large sign marks the entry to the 1500-acre preserve. Continue up along the dirt road to the parking lot. The trails head up from here. Unusual for trailheads are a drinking fountain and quality restrooms. Also here is a walk-in campground for tenters, with a dozen spaces separated by thick bushes. You're likely to see more equestrians than people and dogs on leash are O.K.

Mt. Gower is that obvious peak off to the right, sticking up 3,103 feet above sea level. Head out along the trail by the information kiosk and a short distance in you'll have some choices. Take the branch to the left and the trail winds down and up along several prominent ridges, up to 2200 feet above sea level. Take the straight ahead choice and you're on the obvious main peak trail, which will wind around through mostly chaparral terrain 6 miles one way. You'll be advised about your progress with markers every so often.

At mile 1 is a bench, right beside a huge boulder. Here you have two choices. Keep going straight ahead for a quarter mile to an overlook of the valley, with some more benches. Or go left and continue up toward Gower. The trail winds past the large water tower, has some up and down with great views all around. The official trail doesn't go to the peak as the bailiwick changes to BLM land, but several options can get you up there. On hot days, choose another hike.

Back at the Estates on San Vicente Road will be a marker noting the famed tennis match between Bobby Riggs and Margaret Court. This was a milestone in women's tennis, with Riggs loudly denigrating women's tennis, though his volume reduced significantly when he then lost to Billie Jean King. The Gower name comes from an early surveyor in the district.

How to get there: (a) Highway 67 to Ramona to town center, right at light to 10th St./San Vicente Road and 6 miles south to Gunn Stage Road, left 1.9 miles to entrance. (b) Drive out Wildcat Canyon Road, past Barona, and to dead end at San Vicente Road. Turn right, drive 1.6 miles to Gunn Stage Road and take a left.

24. Lake Poway (Poway)

This is a popular regional park, located at the reservoir created by the 165 foot wide dam. It offers picnic tables overlooking lake, ball field, fishing, sailing, and boat rentals. From the picnic area, a trail circles the lake. The most interesting is to take the trail heading around the east side of the lake (right as you face the lake). This winds right along the shore and across a small sandy spit, which may be wet after rains with a fast-flowing waterfall coming off the hillside. Picnic at several spots including amidst pines at one. Boaters can come ashore as well at a couple spots. The full 3-mile hike around the lake takes about two hours. Dogs on leash O.K., but must be kept 100 feet from shore.

A sign directs you away from the lake along a good path which winds about a mile down to a well-shaded improved picnic and campground, with tables, fire pits, an amphitheater and restrooms. Kids have a fine time climbing along the oak branches. Enjoy a stroll among the trees of the **Blue Sky Ecological Preserve**. Looking north you'll see the **Ramona Dam**, with a road leading up to it. Return on the trail heading up the west side of the dam to the lake and main recreational area.

At the east side of park is the start of **Mt. Woodson Trail**. This is a sturdy hike over to Woodson and back, or do a 2-car caravan.

How to get there: I-15 to Ted Williams Parkway. East to Twin Peaks Road right 2-3 miles to Espola Road, left to Lake Poway Road, right. From north, I-15 to Rancho Bernardo Road, east, becomes Espola Road, 2-3 miles to Lake Poway Road, left. Large parking area.

25. Blue Sky Ecological Preserve (Poway) ❖❖

This preserve is a joint effort of the California Wildlife Conservation Board, San Diego County, City of Poway and Trust for Public Land. It's 700 acres set amidst bustling humanity and provides a fine getaway. Start in along the access road, and then get off on the trail among the oaks and sycamores. The hike is about 1.5 miles round trip within the preserve or you can keep on trekking south into a picnic and camp area (shaded, tables, with facilities). Here you'll be near the **Lake Poway Dam** with trails lead up either side to the top and the lake recreation area. An alternative is to start at **Lake Poway**, hike out either side along the lake and take the trail down to Blue Sky. To get up to the Ramona Dam and reservoir, look for the trail heading to the north.

How to get there: I-15 to Ted Williams Parkway to Twin Peaks, right to Espola Road, left. First is Lake Poway, then Blue Sky.

26. Sycamore Canyon/Goodan Ranch Open Space Preserve (Poway)

This 2,000+ acre preserve is under joint management of Poway, Santee, California Fish & Game and San Diego County. Here are 10 miles of hiking trails, from 2 staging areas. This is horse country so trails are open to them as well. The environment is primarily chaparral, with some significant oak groves as well.

NOTE: This preserve was particularly heavily hit by the October 2003 fires, with much of the open area burnt and many structures damaged. The descriptions will need to be adapted to recovery plans.

From either parking area hike down to the **Goodan Ranch**, where the ranger office is located. Take in the exhibits and live critters on display. The several structures and windmill date back to the 1930s when this was a working ranch. You can take a 2-mile hike around the grassland and wooded area. By the main ranch house is a good rest stop under a huge spreading oak.

From the Poway side, take the **Martha's Grove Trail**, starting along an open hillside, then into an oak grove with a bench. The trail loops back to the staging area for a 3-mile hike.

From the Highway 67 side, head down from either a trail just east of the parking area, or right at the parking lot. Combine these 2 trails for roughly a 4.5 mile hike through a variety of rough and easy terrain (lug soles recommended).

How to get there: (a) I-8 to Highway 67 north. Six miles from the Highway 67/Willow Road intersection, look to the left for the preserve entry. Drive in 1.5 miles to the parking lot, (b) I-15 to Poway Road east to Garden Road to Sycamore Canyon Road.

27. Iron Mountain (Poway Area) ✤✤

This is that dominant peak on Highway 67 right at Poway Road, with usually many cars parked right beside the road. This is one of our most popular areas for families as well as heavy-duty hikers. It provides a delightful easy hike alive with chaparral, flowers, oaks and manzanita along way, then the option of a moderately-challenging trail heading upward to the peak, and super scenery from there. Take the kids, bike, or even the hound (on a leash and with poop sacks please).

Iron Mountain provides an example of the power of nature to recover. It was severely burned in the summer of 1995 (and again in the October 2003 fire). The following spring saw a profusion of wildflowers among the blackened terrain, and by fall much foliage had returned. It has been one of our most visited hiking areas ever since.

Hike in as much as you're comfortable, a half mile in to a stream crossing, 1.5 miles to where the trail heads up 2 miles more to the peak. The trail upward is open country, mildly strenuous, with views of rolling hills, San Vicente Reservoir, Black Mountain and the Pacific Ocean. You'll enjoy the sign-in register at the peak as hikers leave flowing and witty messages (so add yours). It's about 3 hours round trip. Skip the hot summer months, unless you go early or late.

An alternative trail heads in a mile north of the main trail from the **Ellie Lane turnoff**. This is a longer hike along a good trail through chaparral and boulders to where it meets the main trail. From here it's on to the peak. Return to Ellie Lane either the same way you came up or head back on the main trail and near Highway 67, pick up the marked trail to the right heading along flat ground past a pond back over to Ellie Lane. Allow 4-5 hours up and back.

Iron Mountain is under the jurisdiction of the City of Poway. A support group is the **Iron Mountain Conservancy** which is working to increase public awareness and extend the open space.

How to get there: From I-8, take Highway 67 north past Lakeside. Just before the Poway Road signal light, see the parking area and signs on the right. Park on either side of the highway. Ellie Lane, is 0.75 mile further north.

28. Mt. Woodson (Poway-Ramona) ❖❖

Continue further east on Highway 67 and you can't ignore Mt. Woodson, the major peak to the left bristling with communication antennas. Mt. Woodson got its name from Marshall Clay Woodson and his family, who homesteaded here from 1873-1900. They were early planters of eucalyptus trees, most of which are still standing.

Three miles from Poway Road you'll see vehicles parked along the highway near the entrance to the **Department of Forestry Fire Station**. From here you have several hiking choices:

A. The most popular route is the one straight up. Locate the trail entry, signed, about 15 feet past the Fire Station sign. Hike to the left along the footpath through an oak grove about 0.25 mile to the paved road. Turn right and follow the road up 1.8 miles to the peak. You'll see fellow hikers & pooches on this trip, and possibly some rock climbers. As you walk, always upward and with little shade, the most dominant features are boulders, with patches of flowers along the way. Hike up to the many communication towers and enjoy the view all around. Return the same way or see option D.

B. For this trail you walk from the Fire Station parking area up Highway 67 toward Ramona about 1000 feet (lots of traffic so be careful). Turn left onto **Archie Moore Road** (recall that quiz question?). About 100 feet before the entrance to the Mt. Woodson Country Club is the entry to the **Mt. Woodson Trail System**. This is probably as pretty a trail start you're likely to find anywhere. Those looking to commune with nature will mutter a lot for the first half-mile as the trail passes right by the golf course, back yards of fancy houses and large water tanks. Once past the developed area you'll be on one of our most pleasant trails, the **Fry/Koegel Trail**, and on the north side of Mt. Woodson. Here are wild flowers, oak groves, manzanita, frequent shade (and no houses). Off to the right you'll see Lake Ramona and Blue Sky Preserve, ahead Lake Poway with lots of rolling hills in between. You can (a) hike all the way over to Lake Poway (3 miles); (b) turn around and retrace your path for a modest, yet pleasurable, roughly 3-mile stroll; (c) catch the marked side trail up to Mt. Woodson, about 1.5 miles in from Highway 67.

C. To continue to the peak (option 3), you have some work to do as it's a steady upward climb, the first leg about 0.5 mile. At the main **Lake Poway-Mt. Woodson Trail**, take a left, and keep heading up to the communication towers. Return via the same trail or walk down the paved road to the parking area.

D. If you came up the paved road, a pleasant loop hike is to return via the **Fry/Koegel Trail**. To catch it, come up the paved road to the first tower, take the road to the right, pass the other towers and buildings to the end. Keep going right onto the trail. Now hiking down, look for the trail off to the right about 0.75 mile down and marked with some stacked rocks (needs a sign, trail team). Take that down to the Fry/Koegel Trail, turn right and back to Highway 67.

Some alerts. Start hiking by 9 a.m. as the steady uphill climb is a workout. Options B and C call for good boots with lug soles. With any route, for a pleasant wind-up, go into the Country Club, passing the historic Amy Strong rock "castle" to the club house. Enjoy some refreshment and take in a great view of the peak you just climbed. Ah, life is good!

How to get there: Highway 67 north of Poway Road 3 miles.

29. Dos Pico County Park (Ramona)

Past Mt. Woodson a few miles more will be the entry to this popular spot for campers and picnickers, with an interesting scenic trail up to one of los dos picos. It's easy to get to, has lots of space and most importantly is heavily wooded with plenty of oaks and other trees.

For a modest stroll, take the short trail out around the park and through the woods. (Note; no dogs on trails here.) For a workout, with reward, look for the trail near the campground. It's an obvious side trail at marker #2. Definitely wear your lug soled boots and take a walking stick as this trail is steep. You'll pass by large boulders, oaks and manzanita to finally arrive at the peak, actually several huge rock formations. From here the view is terrific as you peruse Mt. Woodson across the valley and Highway 67, El Capitan mountain to the south and the rest of the county elsewhere.

This is also a good place for just poking around – kids will love it, after they finish griping about the steep trail. The trail needs some work as the steepness is sure to lead to lots of erosion with winter rains. Up and back is about a one hour trip.

How to get there: Highway 67 toward Ramona, several miles past Mt. Woodson. Turn right (south) at Mussey Grade Road, then right at Dos Picos Park Road.

30. Lake Sutherland Reservoir (Ramona)

Lake Sutherland sits in the rolling hills northeast of Ramona and is fed by **Santa Ysabel Creek**. It's a pleasant place for an outing, with recreational facilities, food and a picnic area on the south side. Hike east up the creek and perhaps you'll see some wild turkeys. Look for a guided hike below and across the dam for a close look at how a dam looks and functions.

The **San Dieguito River Park** regularly conducts hikes from south of the dam along the **Santa Ysabel Truck Trail** over to **Pamo Valley**. This is a pleasant several hour hike with return via a 2-vehicle shuttle. Joining them for a guided hike is a good way to experience this region.

Here are some of the enjoyable aspects along the way. A mixed terrain with chaparral, lots of wildflowers, several heavily forested sections. Passing by the discontinued **Black Canyon Campground** and a potential dip into the creek with likely locals jumping into the pools and dousing under several cataracts. Crossing Black Mountain Road as it heads up toward Mesa Grande Indian Reservation. A welcome oak cluster and finally a grand view looking down into lovely **Pamo Valley**. Finally the trail winds down to Pamo Road where your shuttle vehicle will be waiting.

How to get there: Highway 67 to Ramona. Continue east on Highway 78 for 6 miles to Sutherland Dam Road. Drive to end. Take right fork down to the lake docks and recreational area; left fork past the dam to marked Forest Service staging area. For the shuttle return vehicle, Highway 67 to Ramona, left on Pine to Haverford Road, then left on Pamo Road. At 2.6 miles look for the trail coming down from the east.

SAN DIEGO INLAND - NORTH

In this section we start with Lake Hodges and San Pasqual Valley, part of the **San Dieguito River Park**. This is a multi-agency encompassing the **Coast to Crest Trail**, a 55-mile stretch of park, preserves and open space running from the sea at Del Mar up to Volcan Mountain and beyond. This is an ongoing project, constantly adding further segments toward the eventual goal. As of 2003, over 17,000 acres have been preserved, with many public agencies, non-profit finding groups and many dedicated citizens organizations all pitching in.

Mention the name **San Pasqual Valley** and most people know it for the Zoo's **Wild Animal Park**. For outdoor enthusiasts, and history buffs, the valley has plenty more to offer that many are unaware of. Located east of I-15, between Escondido and Rancho Bernardo, it provides one of our most pleasant drives close-in to the city as it's primarily an agricultural preserve largely owned by the City of San Diego, and an area with important historical and environmental significance.

31. Lake Hodges South (Rancho Bernardo) ✤✤

The Lake Hodges area is one of the main sections of the River Park for public activity. Here you'll find a variety of developed trails on both sides of the lake, with many informational kiosks, footbridges, superb bird-watching and even a small waterfall. Many of the projects have been done by local youth groups as you'll see on the plaques.

On the south shore of the lake in Rancho Bernardo is the **Piedras Pintadas Trail**, with many educational markers about Native Americans and the natural features of the area. Hike out and back for a nearly 4-mile trip. Pick another trail and hike along the lake.

Also on the south shore and along the San Dieguito River is the **Highland Valley Trail**. This starts east of I-15 and is an enjoyable, mostly level hike through varied habitat - lots of trees for shade. Good hike for kids and kids have helped develop this trail. A short way in, you'll cross over a wooden footbridge, a Boy Scouts project. Full hike is 4 miles round-trip.

How to get there: I-15 to the West Bernardo exit. Piedras Pintadas - cross over freeway to marked entry and parking lot on the right. Highland Valley Trail - from West Bernardo exit, drive east short distance to Highland Valley Road and into marked parking lot.

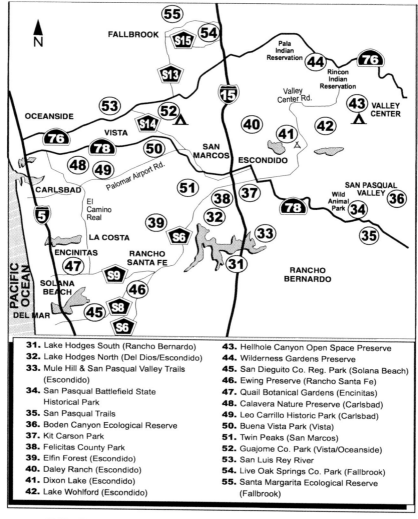

N

FALLBROOK

55
S15 54
S13
Pala Indian Reservation
44
76
Rincon Indian Reservation
Valley Center Rd.
15
53
OCEANSIDE
52
43 VALLEY CENTER
VISTA
S14
40
41
42
76
78
50
SAN MARCOS
ESCONDIDO
48
49
Palomar Airport Rd.
CARLSBAD
El Camino Real
51
39
S6
32
38 37
SAN PASQUAL VALLEY
Wild Animal Park
78
36
34
5
LA COSTA
33
35
RANCHO SANTA FE
31
ENCINITAS
47
RANCHO BERNARDO
SOLANA BEACH
S9
46
45
S8
DEL MAR
S6
PACIFIC OCEAN

31. Lake Hodges South (Rancho Bernardo)	**43.** Hellhole Canyon Open Space Preserve
32. Lake Hodges North (Del Dios/Escondido)	**44.** Wilderness Gardens Preserve
33. Mule Hill & San Pasqual Valley Trails (Escondido)	**45.** San Dieguito Co. Reg. Park (Solana Beach)
34. San Pasqual Battlefield State Historical Park	**46.** Ewing Preserve (Rancho Santa Fe)
35. San Pasqual Trails	**47.** Quail Botanical Gardens (Encinitas)
36. Boden Canyon Ecological Reserve	**48.** Calavera Nature Preserve (Carlsbad)
37. Kit Carson Park	**49.** Leo Carrillo Historic Park (Carlsbad)
38. Felicitas County Park	**50.** Buena Vista Park (Vista)
39. Elfin Forest (Escondido)	**51.** Twin Peaks (San Marcos)
40. Daley Ranch (Escondido)	**52.** Guajome Co. Park (Vista/Oceanside)
41. Dixon Lake (Escondido)	**53.** San Luis Rey River
42. Lake Wohlford (Escondido)	**54.** Live Oak Springs Co. Park (Fallbrook)
	55. Santa Margarita Ecological Reserve (Fallbrook)

INLAND, CENTRAL (&NORTH) - HIKING

32. Lake Hodges North (Del Dios/Escondido) ✤✤

On the north shore, you have several options for pleasant hiking, from gen-
teel to heavy duty as the trail runs all along the north shore for 8 miles from
I-15 to near the dam in Del Dios. A good staging area from the west end is the
Del Dios Community Park. From here hike west to the dam for a look at the

community of Del Dios, the many waterfowl in the lake, and observe a few fishing boats. If you can get here after a major rainy season when the falls is overflowing, you'll enjoy a memorable experience. Any time is a fun hike, and you can recover with lunch or a margarita at the well-known Hernando's Hideaway.

From the park you can also head east out to the **Lake Hodges Boat Docks**, with restrooms, boat rentals for fishing or canoeing, picnic tables and a store. Also you can continue east along the lake which is the trail described next. You can modify your directions by starting at the Boat Docks and heading either toward the dam or east toward I-15.

How to get there (west end): Community Park - I-15 to Via Rancho Parkway, west to Del Dios Highway west to Lake Drive. Boat Dock - from Lake Drive take marked road to left or south.

Another staging area is located by the lake just east of I-15. From here you can cross under I-15 for a pleasant and scenic stroll, as you're passing the lake (even better when it has water), many stands of beavertail cactus, and a variety of other greenery along the way. This is the usual trail for the River Park's annual May run/hike fundraiser, with a thousand or so people making this morning jaunt at various paces over to the boat launch area; turn around or keep going over to the Community Park (good place to leave 2nd vehicle for shuttle back) or all the way over to the dam. That would make an 8-mile one way hike, or if you're up to it, turn around for a 16-mile round-trip journey.

That natural hill to the north is **Bernardo Mountain**, a recent park acquisition. A hike up here gives you a much different experience from the walk along the lake. From the staging area east of I-15, hike along the main pathway about 30 minutes. Just after crossing **Felicitas Creek**, you will see a trail heading off to the right (marked by wooden fencing). Head in here along the creek and you'll be in riparian country, with oaks, sycamores and palm trees along the bubbling Felicitas Creek. This heavily-wooded area continues for another 0.25 mile, with some good spots to settle in for some repose and a snack. Then the trail leaves the creek area and heads outward and upward to Bernardo Mountain. Soon you'll enjoy an expansive view overlooking Lake Hodges, Mt. Woodson and the communities below. Come back the same way and head home for about a 4-hour well-spent getaway.

Also from the east parking lot is access to the **Mule Hill Trail**, described next.

How to get there: I-15 to Via Rancho east, then first right turn onto Sunset Drive to dedicated parking lot on the left or on the street.

33. Mule Hill & San Pasqual Valley Trails (Escondido) ❖❖❖

Starting just east of I-15 and Lake Hodges is a joined set of trails heading 10 miles east into San Pasqual Valley out past the Wild Animal Park. This is also the area of San Diego City's extensive Agricultural Preserve, an important part of keeping significant open space for other use than residential development. (We could use about 3 more of these in the county.) Included here is the **Orfila Vineyard**, an enjoyable spot anytime for a wine-tasting and picnic, and even more so as a reward for a long hike.

The first segment is the **Mule Hill Trail**. Along the way are several informational displays which provide background about the history, current use and natural aspects of the valley. A little over a mile in is a detailed display with flags marking the historical nature of Mule Hill.

Why the name, you ask? Well, even if you didn't, here is a summary version. A few miles further east of here is the **San Pasqual Battlefield**, where the U.S. Army came in as runner-up, or got shellacked by the Californios for whom this was briefly a separate nation, not in total appreciation of a bunch of U.S. troops coming in to their territory, not on a diplomatic visit. Chief U.S. scout was a chap named Kit Carson. Leading the U.S. troops was General Stephen Kearny, a name well-known here. After suffering heavy damage from the Andres Pico-led local forces, Kearny's now bedraggled troops headed further west. Still under siege and low on food they cooked up a few of their mules, thus the name Mule Hill. Looking for help from U.S. military in San Diego Harbor, Kit Carson and a couple of others snuck their way over to Los Penasquitos Canyon where a sign marks where they crossed the creek.

Walk a hundred yards more and you'll find one more display. If you want to have a pleasant easy hike on a level trail, with some history thrown in, you can make a 2.5 mile round-trip hike just this far.

The **San Pasqual Valley Trail** continues eastward on a wide level trail. The next marker at the **San Dieguito River Crossing** makes a good resting spot as a large stand of eucalyptus trees provides welcome shade. Just past the shaded section is a trail marker at 2.5 miles and short walk over to **Highland Valley Road**, providing a good pickup spot for those who want to hike a short distance.

From here continuing east it gets to be a workout, so avoid the full segment on a hot day. The next leg continues through still-level, mostly open terrain along the creek, passing willow and oak trees. Around 4 miles the gentle nature of the hike changes to a steady uphill segment. As you climb, you have expansive views of the **San Pasqual Valley** and the **Agricultural Preserve** (locate the ostriches over by Highway 78), across to the **Wild Animal**

Park, and east to the rolling hills. At the top, 5 miles along, is the **Raptor Ridge** view area, another good resting spot.

Continue east passing by the agricultural fields and arrive at another staging area and kiosk at mile 7.5, right at **Bandy Canyon Road** and **Ysabel Creek Road**. Here a large parking lot makes this a good entry or departure option. One more stretch ahead, now mostly adjacent to the road, passing a variety of farming products, from sod fields to dairy farms (you'll know when that is). With low road traffic, this makes a pleasant hike (though with little shade) as you pass the eastward hills. Finally the trail ends (or begins) at a large parking area at Highway 78 and Bandy Canyon Road, with restroom. For those who want to hike the full 10 miles, a 2-car shuttle will be a good option.

How to get there: Take I-15 to the Via Rancho exit, at the south end of Escondido. Head east and turn right at the first light to Sunset Drive just past the Shell gas station. Park on the street or in the large lot on the left. Marked trail entrance is just south of parking lot.

34. San Pasqual Battlefield State Historic Park (San Pasqual Valley)

Just east of the Wild Animal Park is the site of the battle which occurred in 1846, mentioned above in the Mule Hill trail segment. Get all the details at the **Battlefield Visitor Center**, open only on weekends. Take in the displays and maps at the center to get the scoop on the battle, then take the trail up to the monument. This is a pleasant 2-mile meander around the hill behind the center.

The park hosts regular historical events on each first Sunday in summer. These include people in costumes of 150 years ago, music, exhibits and cannons firing. Then each December the 2 sides go at each other again in full costume and with lances flying (sort of).

How to get there: I-15 to Highway 78 east, just past Wild Animal Park.

35. San Pasqual Trails (San Pasqual Valley) ❖❖

Two trails head up from both sides of Highway 78. As you head east from the Wild Animal Park, the first one is on the south side, with a marked parking area. From the kiosk sign and trail map, you can trace the trail. It's not especially complicated as the trail goes up and comes back down for a roughly six mile round trip hike. The terrain weaves across several hills through mostly open chaparral, with an oak grove as you cross the creek via a footbridge. Upward along the creek is **Clevenger Canyon**. As you amble along you'll gain some altitude to enjoy views of the valley and, to the east, the Cuyamacas. An option, about 0.5 mile up from the road, is to take the trail off the right. This goes up 1.4 miles to Vista Point, overlooking the battlefield site.

How to get there: I-15 to Via Rancho exit south. Drive a few blocks to San Pasqual Road. Turn right, then right on Highway 78. From the Wild Animal Park, drive 5.6 miles to marked parking lot on right.

Keep going further east on Highway 78 and you'll find another good hiking area, more challenging than the south side trail. From the parking area you'll see the trail heading down through the boulders. Hike down into a forested section and take 2 footbridges across the Santa Ysabel creek. Enjoy the shade as this is the last you'll see for a couple of hours as the trail winds up the side of the hill. You're likely to see wild flowers along this stretch and above where a serious fire occurred a few years back. Toward the ridge, the clarity of the trail fades though you'll likely see some ribbons marking a trail over to an overlook – peaceful lunch spot with views all around. This full hike will be about 6-8 miles round trip.

How to get there: From the Wild Animal Park drive 6.2 miles to the marked parking lot and trailhead on the left or north side.

36. Boden Canyon Ecological Reserve
(San Pasqual/Ramona)

Keep going east on Highway 78 to one end of this beautiful and lightly explored canyon. In recent years over 1200 acres were acquired to put the Boden Canyon Reserve into public land. The canyon has long been a prime target for preservation by the River Park. It's a lovely place, with lots of trees, 128 (identified so far) species of birds, a pond and the year-round flowing **Clevenger Canyon Creek**. The canyon provides an important corridor for wildlife, continuing all the way over to **Pamo Valley**, with a total of 2000 acres.

Boden has a complicated multiple agency involvement (such as San Dieguito River Park, San Diego City, California Fish & Game, US Forest Service, maybe even more) as you will see with a visit. It can be entered both from the lower, Highway 78, end, and the upper, Ramona, end. However, the upper end is more visited by hunters and off-road vehicle fans than hikers, so I recommend you skip it for now.

Starting your hike from the **San Pasqual Valley** lower end, walk around the locked gate and down the road (**Orosco Truck Trail**). The first 2 miles are mostly open terrain, with, fortunately on a hot day, several shaded sections (oak, sycamore). This is pleasant terrain, with hills rising up all around from the canyon. About 0.5 mile along keep downhill to the left where the other dirt road comes in from the right (**Santa Ysabel Creek**). You'll see signs from the different agencies, some noting whether hunting is allowed or not, and you'll pass around more gates along the way. Once you hit the major wooded section, it's shade almost all the rest of the way, a lovely stroll. Pick as much as you want up to roughly 5 miles, with a return trip back the same way. (Remember, the last 2 miles are open so take plenty of water).

How to get there: (Lower section) On Highway 78 from Escondido to Ramona, at 6.8 miles from the Wild Animal Park entry sign, turn left onto a dirt road. There's room for a half-dozen cars in the area before the locked gate. This area is San Diego City land. Or coming from Ramona, take Highway 78 north turning west from the center of town to meet the dirt road at 4.7 miles.

(Upper section) I-8 to Highway 67 to Ramona. Turn left at 7th Street, right at Elm, right on Haverford and onto Pamo Road. At 2.7 miles from Pamo Road look for the Forest Service sign and turn left on Orosco Ridge Road. After 0.5 mile the road gets very rough (4WD recommended). Because you are on Forest Service property, you will need a USFS Adventure Pass.

37. Kit Carson Park (Escondido)

The namesake of this 250-acre Escondido park is known mostly for his exploits in the so-called Wild West, but he made some history here as well.

Today, picnics, ball games, and Frisbee-throwing are among the many ongoing Sunday afternoon activities. A pavilion and amphitheater make this a good location for concerts and festivals. In the fall, the annual Felicita Pageant is held here, recalling a love affair between an Indian princess and a soldier wounded at San Pasqual. Trails through the trees, and a stream which leads into nearby Lake Hodges make pleasant strolling areas to walk off the barbecue and potato salad.

How to get there: Take Interstate 15 north to Escondido, turn east at Via Rancho Parkway.

38. Felicita County Park (Escondido)

This is a busy park, given its location in the middle of heavy populated residential areas and its heavily wooded location along **Felicita Creek**. Lots of picnics here for families and groups. Of interest to many is the annual fall **Renaissance Fair and Shakespeare Festival**, with booths, entertainment, troupes acting out Shakespeare scenes, and each day's grand finale, the battle royale with two groups in middle age battle garb having at each other, with dead bodies lying all around (and getting back up when the water brigade comes around). Lots of fun.

How to get there: I-15 to Via Rancho Parkway, west over freeway 1 mile to Felicita Road, north.

39. Elfin Forest, or Is That Mt. Israel? (Escondido) ❖❖

Nestled among the bustling communities of Escondido, Del Dios, San Marcos, and Carlsbad is this island of relative tranquility. Within the 750-acre open space park are a year-round stream, picnic areas, riparian forest, great views and 17 miles of trails available to hikers, bikers and equestrians. If you want to get either away from or above it all, go check out the Elfin Forest, a project of the Olivenhain Water District in cooperation with BLM (Bureau of Land Management).

About the name confusion, here's some background. "Elfin Forest" traces back to the religious retreat located there since the 1940s. Dr. Harvey Urban was affiliated with the Questhaven Fellowship and his children started calling the area the Elfin Forest after a novel and because it seemed to fit the miniature nature of much of the foliage here. "Mt. Israel" is often used to describe this area, yet there is no Mt. Israel on the map. This name came from an early 1840's homesteader, Robert Israel, later the lighthouse keeper at Point Loma.

Hiking and biking starts from the large paved parking lot (with facilities), with room for horse trailers as well as vehicles. Right beside is a picnic area, with trails along the creek, lots of shade, and a true babbling brook as the water courses over the rocks. Even if you don't go any further this is a pleasant spot to explore - except when the babbling becomes racing as winter rains lead to overflown banks.

One hike immediately accessible to the left is the **Botanical Trail**, which makes a modest loop hike upward and back to the picnic area. To the right is the **Escondido Creek Trail**, which follows the creek, then crosses over and continues on to a maintenance road and unimproved trails.

The primary access for most people, however, is the **Way Up Trail** (guess why it got its name). This is the boring, but essential, first phase, 1.6 miles winding upward and about 30-40 minutes.

Once at the ridge, you'll see trails spreading out in all directions, through lots of chaparral and little shade (which is why it's not a good hike in August). Take the 2.7-mile **Equine Incline Trail** to the right, from where you'll look across to the hillsides burned black a few years ago in the major Harmony Grove Fire. Head off to the left along the **Valley View** and **Lakeview Ridge Trails**, which looks down onto Lake Hodges. You can choose a loop of 4, 6 or more miles back to the starting point at the top of **Way Up Trail**. Or for an easier trek, get to **Tykes' Hike Trail** and the **Elfin Forest Overlook** and see the world all around you from the Pacific Ocean to the mountains. High point is about 1350 feet.

This is a hiker-friendly trail system, with many picnic tables, rest stops, toilet facilities (with even trash cans for recycling road apples - O.K., horse droppings— to go with these fine views). Dogs O.K., on leash. Bikes O.K. on trails as marked.

How to get there (not an easy task): (a) From I-15. To west 78 to Nordahl Road, becomes Citracado Parkway south/left. Cross Mission Road, bear right to Country Club Road. 2-3 miles to Harmony Grove Road, right. 2 miles to entrance. (b) From I-5. East on La Costa Road to Rancho Santa Fe Road, left; to Questhaven, right; to Elfin Forest Road, right; to Harmony Grove Road, right. 1.5 miles to reserve.

40. Daley Ranch (Escondido) ❖❖

This 3500-acre park was formally dedicated in 1997 as a City of Escondido park. With its size and location adjoining fast-developing communities, this is a highly-valued park and open space. **It also received considerable fire damage from the October 2003 fire.**

So what's out there in the recreational line? How about 22 miles of developed trails? How about a convenient location right next to **Dixon Lake Recreation Area**, increasing the contiguous natural area for wildlife, plus adding fishing, camping and picnicking to the ranch options? Add in access by bicyclists and horse folk and you've got an all-around top-quality park.

Getting into Daley Ranch, however, is not for out-of-shape hikers. Both parking lots are at least a mile from the ranch house area, from where the trails mostly head out. From the main road (La Honda) parking lot, you'll hike along the access road a mile; from the Dixon Lake trail head, it's about 1.5 miles. So you're biting off a 2-3 mile round-trip hike just for starters.

Park headquarters and Ranger's quarters is the 1928 ranch house with high ceiling and huge fireplace inside, and a large front porch outside overlooking ponds and oak trees. No wonder it was a cherished retreat for generations of the Daley family, starting with Robert Daley who settled there in 1869.

To get out on the trails, pick up a map and then walk past the house where signs mark the trailheads. For a lengthy hike with some strenuous uphill parts head straight out along the **Central Valley Loop Trail** (which you also could have joined a few hundred feet back along the road coming in). This is a 5.5 mile hike through mostly open territory with views of rolling hills all around, plus some wooded sections, a small pond, and monkey flowers and purple mallow plentiful in the spring.

Other options make this a park for hikers of various levels and interests.

A. Take the **Central Valley Loop Trail** in the opposite direction and you'll arrive at the 2.4 mile Boulder Loop Trail, out among those rolling hills (and boulders).

B. The **Jack Meadow Loop Trail** for the first half is the same as the Central Loop Trail, then it heads in the opposite direction across the valley and back to the ranch house (3.2 miles).

C. For a really good workout, about half-way around the **Central Valley Trail** join the **Englemann Oak Loop Trail**, for another 3.8 mile trek among the oaks.

D. If you enter the park from the lot inside the Dixon Lake area, you'll be on the **Chaparral Loop Trail**, which winds past another pond to the ranch house and loops back to Dixon Lake.

How to get there: I-15 to north end of Escondido to Highway 78 east (becomes Lincoln Avenue). At Citrus Avenue, turn left (north), to La Honda Drive, right to end. Park at lot before Dixon Lake entrance or drive into Dixon Lake and on road along left edge of park. A few hundred feet in will be a large lot on left, with marked entrance into Daley Ranch.

Here's a pleasant alternative. Go in the back way into one of the most appealing parts of Daley Ranch — the **Englemann Oak Loop Trail**. At the entrance pick up a map, which shows you're heading along the Englemann Trail. The park says this is a 3.8-mile loop, though you have options to make it a bit shorter or a lot longer.

During this medium-level trek you'll enjoy, first of all, solitude, then a variety of terrain, some oaks, a creek crossing, a pond and a loop around (or optional hike up) **Burnt Mountain**, the highest point on the ranch. Good views of other peaks in several directions, including **Mount Whitney** (O.K., so it's not the one up north). Lots of wildflowers in late spring, such as monkey flower, lilac and lemonade berry. Two-thirds around, in the counter-clockwise direction, you pass a picturesque dead oak tree - a definite Kodak moment. A segment of this trail is also the **Central Loop Trail**, so if you want a real workout you can hike over to the ranch house, and perhaps have a 2-car shuttle out to the main entrance at Lake Dixon.

How to get there: Take I-15 to El Norte Parkway east. At Broadway turn north (left). Shortly past Desmond Dene Park at 4.3 miles turn right onto Cougar Pass Road. About 1 mile along this dirt road you'll see the Daley Ranch entrance. Park either along the road or on the nearby lot.

41. Dixon Lake (Escondido)

Right beside Daley Ranch is the Dixon Lake Recreation Area. It offers a variety of outdoors experiences – fishing, boating, picnics, a scenic setting and a number of trails around the lake. Campers have their pick of 45 sites, including several group sites.

The first picnic area is at Jack Creek, near the park entrance. To work up an appetite, hike up a half-mile along the **Jack Creek Trail**, where in the wet season some falls maybe flowing. From Jack Creek Cove pick up the **Shoreline Trail**, which goes for nearly 2 miles around the lake. For another picnic area drive on Lakeshore Drive, where you can also pick up that Shoreline Trail. The **Grand Loop Trail** provides another 2-mile jaunt around and above the north side of the lake.

From the entry drive straight in to a large parking lot from where you can pick up the trail into Daley Ranch. It's a simple trek over to the ranch house and the many Daley trails. So you have plenty to occupy your time when camping or visiting at Dixon.

How to get there: Same as for Daley Ranch (above).

42. Lake Wohlford (Escondido)

For serious hikers there's not much here. For those who enjoy water recreational activities there's plenty with fishing and boating the main pursuits. It is a pleasant and restful place plus you'll find good dining in the small resort. For a short stroll along the lake drive over to the south side and walk either way from the Oakvale parking lot. A small park is right here also.

How to get there: I-15 to El Norte Parkway; east to Valley Center Road (S6) north, then right on Lake Wohlford Road. The resort and boat docks are on this road. To get to the south side, turn right just before the dam on Oakvale Road and drive over to the parking lot.

43. Hellhole Canyon Open Space Preserve (Valley Center)

Located north of Escondido is this nearly 2000-acre San Diego County Preserve (**nearly 80% damaged in the October 2003 fires**) nestled among surrounding hills and bounded by San Pasqual, Rincon, and La Jolla Indian land (from left to right as you walk in on the main trail).

Here you'll find a well-marked entrance, a large parking lot, toilets, water, space for tent camping (with reservation only) and a resident host. You'll also find at least 11 miles of trails. This is mixed terrain and not easy hiking. Pick a cool day or start early, and carry plenty of water.

Which brings us to how it got its name. According to an article posted at the entrance, a prospector was out here searching for gold in 1864. He picked a particularly hot day and muttered "Now I know this is hell." There's another Hellhole Canyon out in Anza Borrego Desert State Park, near Borrego Springs.

This place has had fireworks as well. In 1906 the Brodys homesteaded here. Mr. Brody came home and found a poacher living in Brody's house - Howard Gore, "a fellow known to be trouble". Brody got Gore evicted, whereupon Gore shot Brody and killed him. Mrs. Brody grabbed her gun and plugged Gore. As he fell, a goner, his rifle went off and shot Mrs. Brody, killing her. Did you follow all that? Shades of Hamlet!

You've got to be intrigued with such a place. From the parking area, the trail heads out and down through mixed chaparral. It's a steady downhill (read uphill coming back) to **Hell Creek**, flowing now but dry most of the year. Now in the midst of Hell comes **Paradise Creek**, with Live Oaks, sycamores, and Engleman Oaks This is an excellent resting place, especially coming back. A large aqueduct, the **Escondido Canal**, comes here off the creek. It was hand-built in the early 1900s, takes water from Lake Henshaw to Lake Wohlford, and is still in use.

From beyond here, the environment changes back to chaparral, plus interesting ornamentals - sugarbush, taco plant (leaves like tacos), manzanita berries (used for tea or poultice). About 1 mile along from the wooded section the trail comes to a "T". This is where the real work begins as it's mostly uphill past here — all chaparral and no shade. To the left the trail heads out to 2 view points with a loop back. To the right the trail either winds over to the left trail, or for the hard trekkers, goes way up and over to other view points. The peaks to the right are at about 3,500' elevation.

An interesting side visit is to **Bates Nut Farm**, reached by crossing from Paradise Road to Woods Valley Road.

How to get there: I-15 to Via Rancho Parkway, east to Bear Valley Parkway, north to S-6 (Valley Center Road). East 6 miles to Lake Wohlford Road, east/right 6 miles (through Lake Wohlford) to Paradise Mountain Road (at Woods Valley Road), east/right 3.3 miles to Las Hermanos (dead-ends), right and quick left to Kiavo (signs may be missing), about 0.5 mile to marked entrance past Santee Road. Horses O.K., no dogs.

44. Wilderness Gardens Preserve (Pala)

This is an 800-acre preserve that got to be one due to determined effort by a small group of dedicated advocates. Go back over 30 years to when **SWAP (Save Wilderness Area Preserves)** decided this area along the **San Luis Rey River** should not be turned over to developers but set aside as a nature preserve. So they put up some money, enough to get it started, then hustled the County to make a commitment to buy it and make it a public place.

We now can enjoy a visit up there to stroll along the ponds and through the oaks and sycamores, enjoy bird-watching, and have a relaxing picnic. The odds are you won't have to worry about crowds as the remote location makes this a little known treasure. It's also only open on weekends. Join up with one of the guided hikes in here and get lots of good info.

This was once owned by Manchester Boddy, known for the **Descanso Gardens** in Pasadena. You'll see some of his plantings here also. Nearby is the Pala Indian community and mission. To switch from outdoors to indoors activity, stop off at either the **Pala or Pauma Indian casinos**, a few miles in either direction on Highway 76.

How to get there: I-15 north of Escondido to Highway 76 east, 10 miles to park entry on right/south.

45. San Dieguito County Regional Park
(Solana Beach) ❖❖

This is a 125-acre haven of nature in the midst of some of the priciest real estate in the county. Nestled between Solana Beach and Rancho Santa Fe, the park offers picnics, playgrounds, hiking and fall colors that will surprise you if you haven't been there lately. You can even get hitched there in a white, gazebo in a mighty pretty setting.

The park has 2 main areas. The **Upper Park** is the first one most people see as they come east from I-5 on Lomas Santa Fe. Turn left on Highland Drive, take the entry on the right and that's the part you're in. There is ample parking, restrooms, lots of picnic tables, and three covered ramadas for group events. Kids will find plenty to do with playground swings and slides. And with eucalyptus trees all around, you'll have plenty of shade. Dogs on leash are O.K. For groups, contact County Parks for reservations.

For the **Lower Park**, keep driving north on Highland to Camino Real and turn right. A short way along is the entrance. With lots of sycamore and liquid amber trees, here is where the colorful red and gold foliage appears in October and November. Here are large grassy areas, picnic tables, even a sometimes stream meandering between two small, one with an island and ducks galore. This area is also popular with groups, especially kids, with ample grassy areas for games and cavorting (or just lying under the trees contemplating the meaning of life and the hectic freeway pace somewhere over there to the west.)

At either entry be sure to pick up the park map. For walking off that huge picnic lunch, or for hikers, trails network all around the park and between the Upper and Lower Parks. The magnets are 3 obvious lookout towers. You can get to the towers easily, though from the Lower Park you'll trek up some steep areas. None are far so you can do an easy hike or combine several trails and get yourself a workout. And for an extra challenge, you'll have to walk about 8 feet along an elevated log to get onto the towers.

Here are some suggestions:

A. From the Upper Park at the parking lot for areas 1, 2, and 3, head east along either the obvious dirt road (near the south ramada) or locate the trail from mid-lot. Keep veering to the left/north and you'll come to a sandstone formation, just made for kids to romp around. Walk nimbly across two suspension bridges and go left to the north tower or right to the mid tower. From either of these you can walk downhill to the Lower Park.

B. From the Upper Park area 4, walk down the paved road passing the Scout Building to a marked trail off to the right. This also goes, with a dip in and up from the canyon, to that sandstone formation.

C. From the Lower Park, locate the tiny south pond. Walk up the nearby dirt road about 100 feet, take the trail to the right and climb up to the mid tower. Also from the pond or the south grassy area, take the trail up to the south tower (also easily accessible with an easy stroll from the Upper Park).

How to get there: I-5 to Lomas Santa Fe Drive east.

46. Ewing Preserve (Rancho Santa Fe)

Just outside the center of this definitely upscale community is **The Nature Conservancy's Ewing Preserve,** donated back in the '70s. Most people drive right past it on Lomas Santa Fe Drive without seeing the small sign marking the entry. Stop and stroll down into a peaceful heavily-wooded canyon with a loop trail around and back. Not a long hike but a pleasant getaway and time to appreciate this special gift to the public.

How to get there: I-5 to Lomas Santa Fe Drive, continue east to just past La Sencilla, look for the small sign marking the entrance (and parking for 4-5 cars).

47. Quail Botanical Gardens (Encinitas)

In Encinitas is this tranquil 30-acre county park just east of and out of earshot of I-5. If you like foliage and shade, this is your place. You can stroll along the pathways, savoring the outstanding plant collections (3,000 species) and waterways. Have a quiet picnic. Take some plants home from the well-stocked nursery to perk up your personal garden. On Saturdays join a guided tour. Get married under the gazebo. Come December, Quail Gardens sparkles with lights and entertainment.

How to get there: I-5 to Encinitas Boulevard east to Quail Gardens Drive, turn left (north).

48. Calavera Nature Preserve (Carlsbad)

This is a work-in-progress, with several agencies involved in establishing an important preserve and open space in the Carlsbad-Oceanside-Vista area. The central element is **Mount Calavera**, an old volcano, with a small reservoir and a variety of habitat. It is in the heart of major development and a determined band of citizens called Preserve Calavera is leading the charge to keep the largest possible preserve area for a valuable wildlife habitat and corridor linking to other natural areas. Three creeks flow through here, including **Hedionda Creek** which continues on to the lagoon. Two segments so far are the **Calavera Nature Preserve**, managed by The Environmental Trust and the **Carlsbad Highlands Ecological Reserve**, under California Fish & Game.

For a foray onto the preserve, start at **Oak Riparian Park**, a pleasant community park. Cross over Calavera Creek under the spreading oaks and continue on the trail. Away from the creek you'll be passing lots of shrubs and ground plants which provide a rich display of wildflowers in the spring. Pass by the lake and up to the peak for roughly a 2.5-mile trek. This area is managed by The Environmental Trust. Allow about 2 hours round trip. Other shorter trails from the west side head over the dam and up to the peak.

How to get there: Highway 78 east to College, south to Lake Boulevard, left to park. From west side, continue south on College to Tamarack Avenue right to Saddle Drive right and see trail heading east.

49. Leo Carrillo Historic Park (Carlsbad)

Opened in mid 2003, this is the former home of the actor best known as Cisco Kid's sidekick, Sancho and his family. Carrillo bought the 2,500-acre ranch, known as Rancho de los Kiotes, and built his weekend retreat, guest homes for Hollywood friends and others, buildings required for his working cattle ranch (at peak 600 head), and a cantina for winding down. He spent many a weekend here until 1960, and wife and daughter lived here until 1978.

Now under aegis of Carlsbad City Parks (760-434-2924), docents lead tours each weekend, giving lots of tidbits about their life, the architecture, and the plush foliage. Popular camera attractions are the 60 peacocks strutting the grounds. While the park is only 27 acres, it adjoins the Carlsbad Trail System, making hikes of 4-5 miles feasible.

How to get there: I-5 to Leucadia Boulevard east, cross El Camino Real onto Rancho Santa Fe Road, past La Costa to Melrose turning north/left, to Carrillo Way left/west, then first right on flying L-C Lane and into the park. Alternative is I-5 to Palomar Airport road east to Melrose south. Plenty of parking, with wheelchair access down to the tour area.

50. Buena Vista Park (Vista)

The City of Vista has created a gem here. As you enter the park, you're greeted by a small pond, lots of trees, and spacious lawns with many picnic tables. For a stroll (and the pooch can go along on leash), head out on the **Arroyo Vista Trail**, dedicated a dozen years ago on Earth Day. The wide, flat dirt trail heads along a stand of eucalyptus, with many large oaks at the creek. Cross over the creek on a footbridge and continue along the creek to the right. Some huge oaks here. The first part of the trail ends at the underpass at Melrose (at Green Oak if you want to start at that end). The trail keeps going. A separate pocket park, **South Buena Vista Park**, is also quite pleasant with more shade, picnic tables, and a short paved walking loop, is located further south.

How to get there: Highway 78 to Melrose exit south. To Shadowridge Drive, right and then left into park. For the southern park, continue on Melrose to Mountain Pass Circle, right and immediate right down the road to the park.

51. Twin Peaks (San Marcos)

The City of San Marcos is developing a trail plan with the goal of 72 miles of multi-use trails. One challenging and rewarding hike heads up from **Discovery Lake**, a small pocket lake near California State University-San Marcos. On this hike of roughly 3-4 hours, you can take in 2 peaks on one hike, if you want to work a bit. Wear good lug-soled hiking boots and take water as you'll want a few swigs along the way. This will be a lot of uphill. (Don't try this in August.)

If you want to do a pleasant warmup, or just want a modest hike, stroll around the lake, enjoying a pastoral setting. Otherwise cross over to the road heading up toward **Double Peak Trail**. About 0.75 mile up, the road ends beside a huge water tank, managed by the Vallecitos Water District. Look for a dirt trail off to the left of the road. You'll appreciate those lug soles as this section is rocky. It will take a sharp turn to the right.

Soon you'll come to a "T". The left leg heads up to **Double Peak**, which you may want to make your first choice as you'll then take on one very steep segment while you're fresh. Look up to the peak and its cluster of eucalyptus and oak trees, the only ones you'll get to on this day. The first part is an easy jaunt; then as the trail heads upward it also gets dusty, the result of years of vehicles churning up the dirt. At the top you'll see the remnants of a stone house. This is a good spot for a break, as you can sit on a stone wall under the shade and take in a 360 degree view of the developing State University campus, plus North County's best peaks–Palomar, the Cuyamacas, Iron Mountain, Mt. Woodson, Mt. Israel, and continuing around to the Pacific Ocean.

Back at that "T", you can head west along a ridge over to the 2nd peak at the San Diego County Radio Transmitter Facility. This area was heavily burned a couple of years back, but the chaparral is fully regrown. As you near the tower you'll look down on Lake San Marcos, and westward toward La Costa, Bataquitos Lagoon and perhaps Fiji. You can walk down the paved road to Lake San Marcos and over to your starting place, or return the way you came up.

How to get there: Highway 78 to Twin Oaks Valley Road south, right at Craven Road to Foxhall Road, left and into the small parking lot next to Discovery Lake.

52. Guajome County Park (Vista/Oceanside) ❖❖

This nearly 600-acre county park is part of a land grant given in 1851 to Ysidora Bandini, of Old Town's Casa de Bandini fame, when she married another well-known figure of the day, Colonel Cave Couts.

Guajome is an old Indian name meaning "frog pond." When you go to the northern, main section of the park, you'll see the appropriateness of the name. This is a paradise for frogs, birds, and kids. The marsh trails and cattails along the stream are tailor-made for turning the kids loose to poke around or drop a line.

Guajome has 2 excellent picnic areas, several popular fishing holes, and several miles of hiking trails. You can get a good workout over a varied terrain, along the ponds and streams, across open meadows and into some pleasant wooded areas. One short trail goes through the woods paralleling the stream and has markers describing natural features.

Here also is a first-rate county campground for RVs or tents, in a pleasant wooded and peaceful area, with full facilities. From here enjoy a hike around the nearby lake or park trails.

Further south and separated, unfortunately, by residential areas, is the **Rancho Guajome Adobe**, built by the Couts-Bandini pairing starting in 1852. Their adobe home, one of the best (and fewest) examples of Anglo-Hispanic domestic architecture, has been nicely restored and is listed in the National Register of Historic Places. Every weekend docents will give you a detailed story about the adobe, its history, and the desk where Helen Hunt Jackson penned her tale of Ramona. Look for the special events with historic costumes and music.

Across the way from the adobe is the **Antique Farm Equipment Museum**, where you can chat with farmer-types about plows and steam engines, and enjoy the annual fall harvest, done with equipment from the old days.

How to get there: I-5 north to Oceanside, turning east on Highway 76. Go 7 miles to Santa Fe Avenue; turn right and see the park entrance. Continue another mile to the adobe on your right. The Farm Museum is just past that. To get to the park's eastern entrance stay on Highway 76 another 300 yards and turn in to the right. Alternative is to take I-5 north to Highway 78 east, to Vista Village Drive north/left to S14 (Santa Fe Avenue) to park, right to Adobe.

53. San Luis Rey River   (Oceanside)

On your way to Guajome along Highway 76 you will have passed the historic **San Luis Rey Mission**. Take a stroll through the peaceful grounds and into the mission. You can reserve a room and enjoy one of the quietest night's lodging you're likely to have. It's a popular place for retreats.

Walk behind the mission and over to the interesting **Heritage Park** on Pala Drive with restored buildings and displays, including a school house from 1893. The park was dedicated on July 4, 1976 as a Bicentennial Project. (If you grabbed a snack at the San Luis Rey Bakery & Restaurant on your walk over, you can have your picnic right here in this pleasant setting.)

Continue on to Douglas Drive and onto the paved walkway on the river's south side. This makes an interesting level stroll as you're right at the river with lots of waterfowl. Stroll a couple miles in either direction. And you can take your pooch, on leash.

How to get there: I-5 to Highway 76 east to the mission. To Heritage Park directly, turn north from Highway 76 on Douglas Drive, then right on Pala. To the river walkway, stay on Douglas Drive.

54. Live Oak Springs County Park (Fallbrook)

If oaks and shade are your thing, here's the place for you, and the kids or grandkids at this favorite North County picnic spot. Drive in along a tree-lined road, visit the colorful flower garden. A stream runs through the park, thus lots of live oaks. Once it was a popular Indian community as seen with the many morteros or grinding stones.

How to get there: I-15 north to Mission Road, west to Live Oak Park Road.

55. Santa Margarita Ecological Reserve (Fallbrook)

Way up here in North County, San Diego State University maintains the Santa Margarita Field Station at the Ecological Reserve. For over 30 years SDSU teams have conducted research along the 5-6 miles of the river within the 4500-acre reserve. The **Santa Margarita River** forms near Temecula and Murrieta, then travels here through the **Temecula Gorge**. This is a key area for predator movement, especially mountain lion and is claimed to be the only river in Southern California that still floods. In 1998 a key parcel added a half-mile of river frontage with a 160 acre purchase by the team of The Nature Conservancy and SDSU Foundation.

To visit here, you need to accompany a group that has received a visitation permit from the Reserve. It is well worth a visit, as you hike in along above the Santa Margarita River, with fine views of this large undeveloped terrain, then into the river gorge, with a variety of water pools, small falls, and surrounded by the canyon walls. This large preserve is a vital natural area surrounded by increasingly developing areas, thus it's critically important to keep this Reserve intact. The river continues west through Camp Pendleton and meets the ocean just north of Oceanside, completing its 27-mile journey.

How to get there: I-15 to Mission Road (S13) west, to Willow Glen right/ north, to Stage Coach Lane, right/north to gate. Hikers will need a pass beyond this point (e.g from the group leader).

Leo Carrillo Historic Park - Residence

Hiking - San Diego Inland

San Dieguito River Park...
South of Lake Hodges

Blue Sky Ecological Preserve

Daley Ranch

Hiking - San Diego Inland

San Dieguito
River Park-
Highland Valley

Santee Lakes

Otay Dam

Easy hiking at
Boden Canyon

San Dieguito
County Park

A day of fishing at
Lake Poway

CHAPTER 5

HIKING
MOUNTAINS
& BACKCOUNTRY

OVERVIEW

SOUTH

CENTRAL

NORTH

Hiking - Mountains & Backcountry

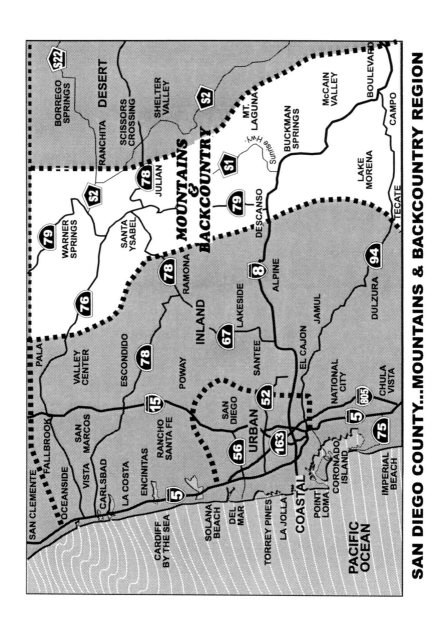

SAN DIEGO COUNTY...MOUNTAINS & BACKCOUNTRY REGION

MOUNTAINS & BACKCOUNTRY

HIKING OVERVIEW

Climb the mountains and get their good tidings.
Nature's peace will flow into you as sunshine flows into trees.

John Muir

A frequent comment by recent newcomers to San Diego is, "I love it here, but I sure do miss the seasons." By driving a bit, San Diegans can actually enjoy, if only for a brief while, each of the four seasons. Several 5 to 6 thousand foot mountains in the northern and eastern parts of the county cover the complete cycle of climatic conditions.

The mountains provide recreational opportunities of many forms for San Diegans, and make a dramatic contrast to the surfing and sailing scenes so commonly associated with the area. Picnicking, romping in the streams, hiking through the woods with walking stick or backpack, exploring Indian haunts, and discovering more about nature are some of the many varied activities furnished by the mountains.

In January the meadows and trees are often covered with snow. Locals head up for sledding and snowball fights, and the hardy ones trade their hiking boots for snowshoes and cross-country skis. In the spring, flowers of many colors make their annual appearance, and animal life rejuvenates. The altitude and ample shade can make for a cooler environment than down below. And in the fall, the colors are memorable.

Part of the Peninsular Mountains Range, much of the area is included in the **Cleveland National Forest**, part of U.S. Forest Service (USFS). The U.S. Bureau of Land Management (BLM) controls sections mainly farther east.

Many places have self-guiding nature trails, ranger hikes or campfires, and museums. Those new to the mountains might add measurably to their appreciation of the mountain life and their own experience by taking advantage of these learning opportunities, plus getting a map and descriptive pamphlets. Being able to identify flora and fauna add much to an outing. Not much of a naturalist, I take pamphlets along and have been able to spot some of the obvious. On one hike a newcomer was curious about what a red-blossomed flower was called. "Scarlet Bugler " I said. A little later, she asked about a blue one and I said "Lupine." Impressed, she asked if I were a botanist. See how little it takes? Had she asked one or two more questions, my knowledge base would have been exhausted.

Now try your hand at our mountains & backcountry quiz.

1. What does "Noble" in Noble Canyon refer to?

2. You've probably hiked in Cuyamaca Rancho State Park. So what does "Cuyamaca" mean?

3. Where were POWs from Germany and Italy kept in our local mountains?

4. If the western end of the San Dieguito River Park is at the Del Mar race track area, what's at the eastern end?

5. Why does an old airplane engine sit up on Cuyamaca's West Mesa?

6. How did the name Kelly end up associated with one of the premier hiking trails in our county?

7. What is the tallest peak in the county?

8. What county park made Sunset Magazine's list of 100 Top Campgrounds in the country?

9. Where is Thing Valley and how did it get that name?

10. Where can you visit one of the world's greatest telescopes and then go fishing ten minutes away?

Author, Tom Leech...Trail at Corte Madera

Hiking - Mountains & Backcountry

MOUNTAINS & BACKCOUNTRY SOUTH

1. Potrero County Park

This is a secluded park down near the border, with an excellent campground, recreational facilities, wildflowers and exploration opportunities. Because of its location in the southeast, it is generally uncrowded (except for certain weekends when the entire campground is booked well ahead by groups).

Get a park map from the ranger check-in office. Stroll along the trails through the park, with much of your hike under spreading oak trees. For a serious workout, hike all around the park perimeter; I suggest you definitely wear lug soled boots and carry a hiking stick as there are some serious up and down sections. For a taste of Mexico, drive over to Tecate, with its pleasant central square and major brewery.

How to get there (an experience in itself): Highway 94 past Jamul and Tecate, then left on Potrero Valley Road and right on Potrero Park Road.

2. Campo

Historic Campo is the site of our most famous shootout, plus the **Railroad Museum** with train expeditions over to Tecate or into the backcountry. Campo has an interesting military history as well, so much so that a serious effort is underway to create a state park here at Camp Lockett. Early in WWII, this was created as an Army training site for first an all-white cavalry unit, then for the Buffalo Soldiers, the historic black cavalry unit. Later, as the U.S. troops shipped out, this became a camp for German and Italian Prisoners of War (POWs). The latter group placed a shrine there in 1944 that is still here (on land leased from Archie & Gwen Leach). Get an overview of the area from the foot path behind the old stone store.

How to get there: (a) Continue on Highway 94 past Potrero and into Campo; (b) I-8 to Buckman Springs Road south.

3. Morena Valley & Lake ❖❖

Out about 90 minutes from the city is this lovely valley. Here Cottonwood Creek (joined with Kitchen Creek and La Posta Creek) comes down from the Laguna Mountains, passes through a wide mostly-flat valley and creates the

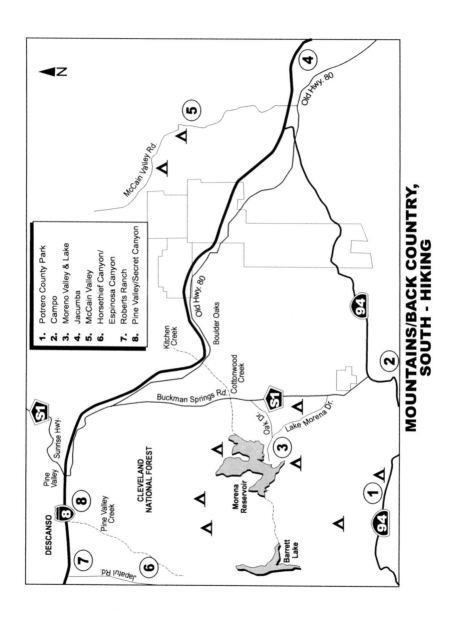

lake. It's a bit of mountain, high desert, grassland and woodland. Here outdoor opportunities abound, in a climate that is mostly on the palatable side.

Lake Morena Regional Park sits at the south end of the valley beside the reservoir and amidst 3,000 acres of oaks, chaparral and boulders. The County operates a developed campground in the shaded area at the southeast edge of the lake. Edge is used with caution as closeness to water varies with the water level of the lake which changes with water demand in the cities. You don't camp? How about a picnic? Fishing? Boating? Wind-surfing? All easily attainable from the campground. This is a truly fun spot for families, with tree-climbing, boulder-hopping and shorebird-perusing beating TV-watching any day.

This is also one of the most versatile hiking regions in the county. Fall is especially good for a visit, with good weather and colors on display. Hikers will be out on these trails all winter long, except when chilly or rainy days make them not so enjoyable. In spring this area is loaded with wild flowers. Dogs are O.K. on trails, with leashes.

From the campground, families can enjoy short or long hikes along the lake, through the oaks and pines and out to the dam (4 or 6 miles round trip, depending on route). Cottonwood Creek continues west from here, leading into and creating Barrett Lake. (Have you tried the fish at Barrett's Junction Café?)

The 2,500-mile **Pacific Crest Trail (PCT)** goes right through here, with its starting point 15-20 miles south at the border. Only 0.25 mile goes through the park proper. From the campground the PCT southern leg heads to the west along the lake. The trail is good as it passes through mostly chaparral and boulders. It can be a modest hike or heavy-duty workout as you choose, eventually dropping into **Hauser Canyon**. About 2.5 miles along, and just before the decline, look for a trail upward to **Morena Butte**. This trail winds upward another 2 miles to the plateau lake overlook. Allow 5-6 hours for this complete hike.

From the lake, the PCT continues north through some rocky sections, crosses under the bridge and then into Cottonwood Meadow. From here it's a pleasant, slightly upward hike paralleling the creek through the meadow and trees over to Boulder Oaks and I-8. Try this as a 4-5 hour 2-way hike from either the lake or Boulder Oaks, or do as a car pool, hiking one way only.

One more option, again for strong hikers, is the trail up to **Corte Madera**. This trail winds through similar country as Morena Butte but is on the north side of the lake. Plan for a 4-5 hour round trip hike up to the viewpoint overlooking the lake.

How to get there: Take I-8 east, passing Sunrise Highway a dozen miles to Buckman Springs Road. Drive south 4 miles to Oak Drive, then west 3 miles to Lake Morena Drive and the park entrance. To get to the primitive camp-ground or the Corte Madera trailhead, turn off Buckman Springs north of the lake on Morena-Stokes Valley Road. Turn into the camping area near the lake or continue on the dirt road about 7 miles to an obvious parking area from where the trail starts.

4. Jacumba

Even if you don't go out there isn't that a fun name to speak? Hah-kum-bah. If you've driven out I-8 past the Lagunas and Boulevard and arrive in the Jacumba area, you come to a dry rock- and boulder-strewn area that just calls out "Hey, there. Stop awhile, get out of that car, and come poke around." This is the high desert: nearly low desert conditions, but add 2,000 feet in altitude. If you continue east from here the highway drops continuously as it winds through the boulders, leveling off toward Ocotillo.

To explore it, walk in from the parking area along the dirt road. You'll have plenty of company out here in BLM (Bureau of Land Management) territory. It's popular with 4-wheelers, rock climbers and hikers. After the first uphill stretch, the road levels off as it continues out among the boulders and into **The Valley of the Moon**. Since you're out here to explore, you'll probably want to take some of the various road options, such as up to an old mine. There's ample desert foliage, frequent bunches of bright orange Indian Paint-brush, an occasional blue lupine, and lots of rocks (or have I said that before).

The road winds down close to the Mexican border (tip - don't cross it). On your return locate a long-abandoned cabin, which had some civilized touches, such as piped-in water, a stone-laid entry, and a healthy 8-foot pine tree (not many of those around here). A popular target, **Smugglers Cave**, is near here. You get the idea. This is an interesting place to spend some time.

How to get there: I-8 east and pass the Jacumba exit (actually just across the Imperial County line). Take the next exit, In-Ko-Pah Park Road, and drive back west a quarter mile to a dirt road. Turn in and park there, or drive in further, depending on your vehicle.

5. McCain Valley

Way out there in East County, just before the Interstate starts its spectacular drop down into the desert is the **McCain Valley Resource Conservation Area**. This is rugged high-desert country with altitude in the 3000 to 4500 foot range. Access is via one dirt road, passable by most vehicles, into this nearly 40,000 acres area in the **In-Koh-Pah Mountains**. A drive through here is itself a bit of an adventure, with some spectacular scenery looking down into Carrizo Gorge (turnoff 9 miles in from I-8) and other desert peaks and valleys.

Camping without crowds is at two developed campgrounds, **Cottonwood**, about 13 miles in from I-8, the more likely one for general camping as **Lark**, 5 miles in from I-8, is popular with ORV (Off-Road Vehicle) people. Cottonwood is quite pleasant, with shade, toilets, picnic tables and water (not the drinking kind).

Here are some definitely interesting hiking trails, though I don't suggest it for novices. Better to start with a group, led by a knowledgeable leader. Hiking east from Cottonwood takes you over to **Sombrero Peak**, a common target, and **Anza Borrego State Park**.

How to get there: I-8 east to Highway 94 exit, drive through Boulevard, left onto Old Highway 80, and left/north on McCain Valley Road, mostly dirt.

6. Horsethief Canyon/Espinosa Canyon ❖❖

Between Descanso and Jamul is this lightly-visted canyon, which is part of the **Pine Creek Wilderness** and under the auspices of the U.S. Forest Service. Trust for Public Land was involved as intermediary for setting aside a large chunk of land here. **Pine Valley Creek** empties further west into Barrett Lake. You may see deer, bobcat and perhaps an eagle. And this is definitely mountain lion terrain. This is the end of the **Secret Canyon Trail** (see #8) which starts up at Pine Valley, roughly 18 miles away. The **Espinosa Trail** (dirt road) continues on east past Corte Madera and the **Corral Canyon off road vehicle area**.

Check the large kiosk and map at the parking lot, then walk in on the trail to the dirt road. About 300 feet in see the marked trail heading down to the right. This is a steady downhill climb past chaparral and some manzanita. This stretch is open, meaning coming back out on a hot day is a workout. For fire prevention, the trail has been cut wide and parts are very rocky (lug soles a must). It continues down into the canyon, well-covered with oaks, thus shade. Proceed another mile or so to a fork (not marked, but obvious). The trail to the right crosses a creek and continues through the woods and along the creek to a large rocky section, a Native American campground with morteros. Back at the fork, if you take the left or north trail, it goes along Pine Valley Creek and eventually up to Pine Valley. A half-mile up from the fork is a swimming hole, with rocks and a small cascade.

This is moderately difficult; allow 2 hours round trip to creek areas. Best times are fall through June, though the extensive shade and water may permit a palatable summer hike. Dogs on leashes are O.K.

How to get there: I-8 to Alpine Tavern Road south, becomes Japatul Road (from the east on I-8 take Japatul south). Right at Lyons Valley Road, then 1.5 miles to turnoff to Japatul Fire Station and Horsethief parking lot and trailhead.

7. Roberts Ranch

A few year ago the ranch was on-track to be a commercial development of ranch estates. Due to a vigorous campaign, O.K., uprising, from a hard-charging citizenry, that development was stopped and the roughly 800+ acres of oak groves, meadows and peaks became part of the Cleveland National Forest.

The area has not been developed and trails that were there before are mostly overgrown. Eventually this will be developed and a valuable close-in resource. It's available to the public now and you can have an interesting exploration here.

You reach Roberts from the same exit off I-8 as for Cuyamaca, except turn right on Japatul Road instead of left. About 300 feet from the I-8 turnoff, park beside the road and enter via the equestrian gate near the Cal Trans facility. Locate a slightly obvious trail to the right along a sometimes wet creek. You're already among the oaks and solitude with the only sound of city life, the freeway traffic noise, which isn't much.

About a quarter mile in, look for a trail to the right over to a dirt road heading slightly uphill, through the forest and eventually arriving at a meadow. From here you have many choices for exploring. Stroll over to another oak grove, ramble through meadows, or climb some hills. Whatever your choice you can get readily back to home base as you can always see I-8.

Another slight trail goes along the private ranch fence and heads south. Hike through mixed terrain, pass a small creek, clamber up a rock-strewn slope and find yourself back on another road. Head north, now on the eastern boundary, tackle the hill on your left for some rock scrambling and vistas, try another hill or head back to the meadow and entrance.

Another option from the entry is to stay on an old dirt road which starts toward I-8, bends to the east and into the meadows.

How to get there: I-8 to Highway 79 exit, right on Japatul Road.

8. Pine Valley/Secret Canyon

Just west of Pine Valley is the entry to a large parking lot. Start from either side of the restrooms. The trail heads south, shortly crossing Pine Valley Creek to the east side. This is a mostly level hike through lots of Kellogg Oaks, to under the tall bridge that takes I-8 over the valley. An impressive scene. Turn around here or continue by crossing over to the west side, then under the bridge for as far as you're inclined. You could take a backpack and hike the entire **Secret Canyon Trail** down to the **Horsethief trailhead** (see #6), about an 18-mile trek.

If you turn north at the bridge you can get to the west end of the **Noble Canyon Trail**. Parking and facilities here, good picnic area under the trees. Head east on the trail to explore the area. (Hikers will be generally headed west along Noble Canyon as that's the mostly downhill direction.)

How to get there: I-8 east past Sunrise Highway to Pine Valley turnoff. Cross under I-8 to red light and turn left on Old Highway 80. Cross bridge and see marked entry at 0.9 miles from bridge. For Noble Canyon turn right just past the bridge.

MOUNTAINS & BACKCOUNTRY CENTRAL

This is the extensive outdoors mountain area north of I-8, encompassing the Lagunas, Cuyamaca State Park, and the Julian area.

9. Kitchen Creek

If you've driven east out I-8 to Arizona, you've passed right over Kitchen Creek about 70 miles out. And you probably didn't realize that just a short hike up the hill is a series of cataracts. One of the ways to get there is by hiking up the **Pacific Crest Trail** (PCT) from Lake Morena through **Boulder Oaks**.

You'll be hiking up into the **Laguna Mountains** through chaparral and observed quietly by a number of Our Lord's Candles, in full bloom in spring. About 2 miles in the PCT levels off and you'll see a trail off to the left. That will take you to the main falls area, at its fastest speed as it starts to make the final drop off the plateau.

Right here or for a mile or so up the creek is an enjoyable break from our mostly arid world. The water flows year round, amidst the canyon it created. This is a fun place to walk along and across the stream, plus clamber over the boulders. When you're ready to head back, be sure you go back up to the PCT via one of the connecting trails; otherwise the cross country route can get mighty difficult. For the round-trip from Boulder Oaks allow a half day, and count on 4.5 miles up/down.

The other way into the falls is shorter and easier as you come in from upstream starting at the bridge on Kitchen Creek Road. Park among the oaks on either side of the road and start hiking in on the dirt road just east of the bridge. About 0.25 mile in the road ends and the creek turns to the right. Look for a trail uphill off to the left. That takes you up to the PCT which follows the creek from high above it. Lots of wildflowers in spring. You'll see several trails down to the creek (be sure you come back up one of those on your way out). This in-and-out hike is about 4 miles and 2-3 hours, depending on your dawdle inclinations.

How to get there: (a) from the south. I-8 to Buckman Springs Road, east to Boulder Oaks and north on PCT. (b) from the north. I-8 to Kitchen Creek Road, north 2.8 miles to creek. Pick up PCT a short distance toward I-8 or start along the creek and look for side trail up east side of creek to the Pacific Crest Trail.

10. Cibbetts Flat

Keep going west on Kitchen Creek Road and you'll come to this Forest Service Campground, popular for camping and also for the falls a short hike west from the campground. Lots of people jump in here and enjoy a splash in and under the falls.

How to get there: I-8 to Kitchen Creek Road north. You can also get here from the Sunrise Highway as Kitchen Creek Road winds up the hillside to end up at Sunrise.

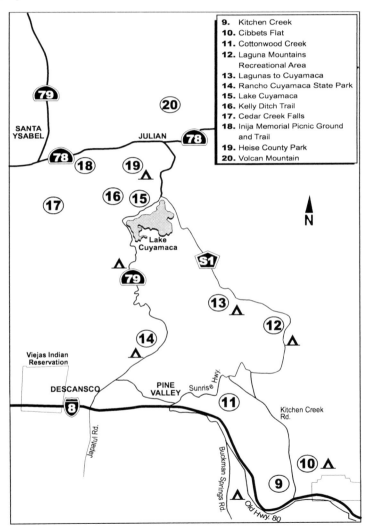

MOUNTAINS/BACK COUNTRY, CENTRAL - HIKING

Hiking - Mountains & Backcountry

11. Cottonwood Creek

When you first head north along the well-known Sunrise Highway, the first good hiking area is this one. It's lightly hiked but has much of interest. From the parking lot just off the east of the highway, head down the narrow trail through high chaparral, and with lots of flowers in spring — mariposa, penstamen, prickly pear near creek. About an hour (2 miles) down, you'll arrive at Cottonwood Creek. Oak, sycamore (but no cottonwood) here. Follow the creek upstream and soon you'll be at a series of small cataracts and pools. It can be hot in summer, but you can cool off in the creek with a couple of small dipping holes. Figure 2 hours round-trip for this 4-mile round trip hike.

How to get there: I-8 east to Sunrise Highway, north 2 miles (just past Mile 15 marker) to parking area. Trailhead is marked.

12. Laguna Mountain Recreational Area (LMRA) ❖❖

The Lagunas. That's the popular name for the area further east of the Cuyamacas, primarily along **Sunrise Highway, a National Scenic Highway**. It hosts a major recreational area and linkages to other locales. The LMRA is one of our richest natural areas. In about an hour's drive from the city, you will have left our typical arid chaparral countryside and arrived at a 6,000 foot altitude region of mountains, meadows, oaks and cedars. And fine recreational opportunities.

Many speak about the Lagunas for its winter joys, as the hillsides and meadows are often snow covered and resounding with shrieks of kids sliding downhill. In spring and summer it is a popular spot for picnics, camping, hiking and biking, with a plethora of wild flowers on display: fields of yellow buttercup, lupine, Indian Paintbrush, lavender and white lilac (ceanothus), scarlet bugler. Perhaps you'll see a deer feeding, and tracks of coyotes or wildcat. You can take your leashed dog with you along the Laguna trails.

The 8,000 acres LMRA is part of the **Cleveland National Forest** and managed by the U.S. Forest Service. Note: you will need to get the Forest Service Pass - either day use or annual. This modest fee is being used to provide some much needed improvements here. Get it at the facilities noted below or call the Ranger District Alpine Office at 619-445-6235.

Most of LMRA was spared during the October 2003 fires, with the primary areas affected north of the Laguna Campground, including Penny Pines, Noble Canyon, and Pioneer Mail.

How to get there: drive east on I-8 to the Sunrise Highway and head north. Or from Julian drive south on Highway 79 to S1 (left/south). Use the mileage markers (MM) to find key spots.

For an introduction, stop at the brand new **Visitor's Information Center** (E), just north of the store and lodge (MM23.5). The helpful members of the **Laguna Mountain Volunteers Association** (LMVA) can give you tips about the area, plus sell you other useful pamphlets and books. (A map is a must, the wild flowers pamphlet handy.) Behind the center, the **Kwaaymii Cultural Trail** is an easy self-guided half-mile loop trail.

LMVA sponsors the annual **Laguna's Living History Weekend**, an event that is great fun for all ages. Step back in time to life in our Laguna Mountains as it was in the early days. Stroll leisurely through a series of camp settings, with re-enactors portraying in costume, paraphernalia, and style many scenes from times past. An early pioneer family might have an encampment where they're cooking, sewing, making butter (maybe they'll share a bite). Next might be cowboys, offering tips about working the ranch (a la 1875). A village of Kumeyaay Indians will be demonstrating crafts (take home a willow basket).

Driving north and off to the right or east are a couple of roads of interest. **Thing Valley Road** is a dirt road off to the east. You might wonder at the name. From the Mountain Heritage newsletter (Spring 2001) comes this version as documented by family member Natella Thing Weaver: "The original (family) name as I recall was Hogg and our ancestors were English and Welsh. Someone wanted to change the name, and so the story goes, went to the judge in England, and the judge asked what name he wanted it changed to. Apparently he had not given much thought to what new name he wanted and replied 'Change it to anything.' So the judge said "THING." The valley and road seem to have been linked to Joseph Thing in the late 1800s.

Kitchen Creek Road (MM 20.5) heads out through the forest and then into open terrain, finally arriving down at the **Cibbetts Flat Campground**, then Kitchen Creek and back to I-8. With a permit, you can find some good secluded camping areas along here, going at least a quarter mile from Sunrise Highway.

Wooded Hill (B - MM 21.7)

Turn right at the road heading up to **SDSU's Laguna Mountain Observatory**, scene of many group astronomical events. Turn left, drive in a short distance to the group campground and entry to a trail heading up and around the hill (at 6223 feet altitude, it's #5 on the highest county peaks list). This is heavily wooded with an easy or tougher workout.

Sunset Trail (A) ✤✤

This trail starts at the large kiosk marking the park's southern entrance. It offers several options, any of which get you quickly among the trees, mountain meadows with panoramic views west toward the Cuyamacas. It's an easy 3-mile loop into the "**Water-of-the-Woods**" (WOTW). This is below the southern end of **Big Laguna Lake**. In spring a series of cataracts as the water continues past WOTW makes this a fun spot. Continue north passing west of the lake and meet the **Big Laguna Trail**, then left to the Noble Canyon Trail and right to end at Penny Pines on the Sunrise Highway. This makes a 5 mile journey. You can head back toward the starting point anywhere along the way, depending on your energy. For just the one way, use a 2-car shuttle.

Desert View Picnic Area (F)

Just past the Visitor's Center and off to the east is this setting for a picnic under oaks and pines, and expansive views looking down over the desert (on a clear day you can see the Salton Sea) or across to the nearby mountains. Off to the northeast is Monument Peak (attitude 6,272 feet, #4 in County). The PCT goes right through here, marking 42 miles from the border starting place. After lunch, take a stroll along the PCT, through chaparral, south to **Burnt Rancheria** (D - 2.4 miles round trip, about one hour easy walk) or north along the trail or up the paved road to Monument Peak, with the large radio towers, and Mt. Stephenson (6,220 feet altitude, #6 in County).

Big Laguna Campground (I - MM26)

This is the premier Lagunas campground, open year round. In addition to many camping facilities for individual or group camping, it has a picnic area all the way in. From here you can take an easy hike out through woodlands of oak, pine and incense cedar to Big Laguna. Explore the area, or hike over to Little Laguna Lake (often dry).

Penny Pines Parking Area (K - MM27.3) ✤✤

This is the starting area for several hikes east or west, reasonably short or significantly long. You'll see lots of action here as hikers, equestrians and bikers all know this well.

The western segment starts along the **Noble Canyon Trail**. A short distance in the **Big Laguna Trail** heads off to the left or south. This is a fun, mostly level trek through the trees, along the meadow and right up to the lake. Return the same way.

Or you can pick up the **Sunset Trail** off to the right from the Big Laguna Trail and head over to the **Water of-the-Woods** (about 3 hours). For a shorter walk loop back over to Big Laguna Trail on a less obvious trail just north of the Little Laguna Lake.

Hiking - Mountains & Backcountry

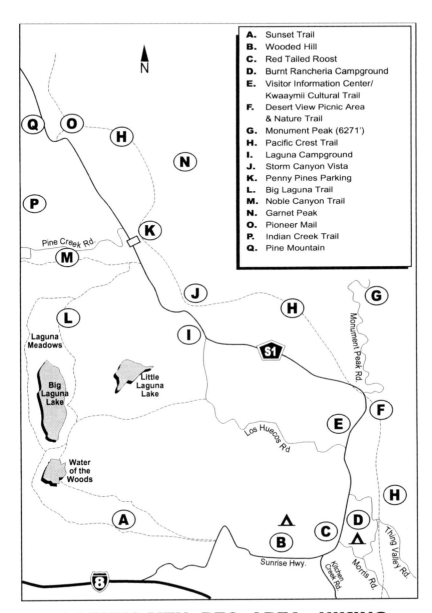

A. Sunset Trail
B. Wooded Hill
C. Red Tailed Roost
D. Burnt Rancheria Campground
E. Visitor Information Center/ Kwaaymii Cultural Trail
F. Desert View Picnic Area & Nature Trail
G. Monument Peak (6271')
H. Pacific Crest Trail
I. Laguna Campground
J. Storm Canyon Vista
K. Penny Pines Parking
L. Big Laguna Trail
M. Noble Canyon Trail
N. Garnet Peak
O. Pioneer Mail
P. Indian Creek Trail
Q. Pine Mountain

LAGUNA MTN. REC. AREA - HIKING

Noble Canyon Trail (M) ✤✤

This is one of our top trail experiences and a **National Recreation Trail**, one of only 47 in the National Forest System. It runs from Sunrise Highway to Pine Valley and is generally done as a one-way, downhill journey. The trail is as close to a major thoroughfare as you'll find, with hikers, bikers, and horses all sharing the turf. And it's turf that has a bit of everything — mountain terrain, forest, chaparral, flowers, and stream. You want to be in shape and wear good hiking boots on this one as it's about 10 miles one way or roughly 4-6 hours hiking. Definitely take water and lunch.

Noble Creek was the scene of gold mining activity in the 1800s, with the Noble brothers among the main miners. Along the creek are some remnants of that era — flume, rock foundations, metal equipment. Don't mess with them as they're all protected by the Federal Antiquities Act.

The trail is well-marked and begins at Penny Pines. Keep straight ahead when **Big Laguna Trail** (L) veers southward 300 feet in. The trail crosses the Forest Service road several times, goes in and out of forest and chaparral, with a wide variety of flowers in spring. About 5 miles in you'll arrive at **Noble Creek**, a particularly pleasant section as the trail goes along the creek and through the woods, while crossing the creek many times. A round trip hike to the creek area is roughly 10 miles, a good day's workout. Finally the trail leaves the wooded area and climbs so you look down on the stream from above while trekking through open country. The trail goes up and down but not arduously and eventually arrives at the Pine Valley parking area.

How to get there: For a two-vehicle shuttle, leave one in Pine Valley. Take I-8 to Pine Valley, turn left on Old Highway 80, then right at Pine Creek Road and 1.6 miles to parking area, restrooms and trail head. Take the second vehicle back through Pine Valley to Sunrise Highway, left to Penny Pines. A single vehicle option is take an in and out hike of whatever distance you choose, recognizing the return will have some uphill walking.

Garnet Peak (N)

This is the striking mountain right at the rim over the long drop down into the desert. Pick up the **Garnet Peak Trail** from the parking area around MM27.8, just before Pine Creek Road. Take the trail east, crossing the PCT over to the peak (5909 feet). Don't be surprised if the wind is swooping up from the desert. Come back down to the Pacific Crest Trail (PCT) and hike north along it to the **Pioneer Mail Picnic Area.** (You can also start here and reverse the route.) Here is more shade, restrooms and a bit of history as the information kiosk will note this was the original mail delivery route from Texas to San Diego, bringing the "jackass mail" here (for the pack animals that carried it). Still on the PCT continue north to Kwaaymii Peak.

A longer way over to Garnet Peak is from Penny Pines, where the PCT goes just east of the parking area.

Pioneer Mail (O)

Pioneer Mail is also a good starting point for hikes to the west. Cross over Sunrise Highway to pick up the **Indian Creek Trail** (P), through the gate. You can take this over to pick up the **Noble Canyon Trail** and on to Pine Valley or back to Penny Pines. Or continue heading west on over to Cuyamaca.

Also across Sunrise Highway, look to the right heading up the hill for a recently opened trail onto **Pine Mountain** (Q). Up here is a small pond, lots of trees, a good picnic spot. Continue on to pick up Indian Creek Trail and back to Pioneer Mail.

13. Lagunas to Cuyamaca ❖❖

This one takes a two-car relay unless you're a whole lot tougher hiker than I. This hike encompasses both these major recreational areas by going from Sunrise Highway over to Highway 79 in **Cuyamaca State Park**. It's actually less forbidding than it appears as the trails are mostly easy to follow, the scenery is magnificent, and knowing that second car is waiting is encouraging. It is roughly in the downhill direction, with a couple of significant uphill treks on a 12-mile journey.

Leave one car on Highway 79 at the **Sweetwater Bridge** (or other end point). Drive back over and park either at **Pioneer Mail** picnic area or the **Penny Pines** parking area by the road. From Penny Pines head west on the **Noble Canyon Trail**. Two miles in, turn right on the **Indian Creek Trail**. (If you started from Pioneer Mail, this is that trail.) Cross the creek, keep on walking and soon you arrive at the sign marking the entrance to the state park. Now you'll be on the **East Mesa Fire Road**, which intersects the **Harvey Moore Trail**. Walk left or south, perhaps with a side trip to Granite Springs, then down to Sweetwater Bridge, where that other car is waiting (perhaps with some energizing drinks in the cooler).

14. Rancho Cuyamaca State Park ❖❖

What the locals refer to as Cuyamaca is the state park of 26,000 acres, with 6,000+ foot mountains, broad meadows, spreading oaks and pines, making it one of this County's most valuable natural areas. It's readily accessible, and offers outdoors opportunities for easy strolls or heavy-duty treks along its 100 miles of trails. Many San Diegans make jaunts to Cuyamaca, a vital part of enjoying nature and restoring sanity to busy lives.

Cuyamaca was especially hard hit during the October 2003 fires. Much of the natural terrain was burnt, and most of the town on the north edge of the reservoir was destroyed. The park headquarters historical building was destroyed, yet the nearby 6th grade camp and main campgrounds were mostly spared. While the trails were obscured, it's likely they will recover to match pre-fire situations. The following writeups will need to be adapted to the conditions as they evolve.

A good starting place is **Park Headquarters and Museum** (M) in mid-park (at 6.2-mile marker), with displays and photos describing Cuyamaca's wildlife and history (the name means "rain from above" or some variation thereof). A "must-have " is the park map, which shows all the trails, picnic spots and campgrounds. Also pick up the pamphlets identifying mountain flowers and shrubs. These apply to any of the mountain areas and can make you sound like a naturalist when you can say "Well, daughter, that's a lupine, not a daisy." You can picnic here and take a short walk north along the creek. It leads to an open meadow, with a fine view of **Stonewall Peak** and possibly some deer. A series of exhibits, built by the kids attending the legendary 6th grade camp, shows how the Native Americans lived.

If you just want to picnic, visit either campground, **Green Valley and Paso Picacho**. If you take your pooch, be aware that they're allowed only in the campgrounds, not the trails.

How to get there: Drive east on I-8 to Highway 79 turnoff, north at Descanso to the park.

What follows are a variety of places to visit or trek, all accessible from the highway. As you drive north, to your left is West Mesa, to your right, East Mesa.

Descanso Entry (A)

The southernmost trail is the **Merigan Trail**. Take the turnoff at Descanso Junction and at 0.5 miles along at the **Sweetwater River** you'll see the sign, kiosk, and stables. This is a little known trail up the river into the park. You may see some horsey groups on the trail, but otherwise you mostly have the place to yourselves. It happens to be one of the most pleasant hikes in the park, with the river flowing steadily downhill, frequent shade trees and flowers. You can hike up and back or continue on over to over to **Green Valley Falls**.

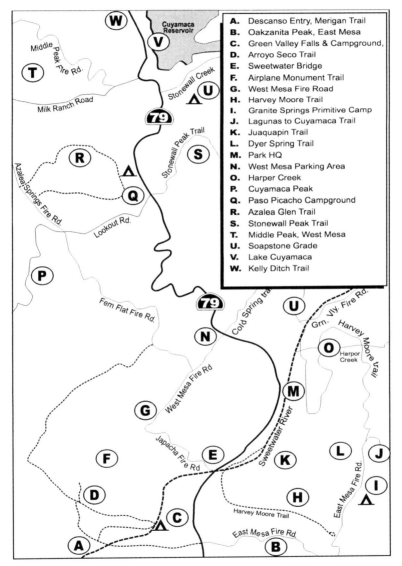

A. Descanso Entry, Merigan Trail
B. Oakzanita Peak, East Mesa
C. Green Valley Falls & Campground,
D. Arroyo Seco Trail
E. Sweetwater Bridge
F. Airplane Monument Trail
G. West Mesa Fire Road
H. Harvey Moore Trail
I. Granite Springs Primitive Camp
J. Lagunas to Cuyamaca Trail
K. Juaquapin Trail
L. Dyer Spring Trail
M. Park HQ
N. West Mesa Parking Area
O. Harper Creek
P. Cuyamaca Peak
Q. Paso Picacho Campground
R. Azalea Glen Trail
S. Stonewall Peak Trail
T. Middle Peak, West Mesa
U. Soapstone Grade
V. Lake Cuyamaca
W. Kelly Ditch Trail

CUYAMACA RANCHO STATE PARK - HIKING

Hiking - Mountains & Backcountry

5 - 21

Oakzanita Peak, East Mesa (B)

This hike starts from the first paved parking lot you'll meet inside the park (before Green Valley Falls). Head east and you'll see the obvious peak just to the south. This trail is well-marked so take the side trails (one is at 2.8 miles in) right up there. An option is to take the trail marked E16 to the left over to the **Harvey Moore Trail**.

Green Valley Falls and Campground, West Mesa (C)

On your left is this popular spot. Some go here to picnic, some to walk out to the falls and splash around, and some to camp overnight. It meets all those interests nicely. Plus it is the starting (or ending) place for some good hiking out onto West Mesa. For a good introductory hike, take the **Pine Ridge Trail** west and loop back on the **Arroyo Seco Trail** (D). Or keep going north on Arroyo Seco to **West Mesa Fire Road**, over to Sweetwater Bridge and back to camp along the **West Side Trail**.

Airplane Monument, West Mesa (F) ❖❖

Just past the campground is the landmark **Sweetwater Bridge** from which many trails emanate, both east and west, and popular with equestrians and hikers. This trail starts at the north side of the bridge, heading west. Turn right at the West Side Trail (which parallels the highway all the way up to the Paso Picacho Campground). A short trek leads you to a left turn onto the **Japacha Fire Road**. Hike gently uphill along Japacha Creek, through oaks, pines and open meadows about 1.5 miles to where it intersects with the **West Mesa Trail** (or it may be identified as heading toward **Japacha Spring**.)

Go left, pass marker for Japacha Spring (likely closed), and then look for a sign marking the **Airplane Monument,** which is the engine from the airplane that crashed here. It's placed in a small clearing and dedicated to the aviators who lost their lives: "December 7, 1922. Col. F. C. Marshall and 1st. Lt. C. L. Webber fell on this spot."

Benches make this is a good spot for lunch and reflection. From here, hike down along Monument Trail through open chaparral to join the cutoff back left to West Side Trail and Sweetwater Crossover. Allow about 3 hours for this hike.

An alternative goes the other way. Start the same way, then walk south along West Side Trail. Near the campground look for the marker to **Arroyo Seco Road**. Take it upward to the west (or right). About 1.5 miles up from the camp pass through **Arroyo Seco Primitive Camp**, one of only two places for backpackers to camp (and for which you need a permit and have to park at the campground, not the bridge).

This was a Native American camping area as you can quickly determine from morteros or grinding stones on the large boulders and under the spreading oaks (thus a likely communal talking and grinding spot). Continue along the trail to a right fork (B12, B13 or **Cutoff Trail**, depending on which map you have). A half mile along (or 1.6 miles from Arroyo Seco Camp) is the intersection for the trail heading down to Monument Trail (i.e. toward Highway 79) and the Airplane Monument (0.1 mile back north along W. Mesa Trail). Take **Monument Trail** back down as noted before. Allow 3-4 hours.

Sweetwater Bridge, East Mesa (E) ❖❖

The East Mesa side offers many options for hiking, from a modest to serious workout.

Head east onto the **Harvey Moore Trail** (H). Hike at a steady uphill pace until arriving at a trail crossing at 2.4 miles, marked by what is known as the "big tree." Keep going east another 1.6 miles and you'll arrive at the **Granite Springs Primitive Camp** (I - useful to know is there's a genuine toilet here). Continue on around for a few more hours and you come out in the Park Visitors' Center region. Take the **Harper Creek Trail** (O) west to that vicinity, grab the **East Side Trail** back to the bridge. You'll have done about 10.5 miles.

For a much shorter hike, at 1.4 miles in take the cutoff over to the **Juaquapin Trail** and back to the bridge. Or a bit longer, at that "big tree" take a left or north along the **Dyer Spring Trail** (L). Take this to the **Juaquapin Trail** (K), turn left and back to the bridge.

Reverse the last option by starting out from the bridge along the **Juaquapin Trail**, from the north end of the parking lot.

Here's one more, mostly level hike that takes you through areas rich in foliage and wildflowers without too much work. From the bridge, take the **Juaquapin Trail**, then the **East Side Trail**. Stop at the park headquarters for a restroom break, lunch by the river and a visit to the museum. Take the short hike north along the river and back. Cross over the highway to the **West Side Trail** and troop back to the bridge. Plan a couple of very pleasant hours.

Park Headquarters Trails

Described earlier, this also is a good starting point for several hikes. Park in the lot just off the road, as parking near the HQ and museum is time limited. For a short, educational hike walk down the paved road to the **Cold Stream Trail** which goes to the left or north along the creek. You can continue north past the trail exhibits on over to **Paso Picacho** or **Stonewall**.

Another fun place is **Harper Creek**, also on East Mesa. Walk past the park headquarters and museum area. This is an easy hike out across and along the creek, about 1-2 hours round trip. The creek is especially lively in spring and early summer. Or, for a heavy duty hike, keep on going onto the **Harvey Moore Trail**, looping around to the south, returning back on the **Dyer Spring Trail** to the headquarters parking lot .

You can also head west from the parking area, picking up the **West Side Trail** either north or south to the **Japacha Fire Road**, looping back to the start. For a longer loop hike pick up the **West Mesa Fire Road**.

West Mesa Parking Area (N)

Next major trail entry is from this lot, the second one north from Park HQ. You have many choices from here, heading either up the **West Mesa Fire Road** and beyond or along **Westside Trail**; east on the **Cold Stream Trail** or **East Mesa Fire Road** over to **Stonewall** and more.

Cuyamaca Peak, West Mesa (P)

West of Highway 79 are three peaks, with two called Middle and North, so logic says that Cuyamaca will be the southern one, the first you pass as you drive in from I-8 and the most prominent. You have many options for making your trek up to the 6,512 feet peak, the 2nd highest in the county. Any of them go right through prime forest territory, along marked trails (mostly). Whichever route you choose will be rewarding and uphill, with roughly 6 miles round trip, so plan about a half-day hike. Take water and extra clothing as the weather may shift as you hike.

One route starts from the **West Mesa parking area**. Head up the **West Mesa Fire Road** (G) to a 3-way intersection. Take the trail to the right, staying on the Fire Road and heading to the Fern Flat Fire Road. Go to the right or north, joining the **California Riding & Hiking Trail**. At **Lookout Road** (or **Cuyamaca Peak Fire Road**), turn left and from here it's a long paved road to the top. Either return the same way or locate a trail to the **Burnt Pine Fire Road** (as you come back down 0.4 miles, it will be off to your right or south). That's a rambling stroll mostly downhill back to the California R&H Trail and W. Mesa Fire Road.

Another route starts from the south end of Lake Cuyamaca. Drive 1.5 miles north of **Paso Picacho Campground** to the parking lot beside the road, generally with cars and hikers coming and going. Head up the paved **Milk Ranch Road** to an obvious ridge and trail intersection with spectacular spreading oaks. Take the **Azalea Spring Fire Road** to the left, then a short way along turn right on the **Conejos Trail**. This heads through more forest and about an hour along you'll arrive at the paved **Cuyamaca Peak Road**. Head right 0.5 miles up to the peak. Come back the same way.

Paso Picacho Campground (Q)

This is a good place for camping, picnicking, exploring and starting place for many excellent hikes.

Azalea Glen, West Mesa (R) ✤✤

Near the restrooms in Paso Picacho, locate the **Azalea Glen Trail** and start up along the trail many people rate their favorite. This is a loop trail, with the Azalea Spring at the top. You can hike either in clockwise or counter clockwise direction, with lots of shade all the way and even a modest creek on the northern section.

The spring has flowing water, an informational kiosk and is a good spot for a rest and snack. Locate the **Azalea Spring Fire Road** and hike to the left (south) to Lookout Road. This is paved and goes steadily uphill, not as much fun as the Azalea Glen, but the views along the way and from the top are worth it. Another good snack spot is atop the boulders right at the peak. Come back down the road and return via the other half of the **Azalea Spring Trail.**

Stonewall, East Mesa (S) ✤✤

This the most obvious landmark in Cuyamaca State Park, and the trail up is well trod from the thousands of hikers young and old who've been making that trek for decades. The trailhead for **Stonewall** starts across the road from **Paso Picacho Campground**. At 5,730 feet, it's not one of the major peaks in the park; yet because it's so obvious it demands to be climbed. Though fairly steep it's a moderate and pleasant climb, with terrific views of Lake Cuyamaca, the forests and meadows below and the adjoining peaks.

Then there's another Stonewall option, hiking around it, not up it. This meets a couple of important criteria on my spouse's list for choosing whether to hike or not to hike, namely it's mostly level and mostly shaded. The hike around can make for a pleasant morning, perhaps followed with a picnic. Or on cool days, a hike later in the day works fine as well.

From the **Paso Picacho Campground**, cross the road and hike south along the **Cold Stream Trail**. The trail parallels the highway and winds through the forest and along the creek. About a mile in the trail heads sharply east or left, and is marked. (The route from here becomes easy to follow, as it's all left turns around the mountains.) Take that another mile, with a short uphill stint here, to the **Stonewall Creek Fire Road** heading north or left. This passes through many wooded clusters, with ample photo ops across the meadows of **Stonewall Peak** and its sidekick, **Little Stonewall** (5,250 feet). About the time you've passed those peaks, you'll see the sign for the **Vern Whitaker Trail**, to the left. That will pass by **Los Vaqueros Group Camp**, and **Los Caballos Horse Camp**. Continue almost to the highway and pick up again the **Cold Stream Trail** back to Paso Picacho.

Hiking - Mountains & Backcountry

Middle Peak, West Mesa (T) ❖❖

This is a moderately uphill trek (peak height is 5883 feet) through some of the most shaded part of the park. Start early from the parking area on the park's northern edge, at **Milk Ranch Road** just south of Lake Cuyamaca, and you'll soon be under thick shade for almost the entire hike. You can come back down the same way, take a side trail over to the lake, or circle middle peak and loop back down to the parking area. Or, to toss in some other variations, hike on over to the **Azalea Spring/Cuyamaca Peak** complex of trails linked to Paso Picacho Campground.

Green Valley/Soapstone Grade (U)

This is a pleasant hike out across the northeastern edge of the park, combining many of the best features of the park. This is about a 4-hour good workout hike with a rich reward in the view overlooking Lake Cuyamaca. From the **West Mesa parking area**, head east a short distance to the **Cold Spring Trail**. Walk right along the creek to the **Upper Green Valley Fire Road**. After a lengthy amble through a mixture of wooded and open terrain arrive at the Soapstone Grade Fire Road, turning left or west. This stretch offers the views of the lake. Turn left/south at the **Stonewall Creek Fire Road**, a mostly open stretch with Stonewall over to your right. Take the **Cold Springs Trail** to the right and you're heading for the home stretch, with the last part in much-welcome shade.

15. Lake Cuyamaca (V)

This modest reservoir nestling in the mountains on the way to Julian serves as a focus of many outdoor adventures. It's well worth a visit for fishing, a pleasant lunch on the deck of the restaurant overlooking the lake (with maybe even an oom pah band), or for a hike around the lake, combined with a picnic among the oaks. There's parking at the restaurant area, along the lake's north side, and just off Highway 79 a short distance south of the lake (no fee here).

You can take your own trek around the lake shore or over to what appears to be an island but isn't and shaded picnic tables overlooking the lake. As you lunch you'll be entertained by the many birds which make the lake their home, even if only on a temporary basis. The lake's recreational group sponsors guided 3.5 mile hikes each Sunday afternoon. Other options:

A short jaunt heads over to the **Old Stonewall Mine** where once gold mining occurred in a big way. The trail leads from the **Milk Ranch Road** lot, just off Highway 79 a short distance south of the lake. From here you can enjoy a pleasant walk along the lake. Or reach the mine trail by crossing over the walkway from the lake's north side. Continue from the mine trail over to a less-crowded way up Stonewall. Across the road from the restaurant, take the trail over to meet the **Middle Peak Trail**.

How to get there: I-8 east to Highway 79 turnoff, north at Descanso and through the state park to the lake.

16. Kelly Ditch Trail (W) ❖❖

This area was heavily impacted by the October 2003 fires, with signifi-cant damage both to the natural areas and to structures at both ends of the trail.

This trail leads you on a mostly downhill hike from the lake over to **Heise Park**. The one-way hike requires a car shuttle (leaving pickup car at Heise), is about 5.5 miles mostly in slightly downhill direction, and takes 3-4 hours. For sturdy hikers the round-trip is an all-day 11-mile workout.

The trailhead, marked with a small sign, starts from the northern end of **Lake Cuyamaca** just west of Engineer Road. The trail follows an old walled ditch, gently upward as it goes just to the west of North Peak. It's a good, well-marked trail through oaks, cedars, pines, and manzanita. Fall colors and views are excellent and lots of wildflowers are on display in spring.

Make an easy crossing on rocks over **Cedar Creek**. There's some more mod-erate uphill hiking, then a long downhill stretch. You'll see a sign directing you to **Heise Park**, with the trail ending at the parking lot, conveniently next to a lovely picnic area. If you left your first vehicle well-stocked with a cooler and snacks, this is a fine a way to end a delightful hike. (Or Plan B, a late lunch and cool drink back at the **Lake Cuyamaca Restaurant** isn't bad ei-ther.)

How to get there: For the 2-vehicle shuttle. Take Highway 67 through Ramona, to Highway 79 to Pine Hills Road, right. To Deer Lake Park Road left to Frisius, left to end at entrance to campground. Pay small fee and leave ve-hicle in lot to right. To drive other vehicle to Lake Cuyamaca, go back to 79 and right to Julian. Stay on Highway 79 (south) to Lake Cuyamaca. Park either at main lot by restaurant or get parking sticker and park in lot just north of the dam. Return back here from Heise.

17. Cedar Creek Falls/Saddleback Trail
(Pine Hills/Ramona)

For a hike to someplace out of the ordinary, take a hike to these picturesque falls in the backcountry. Though hard to reach, this is a popular destination. **Much of this area was burned during the October 2003 fires. In fact the major Cedar Fire started in this area.**

Allow 3-4 hours round trip for either hike. The Forest Service emphasizes the importance of taking plenty of water as they receive frequent calls to send in the Search & Rescue squad to help out a hiker who typically partied too much at the falls and coming back out got heat stroke. Also groups hiking from the Ramona side will need permission (read below). Wear long pants, etc. as this is definitely poison oak country.

Most people visit here from the Pine Hills side, hiking down the river. At the parking area see the Forest Service sign marking the **Saddleback Trail**. You might have some company as this is a popular route (and don't be surprised if there's partying and splashing at the end). Hike down that, with some expansive views as you go (including **Mildred Falls** off to the left). About a half-hour along, take the spur road off the left to the creek and then downstream to the top of the falls. Enjoy the view (and in spring real falls) but use extra care if you're trying this segment as it's steep and slippery. Most accidents occur during this trek down or up, plus from diving into the pools.

An alternative hike heads up the river from Ramona. I was originally alerted about this route from a faithful reader of the **SD Magazine Outdoors Forum**. It is a spectacular trek, with part through Helix Water District land. Groups will need permission from the district officer at 619-667-6268; individuals are requested to also call ahead.

From the parking area, the obvious landmark is the large water tank up the dirt road. Look for an opening (actually two) through the fence on the left of the road about 200 feet before the tank. The further (official) one has a Forest Service kiosk. Hike in on either trail and within 200 feet see the obvious trail winding down slightly to the left through the chaparral. At the rock outcropping, you have a fine view down into the valley and the mountains beyond. Head down and cross the tree-lined **San Diego River** on its way to **El Capitan Reservoir**. Continue straight ahead onto the trail which after a short hike comes to **Cedar Creek**. Follow a sometimes trail and clamber over rocks to reach the bottom of the falls. Return the same way, re-crossing the river and making an arduous hike (especially on a hot day) up this steep hill back to the road.

How to get there: Highway 67 to Ramona, continuing east on Highway 78 passing Santa Ysabel and up towards Julian. Six miles up, turn right onto Pine Hills Road. At 1.5 miles turn right onto Eagle Peak Road. At the "T", stay right (Boulder Creek Road is to left). Continue 8.2 miles on driveable dirt roads to end of Eagle Peak Road. You will need an Adventure Pass.

For the alternative (upriver) hike, take Highway 67 toward Ramona to Dye

Road right, then left on Ramona Street, right at Warnock Drive to San Vicente Road right. (Or from Lakeside, Wildcat Canyon Road to San Vicente Road right). Pass most of the golf course to the left on Ramona Oaks. Take it almost to the end (that's Mt. Gower on your left), then right on Thornbush. Park at the end of the regular street, or continue in a short way toward the water tank. You will need an Adventure Pass.

18. Inaja Memorial Picnic Ground and Trail

Heading east from Santa Ysabel, this is the first park you'll meet up the hill and off to the right. It's a pleasant stop for a picnic and easy stroll along the **National Recreation Trail** overlooking the **San Diego River** (yes, that one going through Mission Valley). The memorial honors eleven firefighters killed in 1956.

How to get there: From Ramona, drive east on Highway 78, replenish your nutrient needs at Dudley's Bakery in Santa Ysabel, continue east and up the mountain.

19. Heise County Park ✤✤

Sunset Magazine included this San Diego County Park on its top 100 list. This jewel of the county park system is more than a premier campground, it's also a place for terrific picnicking and hiking along its roughly 6 miles of nearby trails, plus access to many more. Here you'll see meadows, a creek, and forests of oak, pine and cedar among its nearly 1000 acres. **Sadly, almost 700 of those lush acres were burned in the October 2003 fire**.

William Heise was an entrepreneur (and inventor of a wheeled ambulance stretcher — another reason to appreciate him) who owned and sold the original 500 acres at low cost to the County for this park.

First the campground. Over a hundred campsites are dispersed throughout the area, with two locales permitting recreational vehicles, and one restricted to tents only. Each site has a table and fire ring. Full toilet and (hot) shower facilities. For those without shelter, check into the two cabins, spartan but with bunk beds and tables and good views of the mule deer which may appear.

Picnicking is hard to beat at Heise. One picnic area is right at the entrance, and you may see hikers strolling past here to their cars after hiking the **Kelly Ditch Trail**. Other picnic areas are located further inside the park.

Hiking options range from easy to strenuous. **The Self-guided Nature Trail** is a half-mile loop from the tent campground. Also near there are the **Canyon Oak Trail** (1.25 mile loop) and the 2.25-mile **Desert View Trail** which rises to 5,700 feet at **Glen's View**. From here you can see the Salton Sea or the Coronado Islands, if the clouds cooperate, and they often do in the fall. Back near the RV area is the 1-mile **Cedar Trail** which crosses Cedar Creek and either loops back to the campground or, with a short side jaunt, arrives at the **Kelly Ditch Trail**. Serious hikers can walk along this trail (lovely, shaded, somewhat uphill) nearly 6 miles over to Lake Cuyamaca, though many people do it the other way, leaving their cars at Heise for a two-car shuttle. If you park here, you'll need to display the National Forest Adventure Pass, available from the ranger station.

How to get there: I-8 east to Highway 67 to Ramona. Head east on Highway 78 through Santa Ysabel and before Julian, turn right on Pine Hills Road (south) and follow the signs to Heise.

20. Volcan Mountain ❖❖

This is one of our least known major mountain areas, and yet one of the most pleasant ways to hike along a fine trail, through woods and open meadows, to some of our best vistas. Volcan is just north of Julian, out in wine and apple country. You may have also heard it referred to as the **Rutherford Ranch**, once planned for development. However some stalwart folks known as the **Volcan Mountain Conservancy** started agitating to make it a public park instead. With the help of the Rutherfords and Trust for Public Land, they made it happen. With public funding over the past several years, the preserve is now around 10,000 acres, well along on the target of setting aside the full 12,000.

Today Volcan is the eastern terminus of **San Dieguito River Park**. Because much of it is either recently acquired and still being surveyed, or still privately held, hiking the main trail to the top can only be done with sanctioned groups.

Our best known master of environmental architecture, Jim Hubbell, applied his design talents, and volunteers built a work of natural art for the entryway. You'll pass through it to start your hike.

The hike up is along a wide trail, much of it a dirt road. Unlike most of our mountain trails, you can do this one with tennis shoes. The trail passes by many shrubs and mountain flowers. Part of the time you're among several varieties of oak, incense cedar, then wide meadows. You can go part way along before hitting the locked gate. A guide will point out the Elsinore earthquake fault along the trail. The full round trip might take 2-3 hours. But don't rush this one. Take a lunch, breathe clean mountain air at 5,353 feet and enjoy fine views of the desert to the east, looking directly down on **Scissors Crossing** and **Anza Borrego State Park**. Look south and see the thousands of people milling around trying to find a parking place somewhere near Julian, while your party has perhaps a thousand acres per person to share with the occasional deer. A stop at the Menghini Winery might top off a pleasant day.

How to get there: From San Diego I-8 east to Highway 67 north. Pass through Ramona to Julian's main street and stoplight. Left or north on Farmers Road to the "T", right, then a quick left still on Farmers Road; Pass first apple orchard, see sign and road to right. Parking is limited to along Farmers Road. Entry to park is 300 feet up the road through well-marked gate.

MOUNTAINS & BACKCOUNTRY NORTH

When most people think about or visit the mountains in North County, they generally are talking about Palomar, home of the world-famous Palomar Observatory. And a whole lot more is waiting for you up there. We'll start with the area north from Santa Ysabel on Highway 79. Make a short side trip to the Santa Ysabel Mission and cemetery offering interesting history and an inviting small chapel. An alternative way up to Palomar Mountain is via Valley Center and east on Highway 76.

21. Lake Henshaw

The **San Luis Rey River** starts up in the Bucksnort and Palomar Mountains, is the major source of Lake Henshaw, goes through several important Indian lands, passes by the San Luis Rey Mission, and empties into Oceanside Harbor. State Highway 76 follows the river most of the way from Lake Henshaw to Oceanside, providing one of the most scenic drives in the county.

Lake Henshaw, the County's largest reservoir (except when it's not), sits in a vast valley, surrounded by the Volcan Mountains to the east and Mount Palomar to the west. Fishing is the only recreational activity on the lake. Across the road is a store, cabins and campground.

How to get there: (a) I-15 to Highway 76 east to shortly before intersection with Highway 79 (b) Highway 79 north from Santa Ysabel to Highway 76, left.

22. San Luis Rey Picnic Area

West of Lake Henshaw on Highway 76 a Forest Service picnic area is located in a lovely wooded area just off the road. A wooden footbridge leads across the river so adventurers can explore both sides. Rapids, pools and fallen trees make this fun spot.

How to get there: On Highway 76, 2.5 miles west of Lake Henshaw.

23. La Jolla Indian Reservation and Water Park

Placed nicely along the San Luis Rey River between Lake Henshaw and the Palomar road is the **La Jolla Indian Campground**. Extending 2 miles along the river are several hundred campsites in this heavily wooded area.

Its **Sengme Oaks Water Park** becomes one of the most refreshing places in the County during hot summer months, with long water slides, a huge pool, and inner tubing through the rapids. Fishing is good here, also, where the tubers aren't. Reservations for groups only.

How to get there: From Escondido, take S6 through Valley Center to Highway 76, turn right and drive 9 miles east.

24. Palomar Mountain State Park ✤✤

Palomar is a beautiful spot for enjoying nature, fresh air and fall colors as well as the stars. Palomar offers ample opportunities for an afternoon picnic where you and the family can enjoy the foliage in comfort. The **State Park** is a popular destination, with an excellent campground and many other outdoors options. All of the recreational spots have excellent picnic areas, with parking, tables, restrooms, and easy to challenging hikes. And the **Observatory**, museum and other campgrounds are a short distance away.

Get a map at the park entrance. Less than a half-mile along is the **Silver Crest Picnic Area**, with tables, restrooms, many huge oaks and Ponderosa Pines. A plaque tells the story of the 400-year old incense cedar which spreads broadly. Just behind it you'll see many Indian morteros (grinding holes).

Continue down to the campground, and the parking lot at **Doane Pond**, a popular spot for picnics, fishing and the starting place for several hikes:

A. **Easy hike**, 45 minutes. Right from the parking lot see the **Doane Valley Nature Trail**, off to the right. This goes along the creek and over to the campground. From here walk down the road back to the parking lot.

B. **Another easy hike**, 1-2 hours. Walk past the pond and to the left onto the **Thunder Spring Trail**. This is nearly level and heads along Doane Creek through a heavily-wooded area. About one mile in is an intersection. Take the trail to the left, crossing the creek and over to the **Upper Doane Valley Trail**. This will take you along the wide meadows and back to the parking lot.

C. **Moderate hike**, 2-3 hours. From the lot, walk past the pond and onto the **Cedar Trail**. You'll be in a forest of cedars, thus lots of shade. After a short hike take **Scott's Cabin Trail** to the left. Less than a half-mile along, look for the trail off to the right and over to the **Silver Crest Picnic Area**. Walk out to the paved road and to the left. Pass another plaque honoring the many CCC (Civilian Conservation Corps) members who worked here from 1933-42. A short distance along, spot the marker for the **Boucher Trail**. As you head up this trail, you'll puff a bit, but pace yourself to enjoy the trees, open spaces, and terrific views of the valley below. The trail leads to **Boucher Lookout** observation point and communications tower. A kiosk notes the area is named after early pioneer William Bougher (somewhere the "g" became a " c" and the pronunciation bow-ker, somehow better than boo-ger). Head down the other leg of the **Boucher Trail**, and now you're heading back toward where you started and mostly downhill. After 0.8 mile cross the road (Nate Harrison Grade), continuing now on the **Adams Trail** 0.6 mile to **Cedar Grove Group Campground**. At the **Weir Trail**, you can turn right and go directly to the parking lot, or take a left, walk a short distance onto the **Lower Doane Trail**. This choice takes you through the main campground and down the road to the parking lot.

D. **Serious workout**, 4-5 hours. Start out the same as Hike B, along the **Thunder Spring Trail**. When you come to that "T", continue on to the **Chimney Flats Trail**. This winds through the forest and across the meadows and comes back onto **Scotts Cabin Trail**. Take the same cutoff over to the **Silver Crest Picnic Area** and finish with the final stretch of Hike C.

How to get there: (a) Take I-15 north to Rancho Parkway, east to Bear Valley Parkway, north to S-6 (Valley Center Road), to Highway 76/S6 right (east) to S7 left and up the mountain. At the Palomar Mountain General Store and Mother's Kitchen restaurant (a good spot for restroom break and repast), go left to the State Park. (b) Highway 79 north from Santa Ysabel to Highway 76, left to the Palomar Mountain turnoff (S7 - turn right) up the mountain.

25. Palomar Observatory, Campgrounds & Trails ❖❖

Taking the other road, up toward the Observatory, you'll pass the two USFS campgrounds, nearly across the road from each other and located in heavy conifer and oak forests. From the **Observatory Campground**, take the **Observatory National Recreation Trail** which leads 2.1 miles through well-forested terrain up to the museum with excellent views along the way. Or you can start there and walk down. Allow a couple of hours round trip or one hour one way with two cars. Or stop in at the Fry Creek Campground with plenty of good hiking, foliage and views here too.

How to get there: At the store and restaurant, instead of turning left to the State Park, continue straight ahead for the campgrounds and Observatory.

26. Hot Springs Mountain

On the **Los Coyotes Indian Reservation** near **Warner Springs** is a wealth of outdoors opportunity that is tapped into by only a few people. At 25,000 acres, this is the County's largest Indian reservation. (With its remote location, the tribe is planning a casino not here but in Barstow, where 60 million people traverse yearly on the way to Vegas.) Here is the **tallest mountain in the County** at 6,533 feet, campgrounds with spacious sites under the oaks, and explorations galore. And you'll probably see a dozen people all day. From the entrance, where they collect a modest fee for either day use or overnight camping, get a map and some suggestions (which warn against the rough direct road up). Take the road 2.5 miles to the main campground, a good place to stop for a picnic or amble either in the sunny fields or the cooler shaded areas.

Don't expect many directional signs as you continue further on up the occasionally rough dirt road while enjoying marvelous views of Lake Henshaw, Salton Sea and Palomar. Locate the remote campground (Nelson's) and walk on over, or try the trail to the left. Either way makes for a 2-3 mile hike through the woods and along old roads not used by drivers with any sense (e.g. map identifies one as "Dangerous Road"). It may be cool up here due to the altitude and shade. You'll arrive at **Hot Springs Road**, from where you can make your way over to the actual peak.

How to get there: Take Highway 79 past Lake Henshaw to just before Warner Springs Resort, turning right or east on Camino San Ignacio, then 5 miles to entry.

27. Indian Flats

This is in the high desert just north of **Warner Springs**. This remote area is well-shaded, with water, picnic tables, fire rings and toilets. Pets O.K., on leashes within the campground. Good area for exploring among the rock formations, plus walk a short distance to the creek for a refreshing splash. Easy access to PCT for lengthy hikes to Canada or Mexico. Close by is Warner Springs Resort with its huge warm swimming pools, rustic lodging and first-rate restaurant.

How to get there: On Highway 79, drive 2.25 miles north of Warner Springs, turning right just after bridge onto paved Indian Flats Road. Drive in (not for trailers) about 5 miles to turnoff to right and access to PCT (walk to left through gate up 300 feet to PCT). Continue on another 2 miles to campground.

28. North Palomar

Compared to those who head up on the well-traveled roads, the north side of Mt. Palomar, the **Agua Tibia Wilderness**, sees few visitors on foot. The most-used trail up starts from the **Dripping Springs Campground**. You can bite off as much of a hike as you choose as the trail keeps going upward. From the heavily wooded campground, the trail crosses **Arroyo Seco Creek**, winds through shrub country, then into some of the largest manzanita bushes/trees I've ever seen. On into open country where you'll have long distance views of the San Bernardino Mountains and Vail Lake. And always above you is **Palomar** and that telescope.

How to get there: I-15 to Temecula, east on Highway 79 eleven miles to the campground on the right. Continue further north (25 miles from Temecula) to Oak Grove Campground and the Oak Grove Trail, a shorter trail also heading up the north side of Palomar.

Volcan Mountain - James Hubbell Entry Design

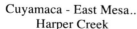

Cuyamaca - East Mesa...
Harper Creek

Hiking - Mountains & Backcountry

Cuyamaca - West Mesa...Airplane Monument

Big Laguna Lake

View from
Kitchen Creek

Hiking - Mountains & Backcountry

Kitchen Creek

Laguna Mountains...
Pacific Crest Trail

Palomar Mountain State Park...Doane Pond

CHAPTER 6

HIKING
DESERT REGION

OVERVIEW

SOUTH

CENTRAL

NORTH

Desert Area

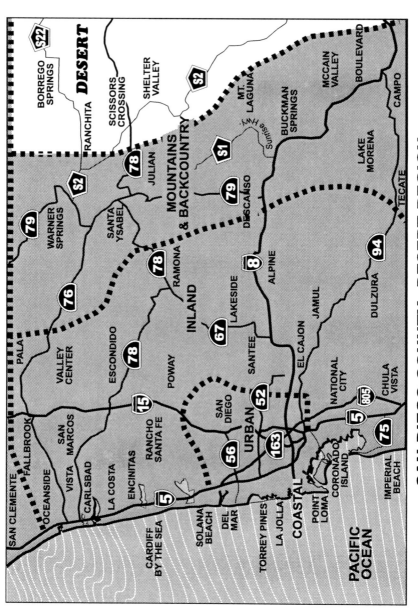

Desert Area

6 - 2

DESERT REGION

HIKING OVERVIEW

*For all the toll the desert takes of a man it gives compensations,
deep breaths, deep sleep, and the communion of the stars.*
Mary Hunter Austin

The desert here means different experiences to different people. For many it's a day trip out to **Borrego Springs** to see the museum, and with luck, see desert colors on display. For some it's a pleasant weekend away from the city's congestion to one of the resorts or campgrounds. For others it's an exploration out in the great open, with the nearest camper a mile away.

The desert evokes reactions that tend to grow on you. When they are on display, the flowers are truly memorable. The air is fresh, the vastness relaxing. (I recall driving out from the city with a backache from a week's hard work, and feeling the pain fade the closer I got to the desert.) Out there, you recall what sunsets and stars really look like on full display.

We are particularly fortunate in San Diego because our desert is almost entirely a state park. At nearly 600,000 acres, it is the largest in the state system. **Anza-Borrego Desert State Park** takes its name from a Spanish explorer of 200 years ago - Captain Juan Bautista de Anza - and the Spanish word for lamb - borrego - from the resident big horn sheep. The park was established in 1933, and except for scattered inholdings and the community of Borrego Springs, the huge area within its borders is all public land. Those inholdings are steadily being bought and added to the park, with the primary impetus group the **Anza Borrego Foundation**. The park was recognized by *National Geographic Traveler Magazine* as one the "Top 10 Affordable Spring Getaways" in North America.

Whether your first time or tenth, the **Park's Visitor Center**, opened in 1979, is well worth a visit. Its many excellent displays, maps, books and slide show will give you an appreciation of why so many people enjoy the desert. Outside is a short trail displaying many of the desert's plants with descriptive markers. The rangers and volunteers are well-informed and will provide tips, camping options, road cautions, etc. Another good way to get smart about the desert is to go with the organizations which offer field trips. These include hikes (easy to advanced) and vehicle excursions, some for 4WD vehicles, others regular.

In **Borrego Springs, Christmas Circle** is a central place for concerts, art shows and other events. It's a good place to spread a blanket, have lunch and later pick up some fresh grapefruit from the nearby stands. Near here is the **informative visitor center for Anza Borrego Desert Natural History Association (ABDNHA)**. For an upscale lunch head over to **La Casa del Zorro Resort**.

When it's flower time, thousands of people will head out to the desert seeking out the many wildflowers that may be on display. Emphasize the word *may*, as sometimes they're hard to find. Most common laments: (1) too many people at the easily accessible flower areas; (2) too few flowers at the other places. Advanced preparation can help. Mail the State Park a self-addressed postcard which they'll return when the flowers are about to hit (Wildflower, 200 Palm Canyon Drive, Borrego Springs, CA 92004), plus call the **wildflower hotline at 760-767-4684** before heading out.

Then pick an area which matches the calendar, as the park's several climates have different flowering conditions. The earliest to bloom and disappear are at the lowest elevations, such as Borrego Springs or Fish Creek. Later they may be profuse where water is plentiful **(Coyote Canyon)**, at higher elevations **(Culp Valley and Yaqui Pass)**, or further south toward Ocotillo (guess what plant abounds there).

To fully experience the desert take a walk along one of the many trails or drive off the main roads. Get a map or ask for tips at the Visitor Center. Remember to be properly prepared. Carry water. Wear a hat and sturdy shoes. Watch out for the tricky cactus, especially those " jumpers", and take along tweezers (just in case). Encouraged so far? Know where you're going, travel with others, watch for rattlesnakes, don't get stuck. If you're driving off road, camping or hiking, you'll also need a $5 per day permit, available at the center and campgrounds.

The desert can accommodate whatever level of outdoor comfort you desire, from air conditioned condos in Borrego Springs to developed or primitive campgrounds to remote camping all by your lonesome. Campgrounds are located throughout the park, and those who don't like company can follow dozens of dirt roads, many driveable with regular vehicles, to their own secluded spot.

How to get to the Visitor Center: Take I-8 east to Highway 67 north. Drive through Ramona to Santa Ysabel. Take Highway 79 north to S2 east. Keep alert for sign to S22 which veers off to the left. Just as you enter Borrego Springs, turn left to park headquarters.

Now try your hand at the desert quiz.

1. Where is Hellhole Canyon?

2. What famous stage coach line ran right through this desert region?

3. Who was Marshall South and what's his connection to Blair Valley?

4. Tamarisk trees provide a tall, green windbreak from desert winds. Is that good or bad for the desert?

5. In what desert campground will you find people soaking their cares away?

6. What was or is Font's Point?

7. The name Sentenac has significance for Anza Borrego Desert State Park. Why the name and the significance?

8. Among the most colorful desert flowers are those of two cacti which look a lot alike - the beavertail and prickly pear. How can you tell them apart?

9. What caused Split Mountain to split?

10. Where are the two heads, also known as Dos Cabezas?

Desert Ocotillo

Desert Area

6 - 5

DESERT AREA - SOUTH

Head east on I-8, and about 90 minutes out, as the road drops down into the desert floor, you'll be driving through some of our most spectacular highway scenery - sparse foliage, sandstone hills, boulders galore and views far toward the Colorado River. Turn north at Ocotillo (just over the line in Imperial County) on County Road S2. After a 10-minute driv of ocotillo cactus, you'll see the State Park entry sign. and you're in a world far different from the city: vast, still, quiet, uncrowded. You're in the south **Anza Borrego Desert**.

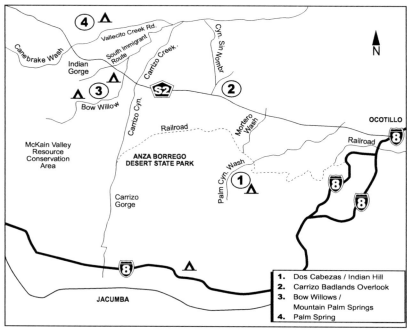

DESERT, SOUTH - HIKING

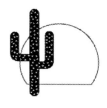

Desert Area
6 - 6

1. Dos Cabezas/Indian Hill ✤✤

The San Diego and Arizona Eastern Railway makes its spectacular descent to the desert over high trestles in this area. An old railroad station, several roads along rocky hills, and a palm grove make this worth exploring. This is where the trains took on water and you can still see the tall water tank and loading ramp. You'll find plenty to do here, under the gaze of the Dos Cabezas — two heads — rocky formations and the **Mortero Palms** oasis. It's a popular camping area with many inviting spots well protected by boulders.

Indian Hill is a short distance north from the railroad water tank. It's an easy 1-mile walk from the dirt road through rich desert terrain toward the obvious huge rock formations. This is the site of a Native American village, well sheltered in a natural cavern under the boulders, This dates back 5,000 years and pictographs record part of that world. Clamber up and around the boulders that make up this large formation. Follow the dirt road along the right side of the hill and you will come to the remains of an old railroad camp. Keep going and you'll arrive at the railroad track and a large tunnel, with no trains now but possibly in the future.

How to get there: I-8 to Ocotillo, then north on S2. At 4.1 miles, turn left onto marked Dos Cabezas dirt road (generally O.K. for regular vehicles). Head west, veering toward the right, and locate the short asphalt stretch crossing over the railroad tracks. Continue straight west toward the rock hills, ending at the oasis, with signs marking camping spots and side road north a half-mile to the oasis parking area. Back where the road crossed the tracks is another dirt road running on the west side of the tracks and northward to the old railroad water tank. Continue 1.3 miles north from the tank to the trail entry under the tracks and over to Indian Hill. For a different way back, preferably with a 4WD or VW bus, from the water tank head east on Mortero Wash to S2.

2. Carrizo Badlands Overlook and Southern Regions

The overlook itself is a worthwhile stop for the scenic view of the rugged badlands, mud hills, and washes. A kiosk here explains that this was once a huge lake, with mastodons, llamas and tapirs (as their bones attest) wandering freely. Over a few million years these former marine reefs ended up as arid desert hills and sculptures.

For a close look, hike down **Canyon Sin Nombre**. To get a flavor of what's out there in those wild lands, here are some notes from an all-day 4WD excursion sponsored by the ABDNHA. It covered several of the main washes and canyons of this southern park area — **Canyon Sin Nombre**, **Carrizo Creek**, **Arroyo Seco del Diablo** (Dry Wash of the Devil... sound inviting?), **Arroyo Tapiado** and **Vallecito Creek Wash**.

As we drove slowly along through mud hills and steep granite or mudstone cliffs we stopped a half-dozen times for further exploration. In spite of the dryness (average rainfall in the desert here is about 6 inches) mesquite trees were surviving well by sending their roots down 150 feet.

Our guide "T" led us up into a narrow channel - **"the Lindeman Slot"** - curving several hundred feet upward through the rock. We examined a seep where coyotes have dug their own water holes. In the midst of this arid country was a relatively verdant section, with a rich stand of agave, a separate cholla cactus grove, a cluster of smoke trees and a green meadow. It would have made a fine home site (except for a few missing ingredients, such as access, electricity, water...). Beside another wash we visited a mud cave, carved about 100 feet into the hills. Then another long, narrow slot -**"Carey's Wind Cave"**, which wound up to the top of a mud hill and an overlook of the terrain below.

Our final leg was along **Vallecito Wash**. This was the route of the Southern Emigrant Trail and the Butterfield Stage Line. Here we passed the Hollywood & Vine street sign (say what?), perched atop a boulder. T's tale is that this was originally stuck there in the '40s by soldiers stationed out here who stole the sign and put it on display. (T: "It's been stolen a few more times and has always been replaced, by the Hollywood Chamber of Commerce." Sure.)

3. Bow Willow/Mountain Palm Springs

Located 17 miles north of I-8 are these 2 campgrounds and hiking trails heading out to lush palm groves with lots of barrel cacti and ocotillo on the way. Hikers start from (a) the **Bow Willow** developed campground, with the trail heading north from parking area at road end, or (b) from **Mountain Palm Springs** with more direct access to the oases.

From the latter, here are three easy hiking options (with water, a hat, lug soles and walking stick): (1) Hike straight west from the parking area and soon you'll arrive at a cluster of palms known as the **Pygmy Grove**. Continue south on the obvious trail toward **Bow Willow** to a trail off to the right and over to the larger **Southwest Grove**. If inclined continue through the grove upward on the marked **Torote Trail**. (2) From the parking area walk north along a wide trail and over rocks about 20 minutes to another significant palm oasis in **Surprise Canyon**. An option is to keep going another mile to **Palm Bowl**. (3) Make a loop by taking the trail joining the two groves. From **Southwest Grove**, locate the trail just as you enter the grove and head up to the right/north. From **Surprise** locate the trail off to the left/south (look for a pile of stones, called a duck, atop a large boulder). Plan about 2 hours for this interesting loop hike over several ridges.

How to get there: From Ocotillo go north on S2, at 17 miles is a small sign for the dirt road left/west to Bow Willow; the camping area is about 1.5 miles toward the rocky hill at the end of the road. A short distance further north on S2 is the Mountain Palm Springs turnoff, west.

4. Palm Spring (yes, singular)

Near Canebrake is a dirt road heading east off S2. It looks intimidating; however most cars can make it out to this old outpost of the **Butterfield Overland Mail**, a California Registered Historical Landmark. This was where the stage folks stretched and enjoyed a drink of cool water. In this vast land of little foliage, here is an oasis rich with plants and birds and a **Desert Pupfish Sanctuary.** Kids of all ages enjoy poking around the hills here. Here is good off-road camping.

How to get there: I-8 east to Ocotillo, west on S2 for 22 miles, take the dirt road, Vallecito Creek Road, heading east, then off to the left.

DESERT AREA - CENTRAL

With a trip of about 2 hours from San Diego, you can be in the central desert. If you don't mind winding roads, head east from Julian on Highway 78 to the well-known intersection with S2 at Scissors Crossing. For the non-winding route, head east from Ramona to Santa Ysabel, turn north on Highway 79, then east on S2 and stay on it down to Scissors Crossing. Heading south on S2 through Shelter Valley, you'll be driving along the Great Southern Overland Stage Route of 1849.

5. Agua Caliente County Park

In this county park and developed campground is a special attraction — a huge warm water pool. Lots of folks will stroll over from their campsites for a rejuvenating soak in the warm waters. The popular **Moonlight Trail** heads out from the campground, and rangers have a steady batch of educational talks and campfire entertainment.

How to get there: On S2, 23 miles south of Scissors Crossing or 25 miles north from I-8.

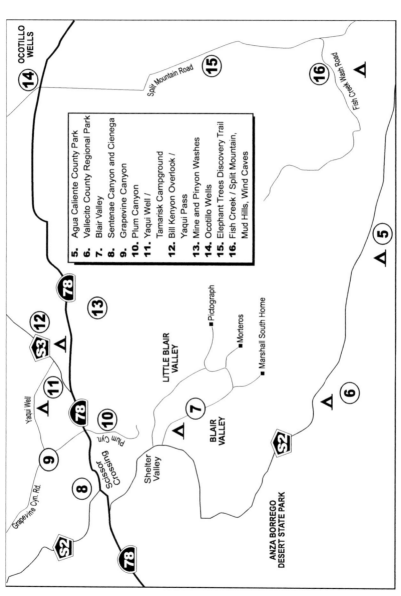

DESERT, CENTRAL - HIKING

5. Agua Caliente County Park
6. Vallecito County Regional Park
7. Blair Valley
8. Sentenae Canyon and Cienega
9. Grapevine Canyon
10. Plum Canyon
11. Yaqui Well /
    Tamarisk Campground
12. Bill Kenyon Overlook /
    Yaqui Pass
13. Mine and Pinyon Washes
14. Ocotillo Wells
15. Elephant Trees Discovery Trail
16. Fish Creek / Split Mountain,
    Mud Hills, Wind Caves

6. Vallecito County Regional Park

Four miles north from Agua Caliente is this modest but historically significant park. Long a camping area for Native Americans, the main attraction is
the reconstructed **Vallecito Stage Station**. It filled several pioneer purposes
150 years ago, with the most activity from the **Butterfield Overland Stage
Line**. In its 71 acres are 44 campsites, a large covered (and appreciated) picnic area, and kids' playground.

7. Blair Valley ♣♣

South from Scissors Crossing on S2 at the 6 mile mark (just past Shelter Valley)
is the turnoff to this popular area with several interesting attractions. It gets its
name from a settler named Samuel Blair, a.k.a. Bronco Sam, per Louis Stein's
"San Diego County Place Names." Orient yourself from the entry kiosk and
note the restrooms (useful when you're out here away from such niceties). Reset
your odometer to zero to more easily follow the directions. You'll be surrounded
by mountains with a wide view across flatland to the south and mountains to the
west.

If you're camping you have your choice of many good sites, all primitive with no
facilities. Just find yourself a reasonably level spot, with perhaps some wind
protection and call it home for the night.

Here 3 interesting hikes combine history, desert foliage and scenery. Sorry no
dogs on the trails. From here in you'll be on good dirt roads that are O.K. for
regular vehicles. Stay on the road to the left, next to the hills with the dry lake to
your right.

7a. Ghost Mountain. At 3.3 miles in you'll be at the parking area, with a kiosk
telling what makes this significant and a sign indicating 1.0 miles to the cabin at
the top, called **Yaquitepec** by its builders, **Marshall and Tanya South**. They
arrived here in 1932, seeking to find a better life than what the depression was
offering. They loaded their possessions into their Model T Ford and took up
residence atop the mountain, raised three kids, and lived here for 15 years until
their divorce in 1947. For the full story of the Souths, pick up Diana Lindsay's
Anza-Borrego A to Z. According to Lou Stein, the origination of the name Ghost
Mountain is not known.

After a half-hour hike you'll arrive at the ruins of the cabin, and get an appreciation for the work involved in living up here. Everything had to be hauled up by
hand, including building materials, metal bed frames, barrels to catch water. As
water was the key to success, they developed a system of catching water and
funneling it into a cistern as you'll readily see.

The hike is pleasant with a good trail steadily climbing up through the rocks. You pass a variety of desert plant life – shrubs, prickly pear, agave, barrel cacti. Up at the house the foliage is thicker with small trees and cholla, plus you get expansive views of Blair Valley and further east.

7b. The Indian Village and Morteros. Return a half-mile back along the road to the sign (located 2.9 miles from S2) leading to the **Morteros** and **Pictographs**. Drive in 0.8 miles from that intersection to the parking area. Hike in 0.25 mile to where a Kumeyaay community existed 1000 years back. Prime attractions are the many grinding holes or morteros in the flat rocks. Used for grinding pinyon nuts and mesquite beans, some are very deep and others have many shallow holes, possibly for ceremonial purposes. These are where the women would spend time together as they prepared a staple of the family meal. To spot the village and morteros, look for the large vertical rock located in the area protected by the hills. Scout around and you'll find a dozen mortero areas.

7c. Pictographs. Continue on down the road from the mortero parking lot and 2.3 miles further in you'll be at the dead end. Here again is a large parking lot and kiosk, which notes this is one of over 50 Native American rock art sites found in Anza Borrego. This is the trailhead into **Smuggler's Canyon**. Per Lou Stein the name came from a popular activity conducted through here way back when, with illegals mostly Chinese laborers.

Hike in about 1 mile and the trail takes you right to a large boulder with pictographs painted on them. If you're into art, this may do it for you, but I strongly urge you to continue along the trail another 20 minutes to the end. You'll be in the middle of a water channel and end up at the place where the water carves through the huge rock formation and then tumbles off as a waterfall 40-50 feet high. It must be spectacular when there is water (though you probably wouldn't want to be standing right there then). The rock formations and views of Vallecito Valley here are terrific.

Finally one more exploration option awaits. Return back along the dirt road to where the road forks off to **Little Blair Valley**. (Or you could have picked this road up from S2, at about 5.5 miles from Scissors Crossing.) There are a few rutted spots along this road section; if your vehicle is a low rider, you may want to skip this one. The environment in Little Blair is very different from the other side of the hill, appearing more meadow than desert. The road goes past another dry lake. This is also good camping as the hills provide protection from coastal winds.

8. Sentenac Canyon and Cienega

Past Scissors Crossing Highway 78 continues east along San Felipe Creek through Sentenac Canyon (named after one of the early owners). Because of the creek, this is a particularly rich area which provides habitat for many endangered plants and animals. It is also one of the newest additions to the park. Parking lot and trail off S2 just north of Scissors Crossing.

9. Grapevine Canyon

From Scissors Crossing Highway 78 heads east along a winding stretch of San Felipe Creek. As you exit the creek area, off to the north you'll see a dirt road coming down from the high desert. That is **Grapevine Canyon**, with the road splitting to either cross the stream to 78 or continue east into the **Yaqui Well** area. Much of Grapevine is the **California Riding & Hiking Trail**.

How to get there: From the north, heading down the canyon, pick up the dirt road from S22 at the east end of Ranchita, look for dirt roads heading south between mile markers 5 and 6.

10. Plum Canyon

Just east of the Grapevine road is a road suitable for regular vehicles, heading south into this canyon. Like many of the side canyons along Highway 78, this heads back several miles along the rock formations. You'll find some good camp sites along the way, well-protected from wind and providing solitude and starry skies. The **California Riding & Hiking Trail** goes through **Plum Canyon**, over to **Grapevine** and you can also hike over to **Blair Valley**.

How to get there: From Scissors Crossing, about 4 miles on Highway 78, dirt road off to the right (south).

11. Yaqui Well/Tamarisk Campground

This is a popular area just north of Highway 78 on S3 (toward Borrego Springs). On the west side of S3 is the dirt road entrance to the primitive campground, also a popular stop for day visitors. This vicinity gives access to some good exploring — to hear the many birds chirping along the **Yaqui Well Nature Trail** (1.6 miles round trip) or to hike up the marked 1 mile **Cactus Loop Trail Nature Trail** across from the developed **Tamarisk Campground**. This is in a grove of tamarisk trees, which as imports unfortunately take water away from native plants, by emulating Ross Perot's famous "sucking sound". More good exploring east of the campground.

12. Bill Kenyon Overlook Trail/Yaqui Pass

Continue a short way further north on S3 to this one-mile trail which winds up and over to spectacular views of the desert plains, canyons and mountains, plus a full range of barrels, ocotillo, beavertail and cholla. A bit further is the barren **Yaqui Pass Primitive Camp**.

13. Mine and Pinyon Washes/Mescal Bajada

Back on Highway 78 and continuing east opens up many possibilities for off-road camping and desert solitude. Immediately to the south is **Stag Cove**. Then comes **Mine Wash**, site of an Indian Village at a small parking area 1.6 miles in. Further east is **Pinyon Wash**. Mine and Pinyon require 4 wheel-drive roughly 2 miles in.

14. Ocotillo Wells

On Highway 78, about 34 miles east of Julian is this center of multi-activities. Right before the small town, you'll see lots of camping activity on the rolling sand dunes to the left of the highway. This is the designated off-road area, Mecca for the devotees. Camp there if you like lots of company and hectic activity.

15. Elephant Trees Discovery Trail

Turn right (south) on **Split Mountain Road** and drive about 5 miles to marked dirt road to right and parking lot. This is an introductory trail which loops around a variety of desert plants, with many informational markers. Pick up a pamphlet at the start and follow the stone guides. Barrels, ocotillo and many others. A half-hour easy stroll.

16. Fish Creek/ Split Mountain, Mud Hills, Wind Caves ❖❖

At the end of the road (8 miles in from Ocotillo Wells) is this fascinating and popular area. A dirt road leads off the paved highway into the usually dry **Fish Creek Wash** and about 2 miles in right through the split. The road has some rough spots but most cars can usually make it unless they're low clearance.

Once in there, get out of your car, look up at 600-foot rock formations and explore. To your right or west is the **Vallecito Mountains**; the left the **Fish Creek Mountains** (the split was created by the stream plus the two ranges rising). The Visitors Center has an exhibit about this area including a recording the ranger made there during an earthquake — not something you want to have hit while you're in **Split Mountain**.

Continue your drive, with about an arm's length of squeeze space on both sides at one spot, and as you exit look for signs off to the left marking trails up to some wind caves. Take the short hike up to see unusual rock formations and major views.

Continue along and you'll arrive at the **Carrizo Badlands and mud hills**-a large cluster of calcite-loaded hills with almost nothing growing on them. The road continues, but without 4-wheel drive don't test your luck. Once more this is a fun place to explore — stay on established trails as this is a fragile area. You might find a camp site here that fits your solitude desires.

DESERT AREA - NORTH

This is the area you'll see as you come down S22 passing through Ranchita and on to Borrego Springs.

17. California Riding & Hiking Trail

A mile past Ranchita you'll find a small sign noting the **California Riding & Hiking Trail**, with parking for a few cars south off the highway by the **Jasper Trail**. Cross the highway onto the hiking trail which heads off to the north and east. It winds through a varied landscape, roughly paralleling the highway off to the south. That's where the noise is; you're missing all that over here. Plenty of bird sounds instead. With a good rainy season, this can be rich in wildflowers, often on display weeks after they've faded down below. Eventually you'll arrive at **Culp Valley**. You can turn around at Culp and head back, or keep on going down and down. A two-car shuttle is recommended, with the second car either at Culp or below.

How to get there: On S22, pass through Ranchita and pass the large state park entry sign. Locate the trail and small parking area about 0.6 mile further along (or 1.7 miles from the Ranchita store)

18. Culp Valley ❖❖

Further down the winding S22 (9.3 miles from the S2 turnoff) is **Culp Valley**. The primitive campground (i.e., has toilets) is surrounded by boulder-strewn hills. Further in, day hikers can park and head out on several trails, including the **California Riding & Hiking Trail**. Many people hike along the trail toward the low desert. The first section is well-watered and will alter your view of "desert" as flora and fauna abound. Trek also the other way, i.e., away from

the desert. This has a more typical desert look, with some climbing and considerable reward. An option is to do a two-car shuttle, as the trail crosses the
highway above Culp. It's clearly marked and provides a mostly downhill 5-
mile, 2-hour hike from Culp down.

19. Hellhole Canyon/Surprise Canyon ❖❖

Now beyond the winding section and almost to Borrego Springs is this canyon which provides a rewarding hike into a variety of desert environments.
Look for the large parking lot on the left (or north). On weekends you'll
probably see other cars as this is a popular hiking area.

In case you're confused, this has the same name as the county preserve near
Valley Center, a considerably different world. Drive into the hard-packed lot
and locate the kiosk. You can read how this one got its name. Back in the days
when ranchers ran cattle down through here — why you might ask — they
noted this was a hell of a hole to get cattle out of.

Here's where the trail starts. You can bite off as much as you choose, and any
part will be rewarding as you'll pass through lots of foliage due to the water
runoff in the canyon. The standard hike up to the palm groves and falls is
about 5 miles round-trip, which will take about 3 to 4 hours, depending on
your mode.

Because the trail goes right up into the canyon, it's hard to get lost. On the
other hand, you'll sometimes wonder where exactly is the trail. The first hour
or so goes gently uphill along an obvious trail. Then you'll see options to the
right, left or middle of the dry wash. (That is, in December it's dry; not so
come rainy season. If it's wet in Hellhole, this latter section of trail can be
slippery.) It doesn't seem to make much difference which side you hike along
on as they all keep heading toward the same region.

For awhile you'll be in typical desert foliage — jumping chollas and ocotillo
— which start to look greener as you hike due to more water underground.
Then you might be surprised to see rich colors appearing, as cottonwoods and
sycamores break the pattern. Finally the palm trees appear and then a palm
oasis, with huge boulders, thick brush, and trails winding here and there. This
may be a good stopping place for a lunch in the shade.

If you continue on and listen carefully, you might hear some water running.
This is **Maidenhair Falls**, which in spring can provide a 20-foot cascade.
Hard-core hikers will probably continue bushwhacking further on to **Upper
Maidenhair Falls**.

For an easier desert sampler, take the trek into **Little Surprise Canyon** from
the same parking lot. Facing away from the back of the restroom see Surprise

straight ahead. This is roughly a one hour in and out stroll; in spring leading to wildflowers on display.

How to get there: Take the S22 down to mile marker 16.5 and into large lot. You can also find the trail to Hellhole and California Riding & Hiking Trail near the Visitor Center parking lot exit.

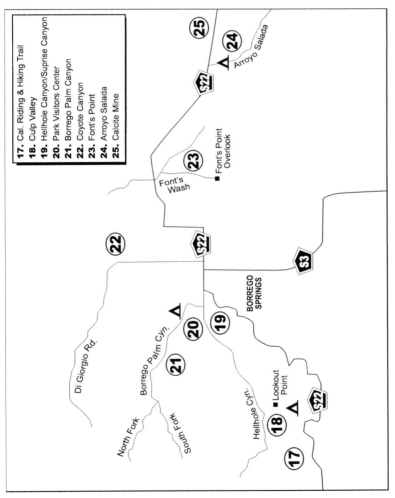

20. Park Visitor Center and Trails ❖❖

As noted before, this is the must-visit center of knowledge for the state park. Right outside the center door is the **Visitor Center Trail**. It's an easy walk through a cactus garden, with plants identified and described. You can learn the difference between those cousins, the prickly pear and beavertail. The prickly pear has large, obvious stickers (and grows edible pears). The beavertail looks almost smooth, but don't run your hand over it. Both can have profuse displays of flowers.

The State Park Full-access Trail is for first-time desert visitors or for anyone who wants an enjoyable, educational meander through the desert. This 0.25 mile trail is wheelchair accessible, with a gentle grade and a series of pull-out view points. Pick it up at the Visitor Center entrance or from the parking lot at the "Campground Trail" marker.

21. Borrego Palm Canyon Nature Trail ❖❖

This is the most traveled trail in the park, located a short distance from the visitor center or at the campground. What you will see on this three-mile round-trip hike is a full-desert array - a running stream, ample foliage (flowers in spring), great rock climbing, and eventually a plush palm grove. To get there, as you enter Borrego Springs, follow the sign to the park campground and pick up the trail there. Also pick up **Panoramic Overlook Trail** at the campground. It's a 1-mile round trip steep hike up to expansive views.

22. Coyote Canyon

Head out from the north end of Borrego Springs along **Coyote Creek**. Regular cars can generally make this dirt road, with creek crossings, wide washes, willows. Generally you'll have lots of company as this is a much-visited area. Lots of places to stop and explore. You'll pass the **Desert Gardens** area, then **Lower Willows**, with a historic marker. These are rich with foliage and wildlife, making for great birdwatching (keep an eye out for Wile E. Coyote). Try the **Alcoholic Pass**, 2.8 miles in, an old path off to the right and uphill used by Native Americans and cowboys. A good workout of 2 miles round trip up to a pass and fine views all around.

How to get there: From the Visitors' Center take the main road (Palm Canyon Road) into town and around Christmas Circle, turning north on DiGiorgio Road. The paved road ends and it's dirt on into the canyon.

23. Font's Point and Carrizo Badlands ❖❖

From Borrego Springs, S22 heads toward the Salton Sea, with many places along the way for camping and exploring. At 25 miles find the **Pegleg Smith Monument**, site of the annual Liars Contest, held close to April Fools Day each year, with no lack of contestants (I've heard politicians and lawyers are prohibited as being established professionals.) Smith was a gold miner who regaled eager listeners about his wonderful mine, located out yonder (as my uncle used to say).

Continuing east is the side road to one of the most fascinating places for a visit, **Fonts Point**. Whether he wanted to make a point or not is not clear, but Padre Pedro Font, the chaplain of the 2nd Anza expedition stood right here in 1775 and wrote about it. From up here at 1229 feet, you're looking out at the broad desert expanse, with the **Borrego Badlands** immediately below. Great place to stop, have lunch and muse.

How to get there: East of Borrego Springs on S22 at mile 29.3, turn off to the south. Drive in 4 miles to the end, generally O.K. with regular vehicles, with care. Call Visitor's Center first for current status.

24. Arroyo Salado Region

Here is a primitive campsite just off the highway to the south. The main activity here is with preferably a 4WD vehicle exploring along the several dirt roads that wind through the washes and canyons. Definitely get a map before driving here (and any other off-roads in the park). **Palo Verde Wash** and **Arroyo Salado** both head out from the camp area, leading to the occasional palms which rise up from the desert world, with names of **Seventeen Palms**, **Five Palms** and **Una Palma** (that's just one).

How to get there: At the eastern end of the park off S22 at 34.8 miles.

25. Calcite Mine

At the far eastern end of the park is this site of an old mine, with little foliage and a challenging hike of 4 miles round trip for stalwarts. Mining of calcite, a form of limestone, was done here until 1944 by Polaroid Company to provide gun sights. There's a scenic overlook (Calcite Mine Overlook or Salton View turnout) near the turnoff, overlooking the **Santa Rosa Mountains** to the north and the **Salton Sea** to the east. The state park ends at the Imperial County line less than a mile further east.

If you don't have a 4WD vehicle, park near the highway and hike on in. A short distance in is the mine kiosk with info. With a 4WD vehicle you can drive in a bit, down a steep road and stop at 0.7 miles in at the parking area. (The road gets mean from here on in, even with 4WD.) Follow the trail along **Palm Wash** to the mine, with obvious dugout trenches, calcite crystals and scenic views. Allow 2-3 hours round trip.

How to get there: Mile 38 on S22, turn off is to the north.

Anza Borrego Desert

Canyon Sin Nombre, Anza Borrego

Hellhole Canyon

Split Mountain

Blair Valley...morteros

Desert Area

Font's Point Overlook

Palms at
Surprise Canyon,
Mountain Palm Springs

Desert Area

CHAPTER 7

BIKING
COASTAL REGION

Point Loma - The Peninsula
Bike Tours
#1, #2, #3

Mission Bay
Bike Tours
#4, #5, #6

Mission Beach to La Jolla
Bike Tours
#7, #8

Old Highway 101
Bike Tours
#9, #10, #11, #12

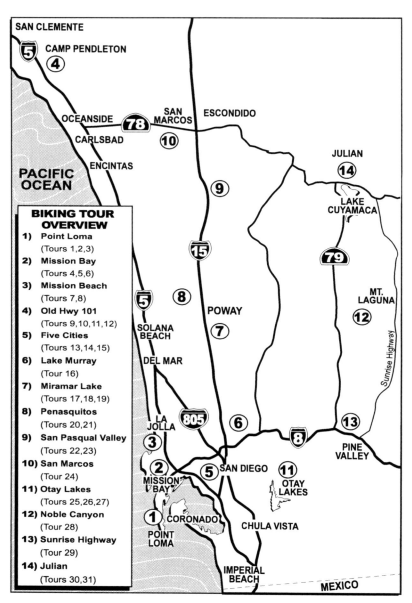

BIKING TOUR - OVERVIEW

COASTAL REGION
BIKING

"Cycle tracks will surely abound in Utopia."

H.G. Wells

POINT LOMA...
THE PENINSULA BIKE TOUR

Equipment: Road Bike, Hybrid or Mountain Bike

Directions to starting point: Exit either Interstate 8 West or Interstate 5 South at Rosecrans Street and proceed west on Rosecrans Street. If coming north on Interstate 5, exit on Pacific Highway and then exit on Barnet Road and proceed through two traffic lights until you come to Rosecrans Street. Turn left on Rosecrans. Proceed west on Rosecrans Street past **Liberty Station** (the old Naval Training Center). Continue through the village of Point Loma and turn right on Talbot Street. Go to the second intersection, which is Catalina and go across Catalina and make an immediate left onto a frontage road that parallels Catalina and runs in front of a residential area. There is always plenty of parking anywhere along that frontage road.

And you're off!

Highlights: Good family trip; Relatively flat and easy; Good bike lanes; Beautiful ocean and bay views; **Old Point Loma Lighthouse; Cabrillo Monument; Great views of Downtown San Diego, Coronado Islands and Mexico**.

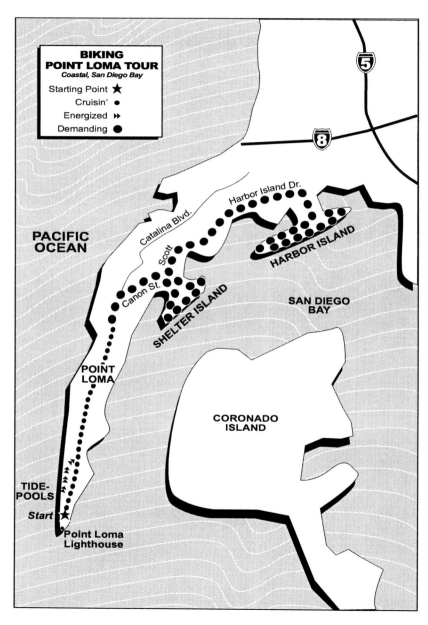

POINT LOMA TOUR - BIKING

Biking - Coastal Region

Point Loma - The Peninsula
Bike Tour #1
Cruisin'...(9 miles)

Continue west on the frontage road, which eventually will move you out onto Catalina. About 1.5 miles from your starting point, you will enter the **Federal Reservation**, which you must go through to reach **Cabrillo National Monument and the Lighthouse**. The road is open from 9 a.m. until 6:15 p.m. The entry time is strictly enforced so don't bother getting there at the crack of dawn – you will not get in. From this point, the Monument and the Lighthouse are only 2.5 miles away. Along the way, there are numerous lookouts that you can pull into for beautiful views of the ocean. There is a wide bike lane that makes this route very child friendly. You will pass by **Fort Rosecrans National Cemetery**. On your left side, at one of the entrances, you will see a concrete stage with a bronze plaque imbedded in the back wall with the Gettysburg Address imprinted on it. This could be a good resting spot for little cyclists-a good opportunity for them to get off the bike, sit down and rest, and perhaps even a history lesson. Behind the plaque you will be treated to lovely views of San Diego Bay, Downtown San Diego, Coronado Island and Mexico. On a clear day you can even see the Cuyamaca Mountains out beyond the city to the East.

Proceed to the Guard gate. Cyclists need to pay a $3.00 admission fee. Proceed to the end of the drive up to the cul de sac. There are bike racks where you can dismount and lock your bike. Walk out to the tall statue of Juan Rodriquez Cabrillo. From this vantage point you can enjoy a lovely view of the Harbor. There is always plenty of boat traffic and on any given day you will see Naval Ships, sailboats, fishing boats, and all manner of pleasure craft. Close your eyes and listen. You can hear the waves crashing below. Walk up to the **Visitors' Center**. There are restrooms here, which may come in handy. But there is also an auditorium where informational shows are held on the hour starting at 10 a.m. and running until 4 p.m. Topics included are: Plants and Animals of the Cabrillo National Monument area and In Search of Cabrillo – about Juan Cabrillo's life and his explorations.. You can leave your bike at the rack and walk several hundred yards up to the Lighthouse. If you are in cleats and want to ride, there is asphalt leading up to and around the Lighthouse. The only problem with riding is that if you want to go into the lighthouse, there is nowhere to lock your bike. And if you have come this far, I would recommend going into this old lighthouse that was built in 1885.

Proceed down from the Lighthouse and out of the guard gate heading back down Catalina to your starting point.

Point Loma - The Peninsula
Bike Tour #2
Energized...The Tidepools (12 miles)

If you would like to add some additional mileage to the Family Trip, I would recommend doing the Tidepools. Before making this decision though, don't let the additional three miles fool you. This side trip includes a significant hill but is well worth the effort. Getting there is easy. Once you leave the confines of the Monument parking lot, look for a road on your left, which overlooks the ocean and begins an immediate descent. Be prepared for an invigorating descent. Even with keeping your speed in check, you can exceed 35 mph.

At the bottom of the hill you will see the **Coast Guard Station** as well as the new Point Loma Lighthouse, which is operational and responsible for keeping boats and ships off of the rocks during foggy days and dark nights. Before going directly to the Tidepools proceed further out the road to the **Point Loma Water Treatment Plant**. There is a parking lot which is invariably empty, visited mostly by seagulls. It is an excellent overlook and rest spot. The site provides an excellent view of the rugged Point Loma coastline which few people have an opportunity to see unless by boat. This will be a good opportunity to grab a Power Bar and some water before heading up the hill. Start heading back but just before climbing the hill, you might want to visit the tidepools. There are no bike racks here but there is a large chain link fence that you can lock your bike to. You can walk down the trail to the tidepools from there. Obviously, there will be more to see if you arrive at low tide, but anytime is a good time to be down that close to the water. Also, on a good day you will be able to see a handful of surfers carving the waves.

Point Loma - The Peninsula
Bike Tour #3
Demanding...The Islands Tour (25 miles)

This add on will give you an opportunity to log a full 25 miles while seeing another dimension of Point Loma - an up-close view of Shelter and Harbor Islands and their numerous marinas.

Before reaching your car on Catalina, there is a split in the road right at a traffic light, before you reach Talbot Street. Stay to the right and take this road which is Canon. Canon will give you a delightful downhill descent with wide bike lanes that will provide you with an enjoyable section to ride. At the bottom, you will enter the **Village of Point Loma**.

Food: If you're ready for a food break, I would recommend **Con Pane** on the corner of Canon and Rosecrans. This is a very casual bakery and eatery. You can eat inside or outside at the sidewalk tables. They have a wonderful sampling of rustic breads from around the world, good sandwiches and a delightful atmosphere. The owner will most likely greet you herself and make you feel like a regular customer.

Continuing on the ride, cross over Rosecrans and stay on Canon.until it ends at Shelter Island Drive. Turn right onto Shelter Island Drive. Once on Shelter Island Drrive you will proceed past **Humphrey's Half Moon Inn** where they hold outdoor concerts each summer. Riding on, you will see the **Tunamen's Memorial**, a beautiful bronze sculpture memorializing San Diego's tuna fishermen who died at sea. It is well worth the stop for an up-close viewing and appreciation of this magnificent work, reflecting back on the time when San Diego was the Tuna Fishing Capital of the World. Out at the end of the island you will see the **Japanese Friendship Bell**. It was presented to the people of San Diego by the citizens of Yokohama in 1958 as a symbol of eternal friendship. As you proceed back along Shelter Island you will be treated to beautiful views of the Bay as well as Downtown San Diego and the numerous sailboats gliding along the water. Proceed back past Humphrey's and continue on Shelter Island Drive until you reach Scott Street. Turn right on Scott Street. This will take you past **Point Loma Sea Food**, which is a San Diego favorite.

Food: If you're hungry, this is a good place to stop for some fresh fish that has just been caught hours before. Take a few minutes to walk around the marina. This is a major sportfishing marina and depending on what's happening at the time, it can be very exciting watching the boats dock and unload their tons of fresh catch.

Just a block past Point Loma Seafood, turn right on Harbor Island Drive. Take this over the bridge and turn into the parking lot at the bottom of the bridge. Follow the sidewalk alongside the water and enjoy the park setting while pedaling along the water. The sidewalk exits the park and takes you to the **Sheraton Hotel**. Just get off of the sidewalk and turn right onto the road which will take you along Harbor Island and its numerous marinas. The road turns around at **Tom Ham's Lighthouse** at which point you are treated to wonderful views once again of San Diego Bay and downtown San Diego as you come back up the Island. Turn left at the Sheraton Hotel and retrace your route back to Scott Street, right on Canon and then right again on Talbot. As you cross Catalina, your car will be on the left, parked on the frontage road.

MISSION BAY...
COASTAL BIKE TOUR

Equipment: Road Bike, Hybrid or Mountain Bike.

Directions: From Interstate 5 exit at Mission Bay Drive. Proceed to the Visitor Center and then park south of it. The parking lot at the Visitor Center is only for one hour which is why you want to park south of it. But there are rest rooms inside the Center as well as snacks so you might want to check it out.

Highlights: All three rides provide the cyclist with beautiful views of one of San Diego's jewels – **Mission Bay**. The Cruisin' ride provides an added advantage in being mostly on the park's sidewalks and then on **Fiesta Island** thus being well suited to beginning or young cyclists who do not want the aggravation of dodging vehicles.

Mission Bay - Bike Tour #4
Cruisin'...Fiesta Island (6.4 miles)

Start your ride on the sidewalk heading south.   This is a family friendly area. It has a wide sidewalk with absolutely no traffic. But you will be sharing the pathway with pedestrians, skateboarders, roller bladers, and other cyclists. The path meanders along the bay. There are several playgrounds along the way if you have youngsters in the group who want to take a break. Out on the Bay you can see jet skis, sailboarders, and sailboats.

When you run out of sidewalk, simply cross the street and continue heading south on the pathway that runs alongside the road. Take this pathway for just a short while and then turn right on the first road that you come to. This will take you out onto **Fiesta Island** which is a fun loop. You will first come to a small part of the Bay that seems to be relegated to Kite Boarders. It is fun to watch these boarders skim across the water at high rates of speed and then launch into the air as their sails fill with air. As you proceed further out onto the island, take the left fork at the first intersection that you come to. This will take you into another portion of the Bay that is relegated to the water skiing set. There is a slalom water skiing course set up here at which you may want to stop and watch some talented skiers fly through the course. There is also a ski jump that is always exciting to watch. This is definitely the happening place for water skiers in metropolitan San Diego.

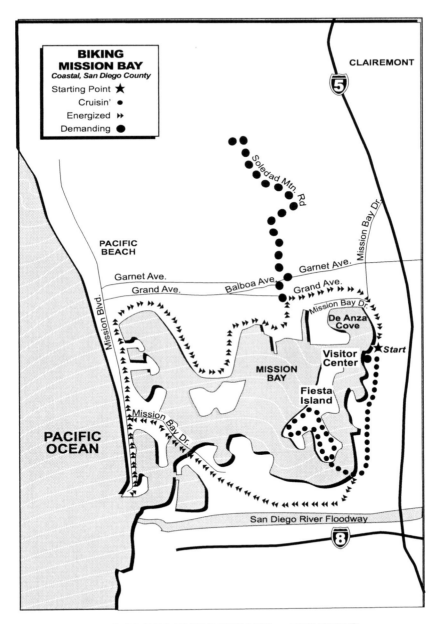

MISSION BAY TOUR - BIKING

You will shortly find that you have completed your loop of the Island. Turn left at the end of the Island back onto the pathway that you took to the Island. This will take you right back into the Park and to your car. There are lots of restrooms and water fountains along the way and barbeque pits if you want to have a picnic lunch.

Mission Bay - Bike Tour #5
Energized...The Bay Loop (20 miles)

Take the Cruisin' ride so that you can check out Fiesta Island then turn right off of the Island onto Sea World Drive. There's a fair amount of traffic here but there is a good bike path. Stay on the bike path and take that over the bridge and turn left on Rivera Drive. At about 8 miles at the corner of Rivera and Mooreland turn left into a little parking spot that only has four parking spots looking directly at the Bay. Make a U-turn across Rivera down the path that takes you onto the bikeway that wraps around the Bay.

At the bottom of the ramp turn right and proceed along the Bay. You will be treated to a lovely pathway occupied only by pedestrians, skate boarders and other cyclists. There are lots of sail boats typically in the Bay. You will pass by volley ball players and lovely homes sitting right along the pathway. This is a very tranquil route.

This path takes you through **Mission Beach**. At the end of the pathway turn around and head back. Instead of exiting the path at Mooreland, where you entered it, stay on the path and it will take you into the **Crown Point** area. When you run out of bikeway, simply follow the Bike route signs through **Pacific Beach**. The route meanders through Pacific Beach until you reach Grand Avenue. Turn right onto Grand Avenue, but you are still following the Bike Route signs. You pass by **Mission Bay Golf Course** heading back to **Mission Bay Park**. Turn right into **De Anza Harbor Resort** which will take you back to the bike path which will return you to the parking lot and your car.

Mission Bay - Coastal Bike Tour #6
Demanding...Mt. Soledad (32 miles)

Take the Cruisin' route plus the Energized route but when you are in Pacific Beach stay on Olney, and pass over Grand Avenue. Do not turn on Grand Avenue which will take you back to your car. Turn right on Balboa which merges onto Garnet and after 0.25 mile turn left on Soledad Mountain Road. This is a long demanding hill. Turn right on La Jolla Scenic Drive and keep heading up towards the antennas which mark the summit of **Mt. Soledad**.

At the top of Mt. Soledad you will see the **Millennium Veterans Memorial Wall** which is a tribute to our War Veterans. Also you will see the famed **Mt. Soledad Cross** which has been the subject of numerous lawsuits over the issue of the separation of Church and State. You are treated here to a beautiful 360-degree view of San Diego county with the ocean to your west and the mountains to your east.

Proceed back down the mountain the same way you ascended. Enjoy the exhilarating downhill - you earned it. At the bottom of the hill turn left on Garnet and then turn right on Mission Bay Drive which will take you back to **Mission Bay Park** and your car.

MISSION BEACH TO LA JOLLA...
COASTAL BIKE TOUR

Equipment: Road Bike, Hybrid or even Mountain Bike.

Directions: From San Diego go north on Interstate 5 and take the Garnet exit which will take you into Pacific Beach. At the second signal light, turn right on Garnet and take that all the way through Pacific Beach until you come to Mission Boulevard. Turn left onto Mission Boulevard which is at the end of Garnet. Mission Boulevard dead ends into North Jetty Road. Turn right on North Jetty. You can't miss this turn since the jetty will block your way, unless you have floats on! Jetty Road leads you into a parking lot with a beautiful view of the ocean and **Mission Beach**. You will see the Board-walk east of the sand. Proceed to the **Boardwalk**.

Highlights: The Cruisin' ride is definitely for cruisers and sightseers. Com-pletely flat, it cruises the boardwalk along **Mission Beach** and **Pacific Beach**. There is no vehicle traffic on this ride. Great kickback ride for adults anvery child friendly, especially with a side stop to the **Roller Coaster**! The Ener-gized ride moves off of the Boardwalk onto city streets but they are side streets primarily through the neighborhoods of coastal La Jolla.

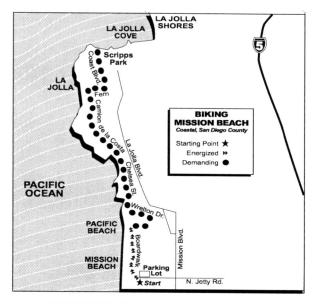

MISSION BEACH TOUR - BIKING

Biking - Coastal Region

Mission Beach to La Jolla
Coastal Bike Tour #7
Cruisin'...The Boardwalk (6 miles)

As you begin along the **Boardwalk** you will be treated to a spectacle of beach volleyball, one of San Diego's popular pastimes. These beaches are wide, sandy and quite beautiful. If there's a swell, you'll be able to see the local surfers carving their boards on the waves.

As you proceed on the Boardwalk, you will feel a bit like a voyeur since the beachfront homes are right next to the Boardwalk. The old Boardwalk has been widened and is much more rider friendly than in years past. There is a lane for pedestrians and two lanes for bike/skateboard traffic, which makes the route much safer and more enjoyable. You will very shortly come to the **Belmont Roller Coaster**. Be sure to bring your bike lock if you plan to take this pleasant diversion. If the kids are along, this is a great carrot to dangle for the end of the trip. There are bike racks in the little park on the south side of the Roller Coaster/Plunge complex. The **Plunge** is one of San Diego's oldest public indoor swimming pools, built in 1925. There are also lots of food vendors in this complex.

As you proceed north on the Boardwalk you will come to the **Crystal Pier** in Pacific Beach which has little hotel cabanas right on the pier. You will also pass by the **Lahaina Beach House** which has been written up in publications as one of the best beach bars in the world. Cruising this route, you are treated to classical Southern California Beach life.

Food: At the foot of the **Crystal Pier** is one of the area's most popular breakfast eateries called **Konos**. Don't be dissuaded by the line pouring out the door. It is well worth the wait and is a local legend for outstanding breakfast food along the Boardwalk. The end of the Boardwalk is just a bit further

north which is the turnaround point for the Cruisin' ride.

Mission Beach to La Jolla
Coastal Bike Tour #8
Energized...La Jolla Neighborhoods (15 miles)

After completing the Cruisin' section along the Boardwalk, turn left when the Boardwalk ends and head north. You're on Crystal Drive. As you approach La Jolla Boulevard, don't go out onto La Jolla Boulevard. Keep going straight and cross over the street and stay on the sidewalk. So you are now on the west side of La Jolla Boulevard heading north. Stay on the sidewalk for two blocks and then turn left on Wrelton which will take you back into quiet residential streets and past some lovely homes. Wrelton becomes Chelsea. Just stay on Chelsea and follow the bike route signs.

The first section that you cycle through is known as the **Birdrock** area. There is a nice viewpoint that you will come to, which is quite obvious, and one at which you may want to stop and enjoy the ocean view. Chelsea finally ends at Camino de la Costa. Take this road which is still the Bike Route. Camino de la Costa becomes Palomar but just keep following the bike route signs down to the shore.

At the shore, the road becomes Neptune and you are right on the coastline at this point. You will pedal by **WindanSea beach** which was made famous by Thomas Wolf in his famous 70's novel, The Pump House Gang. (And yes, there was a pump house!) Neptune will wind up to Monte Vista where you will want to turn left, heading north and following the Bike Route signs to Coast Boulevard which again hugs the coast. Take a minute and stop at the **children's pool**, which used to be a favorite swimming venue for local La Jollans since the area was protected from the pounding of the surf. However, local children have been replaced by local **sea lions** and there are so many sea lions now that the water has become polluted and swimming is no longer allowed. The debate over use of this area continues to rage among local politicians and citizens. But for now the sea lions have the upper hand (or flipper!).

Just past the children's pool, you will come to the **Cove**, one of La Jolla's most popular recreational areas. The grassy park is the home to free Sunday afternoon outdoor concerts during the summer time, a fireworks display on the 4th of July, and the number one open-water swimming location in San Diego county. From dawn until sunset you will see locals swimming either across to **La Jolla Shores** or out to the 0.5 mile buoy and back. The Cove's waters are also ideal for snorkeling and scuba diving because of the rich and varied colorful sea life.

Food: **The Cove** is the turnaround point for the Energized ride. If you're hungry at this point and would like to take a break before heading back, just above The Cove on the hillside is the **Brockton Villa** which is a wonderful addition to your ride. It is housed in an original, lovely, seaside cottage, has great food and an outstanding view. After this respite, just do the route in reverse to return back to **Mission Beach** and your car.

COASTAL REGION - NORTH

OLD HIGHWAY 101...
COASTAL BIKE TOUR

Equipment: Road Bike for demanding & challenging. Hybrid or Mountain for Cruisin' and Energized.

Directions: Go north on Interstate 5. Exit on Las Pulgas Road. Turn right and then take a quick left into a parking lot.

Highlights: Absence of traffic for the Cruisin' ride. This is an excellent ride for beginners, young cyclists or anyone who wants to avoid all traffic. It also affords lovely views of the ocean. The Energized and Demanding rides both also offer great ocean views.

Old Highway 101
Coastal Bike Tour #9
Cruisin'...Old Coast Road (6 miles)

This is an outstanding ride for those looking for a flat, scenic ride with no traffic. Because of each of these elements, it is also an excellent family ride. The lack of traffic and wide cycling paths make this an ideal ride for beginning riders.

From the parking lot proceed north through the barricades. You are now riding on a deserted section of old Route 101. The construction of Interstate 5 rendered this historic old highway relatively obsolete. But only obsolete for cars; it is an excellent thoroughfare for bicycles.

From this road you can see the ocean very well since the road parallels the **coastline**.

To your east is the sweeping panorama of **Camp Pendleton**. At times you will be able to see troops or even tanks conducting exercises.

About a mile up the road you will come to a tunnel that will take you beneath the Interstate. Stop before you enter the tunnel and enjoy the unique view that the tunnel affords you. At the end of the tunnel you are presented with an outstanding **view of the ocean**. Because the tunnel is square, the ocean looks as though it has been painted and is now hanging in a frame. Enjoy this lovely view.

When you exit the tunnel you will be on the west side of the interstate with the ocean still to the west of you. About 2 miles up the road you will come to **San Onofre State Park**. This is a good turnaround point for the cruisers. If you turn around now, the ride will be six miles in length.

Food: Since there are no restaurants in the vicinity, you might want to consider bringing a picnic lunch in a back pack and going into the park and eating at one of the picnic tables. There is no charge for bicyclists entering the park.

Old Highway 101
Coastal Bike Tour #10
Energized...San Onofre State Park (13 miles)

If you are interested in a longer ride, consider proceeding up through the **San Onofre State Park**. As mentioned above, there is no charge for bicyclists. As you come to the 3 mile point of the Crusin' ride, you will be confronted with a fence. Don't be intimidated by it, just proceed around it.

You are now in the park so you will encounter some cars but the traffic is minimal. There are numerous restrooms along the way. You will be passing campers as you proceed north. If your trip is in the morning, you will be tantalized by open wood fires, cooking bacon and myriad other wonderful aromas. At this point you will probably be getting hungry so remember to bring plenty of your own snack food.

There are water fountains so you will be able to fill up your water. If you have brought some substantial food, there are many picnic tables at which to stop and from which you can enjoy an ocean view. If you brought your bike lock with you, you might want to consider locking your bike to a tree and taking one of the numerous trails down to the ocean. The beach here is outstanding and relatively deserted since the access is difficult. But the hike down to the sand is definitely worthwhile. If you proceed to the end of the park, your turnaround point will be approximately 6.5 miles which will make the "Energized" ride just about 13 miles.

Old Highway 101
Coastal Bike Tour #11
Demanding...Trestles (20 miles)

This longer ride is ideal for someone looking for longer miles but is somewhat intimidated by traffic and is looking for minimal encounters with four-wheel vehicles.

If you are still up for more riding, continue north out of the park. Though you will now be on a public road, the traffic is very light. A ways up the road you will come to **San Onofre Nuclear Power Plant** on the west side of the road. When you come to the top of the hill, which will get your heart pumping, look for the signs that say bike crossing and then cross the road to the west side of the road and go through the fence. This will bring you to **Trestles Beach**, known for its outstanding surfing. When it is flat elsewhere along the coast, the waves are usually breaking at Trestles.

Proceeding north you enter another deserted section of Highway 101.

At the end of the bike path you can turn around and head back which will make this a 20.6 mile ride.

Old Highway 101
Coastal Bike Tour #12
Challenging...San Clemente State Park (25 miles)

At the end of the bike path, the turnaround point for the Demanding ride, proceed across Camino del Presidente. This isn't a very attractive street but it gives you a chance to see some of the homes in **San Clemente**. If you are a surfer, look to the east on the other side of the Interstate and you will see the **Rip Curl Factory**. Proceed north past **San Clemente State Beach**. (The entrance is actually a little further up the road.) When you come to the intersection where the on-ramps are located for Interstate 5, turn left, which is Calafia, and take that road all the way down to the beach, named **Calafia State Beach**. At the bottom you can lock your bike up and walk down to the sand and the surf. It is a lovely beach and a good place to relax. This is your turnaround point.

Food: At **Calafia Beach Park** you will find **Schleppi's at the Beach**. Drinks and sandwiches are available here as well as restrooms.

There are interesting sand cliffs down at the beach with names carved into them that the winds have weathered and eroded. Fun place to explore.

As you proceed back up the Calafia hill, if you want to visit **San Clemente State Beach Park** you will see it half way up the hill on your right side. There is no charge to enter the park on your bicycle, so you might want to explore this beautiful park with its ocean views.

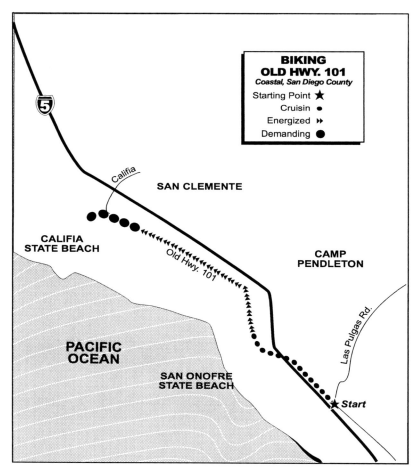

OLD HWY. 101 TOUR - BIKING

Biking - Coastal Region

CHAPTER 8

BIKING
URBAN SAN DIEGO

San Diego Bay...Five Cities
Bike Tours
#13, #14, #15

Lake Murray
Bike Tours
#16

Miramar Lake
Bike Tours
#17, #18, #19

BIKING...URBAN SAN DIEGO

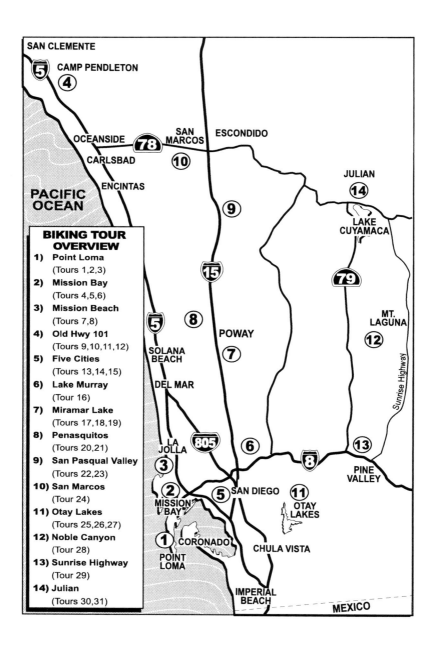

BIKING TOUR OVERVIEW

1) **Point Loma**
   (Tours 1,2,3)
2) **Mission Bay**
   (Tours 4,5,6)
3) **Mission Beach**
   (Tours 7,8)
4) **Old Hwy 101**
   (Tours 9,10,11,12)
5) **Five Cities**
   (Tours 13,14,15)
6) **Lake Murray**
   (Tour 16)
7) **Miramar Lake**
   (Tours 17,18,19)
8) **Penasquitos**
   (Tours 20,21)
9) **San Pasqual Valley**
   (Tours 22,23)
10) **San Marcos**
    (Tour 24)
11) **Otay Lakes**
    (Tours 25,26,27)
12) **Noble Canyon**
    (Tour 28)
13) **Sunrise Highway**
    (Tour 29)
14) **Julian**
    (Tours 30,31)

URBAN SAN DIEGO
BIKING

"Let us travel light on bicycles."
Henry David Thoreau

SAN DIEGO BAY...
FIVE CITIES BIKE TOURS

Equipment: Road Bike.

Directions: Travel to downtown San Diego to North Harbor Drive. Follow the Airport signs and proceed to Terminal 2. Instead of turning right into terminal 2, turn left into Spanish Landing. There is plenty of free parking here.

Highlights: An opportunity to tour San Diego Bay while traveling through five different cities: San Diego, National City, Chula Vista, Imperial Beach, and Coronado. An added benefit is the opportunity to enjoy the ferry ride across the Bay.

San Diego Bay – Five Cities
Bike Tour #13
Cruisin'...The Embarcadero (7 miles)

Before you even begin the ride, you are treated to a lovely view of the **Harbor Island marinas** and the hundreds of sailboats in their slips. There are restrooms located here in the parking area. Proceed up the sidewalk towards the **Sheraton Hotel**. The water will be on your right and the airport on your left. I would recommend a stop at the **Cancer Survivors Sculpture and Plaza**. It is officially called the Richard and Annette Block Cancer Surviors Plaza. It is about Hope. On the various placards one can find tips on how to survive cancer, offering everyone hope. It is the last sculpture created by the world-renowned sculptor, Victor Sallmones. This artwork is well worth the time to view.

Just past the sculpture, take a wide sidewalk out to the street (North Harbor Drive). This is the bike path that you will take all the way past the Embarcadero. A nice wide sidewalk awaits you here and you will be sharing it with other occasional cyclists, roller bladers, joggers or walkers. As you approach the Embarcadero you will see numerous boats anchored in the bay. Some of these boaters are visiting from other parts of the world and others are live-aboards.

Proceed along the Embarcadero. There is absolutely no automobile traffic here but do be watchful of pedestrians.

There are periodic restrooms along this section which is much appreciated. Always remember to bring your bike lock with you though.

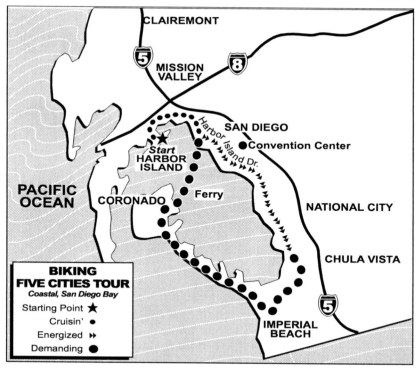

FIVE CITIES TOUR - BIKING

Biking - Urban San Diego

The **Berkeley Maritime Museum** is open daily from 9 a.m. to 8 p.m. The Berkely was an 1898 San Francisco ferry boat that operated commercially in San Francisco Bay for 60 years. One of its propellers is actually mounted beside it with a blade span of about 12 feet. Very impressive.

Next along the path you will see the **Star of India**, an historic old square rigger. Built in 1863 it is the world's oldest ship that still goes to sea. In its prime, it carried British immigrants to New Zealand, salmon fisherman to Alaska and circumnavigated the globe 21 times. It has survived fire, mutiny and arctic ice and has been docked in San Diego since 1927.

Admission to all of the historic boats is $6 for adults, children 13-17 are $4, 6-12 are $3, and children under 6 are free.

Food: Just past the Star of India is **Anthony's Fish Grotto**. This is a fish and chips casual restaurant with patio dining overlooking the Bay.

At this point, you have an option of continuing on the Five Cities Tour, or taking the ferry across the **Bay to Coronado**. The ferry departs from the **Embarcadero** daily from 9 a.m. till 10 p.m. on the hour. Continue further past the Embarcadero another 0.5 mile to **Seaport Village**. This is a fun area to explore. Follow the cobblestone sidewalk into the heart of the village and you will find a bike rack. Be sure to visit the **Carousel**, especially if you have children with you. It is a classic carousel with hand carved animals built in Coney Island, New York in 1890. It came to Seaport Village in 1976. The tokens are $1.00. This is the turnaround point for the Crusin' trip.

Food: Just about anything you could want is here, in Seaport Village. Numerous restaurants of all types will satisfy your hunger or cravings.

San Diego Bay – Five Cities
Bike Tour #14
Energized...Sweetwater River (18.2 miles)

City #1 San Diego
This extension to the Crusin' ride will take you on a nice trip past the new **Petco Park**, home of the San Diego Padres, and out to a lovely picnic spot on the Sweetwater River. From the Crusin' ride, come back out of Seaport Village and turn right on Harbor Drive at the Embassy Suites. Proceed east on

Harbor Drive past the **Convention Center**. On your left you will see the new **San Diego Padres Baseball Stadium**.

On your right will be **Kelco**, the kelp harvesting company and on its exterior wall you can enjoy a colorful mural depicting the history of San Diego. Further down the road you will come to **National Steel & Ship Building Company**, one of the largest ship builders on the west coast. You will continue south past the **Naval Surface Force** of the **United States Pacific Fleet**.

City #2 National City
Just past the **Naval Station** you will run out of road. As you cross the railroad tracks turn right at the stop sign. You will be winding your way through an industrial area. Proceed south on Tidelands. Keep the Bay on your right and you're doing fine. Many people don't realize that San Diego is a major shipping port but as you pedal past the storage yards on Tidelands, you start to understand the magnitude of the goods that arrive by sea in our city.

You run out of road at **32nd Street** so turn left and follow the bike route signs. There is a little park here called **Pepper Park** which is on the banks of the Sweetwater River. If you are interested in a picnic at this point, stop and enjoy the park's amenities.

San Diego Bay – Five Cities
Bike Tour #15
Demanding...Coronado Island (32 miles)

If you have gone to Pepper Park, turn around and proceed a couple of blocks back on Tidelands and turn right on Bay Marina. If you did not opt for the Pepper Park diversion simply turn left on Bay Marina from your Energized ride's directions. Proceed on Bay Marina under Interstate 5 and turn right on Hoover. Take Hoover until it ends and then turn right on National City Boulevard.

City #3 Chula Vista
Stay on National City Boulevard and you will enter **Chula Vista – City No. 3.** Turn right on E Street. Continue on E until it ends. Turn left at the end before you ride into the Bay! Then turn right on Lagoon and it will pull you down closer to the Bay. Follow Lagoon and turn right on G street and then left on Sandpiper.

The Bay Route signs will take you alongside the Chula Vista Harbor. You will pass by the Marina which will have restrooms and then just past the marina you will come to a little park called Marina View. Good place here for a picnic, respite, or restroom break. Just past the park turn right on Bay Blvd. Which is just before you get to Interstate 5. Up the road a bit you will come to mountains of salt. You will think that you are in the Himalayas, with white craggy peaks. Continue until you come to the Frontage Road, which runs alongside the interstate. Take the Frontage Road until you see a bike path just on your right past the salt flats. Take this bike path and it will bring you to...

City #4 Imperial Beach
About 1/4 mile off the bike path turn right on Palm Avenue. Take a right on 13th street and this will dead end into a bike path that will wrap around the tidelands of the south bay area and take you up the Silver Strand all the way into...

City # 5 Coronado
You are treated here to some lovely views of these tidelands as well as an abundance of wildlife. Herons, egrets, seagulls all find nesting areas here. Proceeding up the bike path you have beautiful views of the ocean as well as one of San Diego's most beautiful stretches of beach. The bike path is well used and you will find yourself sharing it with joggers, walkers and roller bladers. Keep traveling north heading towards the **Hotel Del Coronado**, the distinctive old hotel with the red coned top. If you are taking this tour between Thanksgiving and Christmas, you might want to stop at the Del and walk into the lobby to view their annual Christmas tree. Each year they decorate this floor to ceiling tree with thousands of ornaments and lights in a different theme. It is well worth the trip. You can lock your bike out front for safety.

Food: Good time for a rest stop anyway. Walk around the side of the Hotel Del to the **Moo Time Ice Cream Store**. Outstanding ice cream and a well-deserved reward for your cycling efforts.

If you haven't stopped at the Del, and have proceeded down Orange Avenue, there's another Moo Time just down on the right hand side past the Del.

Food: At the corner of C and Orange just as you are entering Coronado, you will find **McPhee's Irish Grill**. It's casual, biker-gear appropriate, especially in the outdoor patio, and a good spot for lunch. There is also a nice little deli, about a half a mile into town on the right side called the **Beach Deli**. Sidewalk eating and great sandwiches await.

Proceed to the end of Orange and turn right on 1st Street. You are treated here to a beautiful view of **Downtown San Diego**. Proceed just a few blocks down the street and you will turn left into the ferry landing. The **ferry** departs from Coronado every hour on the half hour and the tickets are $2.50 which includes the fare for your bicycle. Enjoy the ferry ride across **San Diego Bay**. It is a wonderful end to a Demanding ride. When you depart from the ferry on the San Diego side, simply proceed back along the Embarcadero to your car waiting for you at **Spanish Landing**.

LAKE MURRAY BIKE TOUR

Equipment: Road, Hybrid or Mountain

Directions: Take Interstate 8 East from Interstate 5 and exit on Campus Avenue. Turn left and go north on Campus. Then turn right on Navajo and then turn right on Jackson Drive. Go one mile and turn right on LakeShore Drive. Turn right on Lake Murray Drive and then right on Kiowah Drive which takes you into the Park. There is plenty of free parking. The trail starts on the east end of the Lake.

Highlights: Flat, easy ride. No cars or traffic. Nice environment to be around the lake. Good ride for cruising with the family or for beginning cyclists.

There is no Energized or Demanding rides that coincide with this ride.

Lake Murray
Bike Tour #16
Cruisin'...Lake Murray (6.2 miles)

Lovely bike trail. No cars. The only traffic consists of walkers, runners, skate boarders, roller bladers and other cyclists. Pretty lake. You will be able to see boaters and fishermen casting their lures. You will also have a view of Mission Trails Golf Course, one of San Diego County's public access courses. After 3.1 miles you will come to the end of the trail. There is a bench here with a beautiful view of the lake, so if you or your companions are ready for a short break, this is a good time to take a water break and enjoy the view. This is a short, but pretty ride.

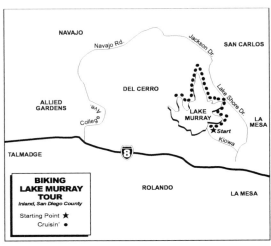

LAKE MURRAY TOUR - BIKING

MIRAMAR LAKE
BIKE TOURS

Equipment: Road, Mountain or Hybrid for Cruisin' but Road for Energized and Demanding.

Directions: From Interstate 15, exit Mira Mesa Boulevard and proceed east. Turn right on Scripps Ranch Boulevard which is at the end of Mira Mesa Boulevard. Then turn left on Scripps Lake Drive and you will find the entrance to the Lake about 0.5 mile on the left side.

Highlights: Lovely, secluded, flat ride with no traffic. Your only other companions will be runners, walkers, roller bladers, and other cyclists. If you enjoy ducks, bring some bread and you can feed the local wildlife. This is an excellent ride for beginners or young cyclists.

Miramar Lake
Bike Tour #17
Cruisin'...Miramar Lake (8.2 miles)

Proceed out towards the eastern end of the parking lot which is where the bike path begins. Unfortunately, the City has closed access to the **dam** so the path no longer circumnavigates the entire lake. Thus, the path is an out and back ride. But, it is a beautiful ride on a wide paved pathway. The path meanders in and out of numerous inlets, providing considerable variety and interest, always in full view of the lake. There are no houses on the lake so one gets a definite feeling of remoteness. You will be sharing this path with other cyclists, runners, walkers and roller bladers, but due to the ample width of the path there is plenty of room for all. The path will come to an end at a chain link fence which will impede any further progress which means it's time to turn around and return to the car. There are restrooms along the way and also picnic tables so you will be able to stretch the ride out a bit with a picnic lunch if desired.

Miramar Lake
Bike Tour #18
Energized...Scripps Ranch (15.2 miles)

To extend the ride, leave your car at the lake and proceed out to Scripps Ranch Boulevard where you will turn left. Take Scripps Ranch Boulevard until it ends and follow the Bike Route signs. Turn left on Sunset Ridge and follow the Bike Route signs. This ride winds through a lovely residential section and is a very mellow ride. Turn right when Sunset Ridge ends on Spring Canyon and take this to **Poway**. At Pomerado Road turn around and head back to the lake parking lot.

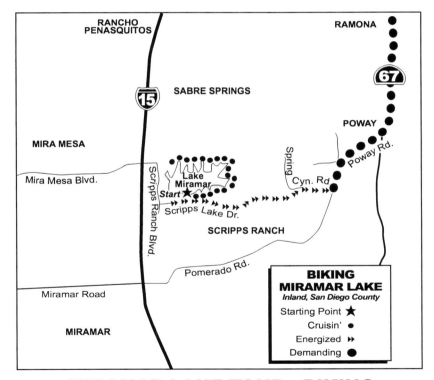

MIRAMAR LAKE TOUR - BIKING

Miramar Lake
Bike Tour #19
Demanding...Ramona (49 miles)

Take the Energized Ride. Stay on Pomerado Road which will bring you down into **Poway** and turn right on Poway Road. Outside of Poway you will start heading slowly up a hill to **Ramona**. There are beautiful views of northeast county backcountry. Huge boulders dot the landscape. Turn left on Route 67 and continue heading up and north to Ramona. This is slow going. There's a bike lane and a great opportunity to enjoy this beautiful part of San Diego County. At the top of the hill you can turn around at the signs for **Mt. Woodson**.

If you use this as your turnaround point, the roundtrip mileage from the parking lot will be 30 miles and if you also did the Cruisin' ride, your day's mileage will be 38.2 miles.

Another option at this point, since you made the climb up the hill is to proceed on into Ramona and ride through the downtown section of this old Western town. If you choose this destination, just stay on Route 67. You will pass by rolling farmlands and then on the outskirts of town you will come to a number of fast food restaurants. If you are starving and haven't brought enough energy supplements along, you will find plenty of food along this strip. Enjoy the next section of the ride as you pass along tree lined streets as well as the Hay, Feed and Grain store. This is an **old Western town** with quaint shops and much history. At the outskirts of town, you can turn around which will make this a 41-mile ride from the lake parking lot. If you also did the Cruisin' route around the lake, you will be logging 49 miles today amid multiple terrains and scenery.

CHAPTER 9

BIKING
SAN DIEGO INLAND

**Penasquitos Canyon
Bike Tours
#20, #21**

**Mule Hill Trail/San Pasqual Valley
Coastal Bike Tours
#22, #23**

**Double Peak / Discovery Lake
San Marcos Bike Tour
#24**

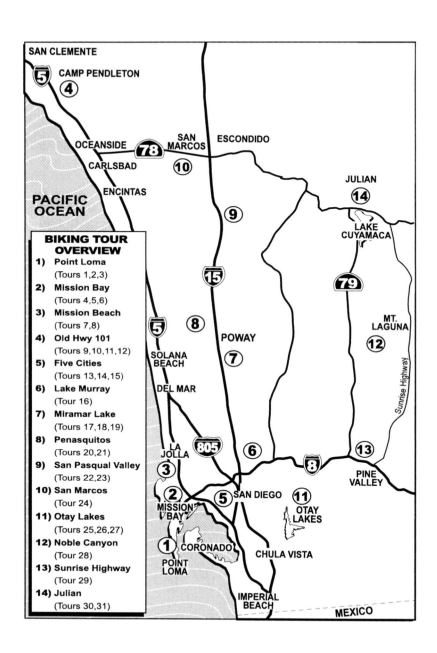

SAN CLEMENTE

CAMP PENDLETON
5 **4**

OCEANSIDE **78** SAN MARCOS ESCONDIDO

CARLSBAD **10**

ENCINTAS

PACIFIC OCEAN

JULIAN **14**

LAKE CUYAMACA

9

BIKING TOUR OVERVIEW

1) **Point Loma**
   (Tours 1,2,3)
2) **Mission Bay**
   (Tours 4,5,6)
3) **Mission Beach**
   (Tours 7,8)
4) **Old Hwy 101**
   (Tours 9,10,11,12)
5) **Five Cities**
   (Tours 13,14,15)
6) **Lake Murray**
   (Tour 16)
7) **Miramar Lake**
   (Tours 17,18,19)
8) **Penasquitos**
   (Tours 20,21)
9) **San Pasqual Valley**
   (Tours 22,23)
10) **San Marcos**
    (Tour 24)
11) **Otay Lakes**
    (Tours 25,26,27)
12) **Noble Canyon**
    (Tour 28)
13) **Sunrise Highway**
    (Tour 29)
14) **Julian**
    (Tours 30,31)

15

79

5

8 POWAY

SOLANA BEACH

DEL MAR

7

MT. LAGUNA **12**

Sunrise Highway

LA JOLLA **805**

3

6

8

13

PINE VALLEY

2

5 SAN DIEGO **11**

MISSION BAY

OTAY LAKES

1 CORONADO

POINT LOMA

CHULA VISTA

IMPERIAL BEACH

MEXICO

SAN DIEGO INLAND
BIKING

"Nothing compares with the simple pleasure of a bicycle ride."

John F. Kennedy

PENASQUITOS CANYON BIKE TOUR

Equipment: Mountain Bike

Directions: From Interstate 5 North exit at Sorrento Valley Road. Turn left at the bottom of the exit and turn right on Sorrento Valley Blvd and then take your first left over the railroad tracks on Sorrento Valley Road. If you are traveling south on I-5, take the Carmel Valley Road exit and then go left off the

exit and turn right on El Camino Real and then right on Carmel Mountain Road which will take you to Sorrento Valley Road. Turn left on Sorrento Valley Road. About a mile up the road turn into Penasquitos Canyon Reserve parking lot. There is a porta potty here for your convenience. If you live inland close to the I-15 corridor, approach this ride from the east parking lot which is off Black Mountain Road half way between Carmel Mountain Road and Mira Mesa Boulevard. If that is the case, the following rides would just be done in reverse.

Highlights: Placid, remote ride along unpaved trails. Excellent get-away from the roar of traffic. If you have beginners and only plan to do the Cruisin' ride, you may want to begin the ride from the eastern end to avoid some small hills on the western approach. The eastern portion of the Canyon is flatter.

Penasquitos Canyon
Bike Tour #20
Cruisin'...The Canyon (5.6 miles)

From the western point of entry, proceed out of the parking lot onto the trail which will bring you directly to a kiosk which will provide some interesting reading for you. You will be following Penasquitos Creek through this park which will take you over to the Equestrian Center on Black Mountain Road. At about the 2.8 mile point you will come to a lovely waterfall which will be your turnaround point for the Cruisin ride.

This is a lovely trail for families or beginners. There is no traffic, no roller bladers, skateboarders or strollers. You will be sharing the trail with hikers, equestrians and other mountain bikers.

The trail is mostly mellow but there are a few hills where beginners may want to get off and walk their bikes. The canyon is completely isolated and is a wonderful refuge from city life, but one can't help but see the houses lining the ridges surrounding the canyon.

At the waterfall, which is your turnaround point, make sure that you stop and take time to climb out to the rocks overlooking the waterfall or better yet, climb down to the stream. This is a great place to eat lunch but since there is no food available, be sure to bring a picnic lunch. There is a bike rack here and your bike is most likely safe but it still doesn't hurt to lock it up, especially if you are planning to go down to the stream. When you are ready to head back, just return to your car the same way that you came, or consider riding the entire length of the canyon on the Energized Route.

Penasquitos Canyon
Bike Tour #21
Energized...The Canyon - Round Trip (12 miles)

Take the Cruisin' ride to the waterfall. As you proceed on further down the canyon, you are treated to a beautiful section of Sycamore trees lining the route. You feel as though you are riding in a beautiful sylvan vale. The trail is very flat for the rest of this section and you will enjoy the serenity of this lovely canyon. At the 6 mile point you will come to the end of the canyon and the Black Mountain Road Parking lot.

An interesting diversion from here is the **Ranch House**. From the East parking lot, proceed west up the trail just about 0.25 mile and cross over the creek. The trail will take you to the old Ranch House which is fun to visit and open to the public.

After the Ranch House cross back over to the main trail on the south of the creek and proceed back to the parking lot and your car.

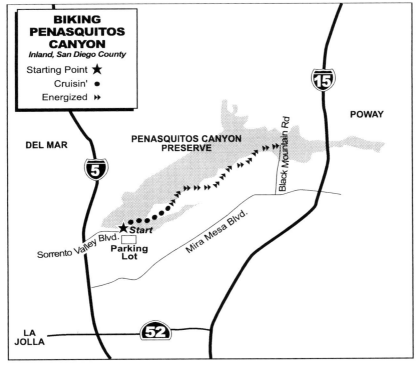

PENASQUITOS CANYON TOUR - BIKING

MULE HILL TRAIL/
SAN PASQUAL VALLEY

Equipment: Mountain Bike

Directions: From San Diego, take Interstate 15 north and exit at Via Rancho Parkway heading east. Turn right at the first traffic light which is Sunset Drive. Take Sunset Drive until it deadends into a small parking lot. If it is full, don't worry because there is plenty of street parking available.

Mule Hill Trail/San Pasqual Valley
Bike Tour #22
Cruisin'...Kit Carson Tour (9 miles)

Mule Hill Trail is part of the San Dieguito River Park Project. This first portion is very flat, wide and easy going. It is an excellent choice for families, beginning riders or if you are just interested in a nice short wilderness ride without automobile traffic and other mechanical distractions. You will share the trail with other mountain bikers, hikers and an occasional horse.

At the beginning of the trail is a port-a-potty which is the only one on the crusin' ride. The trail starts out as a wide dirt trail. About one mile out, you actually come to Mule Hill which is a small hill off of the trail itself. Back in 1846 California's bloodiest battle of the Mexican War took place at San Pasqual, five miles east of where you are riding. On December 7, 1846, American soldiers under the command of Brigadier General Stephen Watts Kearny, whom Kearny Mesa was named after, were attacked from the rear by Mexican forces. This compelled the Americans to withdraw to higher ground which they did, here at Mule Hill. For four days they were trapped by the Mexican forces who were fighting under the command of Captain Andres Pico, younger brother of Pio Pico, a former governor of California.

The Americans were short of food and had to resort to eating their mules, hence the name Mule Hill.

In desperation, Kit Carson, an Indian and another American slipped through the Mexican sentries and worked their way on foot to San Diego to obtain reinforcements.

On December 10 a relief column of American soldiers arrived at Mule Hill and the Mexican troops retreated. Kearny and his men marched on to San Diego, thus completing a 2,000-mile trip from Fort Leavenworth, Kansas.

The trail meanders through the San Pasqual Valley. The hills are beautiful and the trail is quite tranquil. You will be able to ride two or three abreast on this wide, pleasant trail. At about 4.5 miles, you will reach a lovely little rest area at the base of a hill with a picnic table to enhance your lunch stop. This is the turnaround point for the Cruisin' ride.

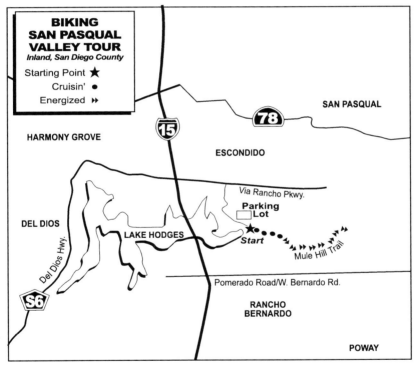

SAN PASQUAL VALLEY TOUR - BIKING

Mule Hill Trail / San Pasqual Valley
Bike Tour #23
Energized...The Valley View (20 miles)

At the Cruisin' turnaround point, the trail changes to a single track and ascends for the next 0.75 miles. It's a good steady climb and the trail is smooth so it is a very doable yet challenging ascent. If you are riding on a weekend, keep your eyes peeled for descending riders, since this is a popular ride. At the top you are treated to a wonderful view of the San Pasqual Valley. There are some benches here which makes it a great place to relax for a moment, enjoy a snack and drink in the view. You'll enjoy the downhill, since you earned it. As you proceed along the trail you will be going through some of the richest agricultural lands in the county. The trail again remains flat until it ends. As you do near the turnaround point for the Energized ride, you will pass by a large orange grove. If the orange blossoms are in bloom, the scent will be intoxicating as you ride past. Enjoy this part of your ride with all of your senses. At about the 10 mile point, you will come to the end of the trail. There are port-a-potties here but no water. Make sure that you bring plenty of water on this trail since it does get hot, especially in the summer time.

DOUBLE PEAK / DISCOVERY LAKE SAN MARCOS
Bike Tour #24
(Mountain Bike Ride)

Equipment: Mountain Bike

Directions: Exit Highway 78 at Twin Oaks Valley Road and go south. Turn right on Craven Road and then left on Foxhall. Follow Foxhall right into the **Discovery Lake** parking lot.

Highlights: Bring plenty of water; there is none along the trail nor at the summit. Demanding ride. The elevation gain is 1,000 ft. Double Peak is 1,644 ft. elevation. The view from the peak is spectacular west to the Pacific and the coastal lagoons, North to Mt. Baldy in the San Gabriel Mountain Range, San Jacinto Peak in the San Bernardinos east to Palomar Mountain, east to the Cuyamacas and southeast to the Harmony Grove and San Dieguito River Valley.

Demanding: (4.5 miles) The **Double Peak Trail** is a very difficult mountain bike ride. Because the trail ascends fairly quickly, I would suggest taking a spin around the lake before you begin. It is a pretty ride and it will loosen your legs up and get your muscles warm. Once you've completed the lake loop head west out of the parking lot on the dirt trail and follow it up, heading toward the water tower. Once you reach the **water tower** follow the well marked trail called Double Peak. This is a good steep section that will get your heart pumping. The City has done an excellent job of trail building in this area. The trail is well maintained and lined by a wooden fence. It can accommodate probably three riders abreast. Follow the Double Peak markers and the trail becomes a single track which then pops out onto a fire road. Turn left on the fire road and keep heading up towards the trees at the top. As you get closer to the top the trail gets steeper and steeper. Don't hesitate to get off and walk at this point. It truly is a lung screamer.

When you reach the summit you are treated to an outstanding 360 degree view that is well worth the trip. To the northeast you can see Mt. Palomar, to the east the Cuyamacas and to the west the Pacific Ocean. You can see **Discovery Lake** below you as well as the campus of **Cal State San Marcos** and **Lake San Marcos**. You will be standing among the ruins of an old San Marcos adobe home that long ago burned and was razed. You will be captivated by the adventuresome spirit of its inhabitants who choose to build their home in such a remote location, and the solitude that they enjoyed. Hopefully you have brought a lunch along or some energy foods. If so, this is a great place to enjoy it.

The return trip is much easier than the ascent. Just follow the same trails back to the parking lot. Another option though is to stay up on the mountain and spend a couple of hours exploring the vast network of fire roads and single tracks that run like a maze around these hills. Since you expended such a great deal of energy to get up here, you might as well maximize your time and enjoy these lovely hills.

The fire road that runs several miles along the ridge line of these hills, named the **Cerro de las Posas Mountains**, will eventually be replaced by a 200 acre regional park. This park will have picnic and camp sites and a soft surface trail will replace the fire road. The **Harmony Grove** fire badly burned this region in 1996 and one can still see the burned skeletons on the mountain side as painful reminders of the devastation that fire causes.

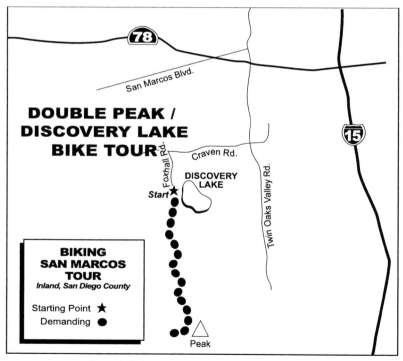

SAN MARCOS BIKE TOUR

Biking - San Diego Inland

CHAPTER 10

BIKING
MOUNTAINS
& BACKCOUNTRY

**Otay Lakes
Bike Tours
#25, #26, #27**

**Noble Canyon
Coastal Bike Tours
#28**

**Sunrise Highway
Bike Tour
#29**

**Julian
Bike Tour
#30, #31**

Biking - Mountains & Backcountry

BIKING...MOUNTAINS & BACKCOUNTRY

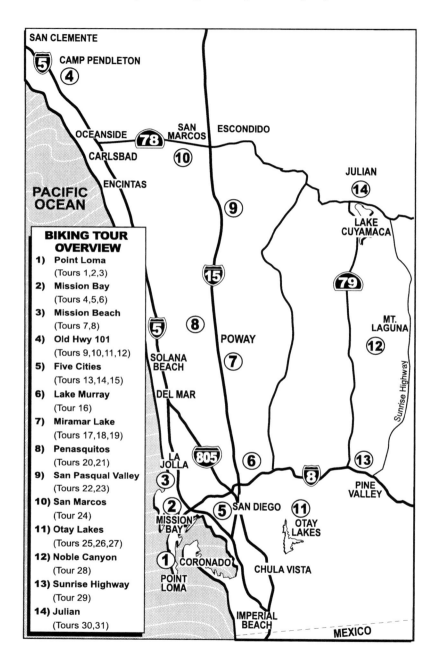

BIKING TOUR OVERVIEW

1) **Point Loma**
   (Tours 1,2,3)
2) **Mission Bay**
   (Tours 4,5,6)
3) **Mission Beach**
   (Tours 7,8)
4) **Old Hwy 101**
   (Tours 9,10,11,12)
5) **Five Cities**
   (Tours 13,14,15)
6) **Lake Murray**
   (Tour 16)
7) **Miramar Lake**
   (Tours 17,18,19)
8) **Penasquitos**
   (Tours 20,21)
9) **San Pasqual Valley**
   (Tours 22,23)
10) **San Marcos**
    (Tour 24)
11) **Otay Lakes**
    (Tours 25,26,27)
12) **Noble Canyon**
    (Tour 28)
13) **Sunrise Highway**
    (Tour 29)
14) **Julian**
    (Tours 30,31)

MOUNTAINS & BACKCOUNTRY BIKING

"Ever bike?
Now that's something that makes life worth living!"

Jack London

OTAY LAKES BIKE TOUR

Equipment: Road, Hybrid or Mountain for Cruisin' ride. Road or Hybrid for Energized and Mountain for Demanding.

Directions: Take I-5 South to Highway 54 East. Then take 805 South and exit on Telegraph Canyon Road. Proceed East. Follow the signs to the **Olympic Training Center**. You're looking for Wueste Road. Turn right on Wueste Road and then turn left at the Stop Sign and proceed to the end of the road where you will find a parking lot.

The **Otay Lakes Park** hours Monday through Friday are 9:30 a.m. to 5 p.m. and weekends and holidays are 9:30 a.m. to sunset. It is a lovely lake and the park at the south end is quite lovely. There are picnic tables overlooking the lake and plenty of parking. There is also a children's playground to provide fun for the little ones as well as restrooms. It is quite a nice park. Be sure to visit the **Olympic Training Center** after your ride. As you are proceeding out of the park on the park road, turn left at the first stop sign and this road will take you up to the **Olympic Training Center Visitor Center**. They have tours every hour on the hour starting at 10 a.m. until 3 p.m.

Highlights: Beautiful lake plus an opportunity to visit the **Olympic Training Center**. Quiet country roads and nice views of San Diego's backcountry.

Otay Lakes
Bike Tour #25
Crusin'...Otay Lake (6.4 miles)

As you proceed out of the park, you are treated to lovely close-up views of the lake and there is a marina on your right hand side. If you bring your fishing gear, you might want to check out the fishing when you have finished your ride. This ride is a nice, easy, warm-up ride. It is completely flat and fairly devoid of traffic. Since it is a park road, the only traffic is that of the park visitors so this is also a very attractive ride for children.

After 3.2 miles you will come to the end of the park road. If you turn around at this point and head back, you will complete the 6.4 mile ride and be ready for a nice picnic lunch at the park.

Otay Lakes
Bike Tour #26
Energized...Otay Extension (19 miles) (24 miles)

Turn right off of the park road onto Otay Lakes Road which will take you along the north end of **Lower Otay Lake**. At the northeast section of the lake you will notice that it is a lovely **bird sanctuary**. Take a pause here and check out the numerous birds reposing in this marshland. The road's shoulders are not particularly wide but there is minimal traffic so the ride is enjoyable. It is a lovely road as it winds through the hills of San Diego's backcountry. In the future, these rolling hills will most likely be covered with homes so get out here and enjoy the countryside while it is still rural. Just past the **San Diego Sky Diving Center** you will be welcomed to Jamul. About 9.5 miles out you will come to the **Thousand Trails Campground**. There is an opportunity here to stop for refreshments at their market and this is the turnaround site for the Energized ride. If you want to put in just a few more miles, keep going another 2.5 miles ahead until you reach a stop sign. Turn around there which is about 12 miles making the Energized ride a 24-miler for you.

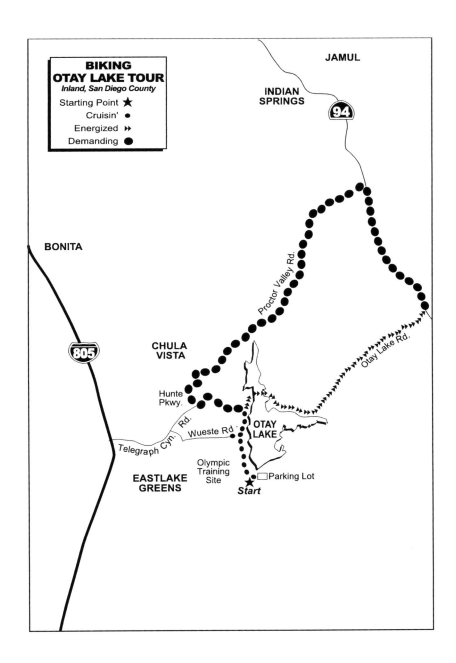

Otay Lakes
Bike Tour #27
Demanding...Proctor Valley (30 miles)

For the demanding ride, it is necessary to have a mountain bike since there is a 5-mile section that is unpaved and completely unsuited for a road bike. The thick dirt and gravel on the road grabs the narrow tires of a road bike and makes it unsafe. But, a mountain bike or even a hybrid bike will do well on this "off-road" section. Proceed past the Thousand Trails Campground until you come to the stop sign at the end of the road. Turn left on Highway 94. This 5-mile section has heavy and high-speed traffic and therefore is not the most pleasant section to ride. If you do not feel comfortable with large trucks and fast cars going by, I would stick to the Energized ride. But after 5 miles, you will turn left on Proctor Valley Road which leads you back southwest towards **Otay Lakes**.

Proctor Valley is a lovely, quiet section that is quite tranquil after the hustle and bustle of Highway 94. After 2.5 miles the pavement ends and the road continues on for 5 miles out through very wild countryside. There are no houses in sight and no signs of civilization except for the occasional dirt bike that might be screaming across the distant hills. Once you get back on the paved road, turn left on Hunte Parkway. After a short distance turn left on Otay Lakes Road and then turn right on Wueste Road which is the park road that will take you back along the lake and to the park and your car.

NOBLE CANYON BIKE TOUR

Equipment: Road Bike, Hybrid, or Mountain Bike. (Whichever has the lowest gears!)

Directions: Proceed east on Interstate 8 about 45 miles from San Diego. It is an easy and beautiful drive through the foothills of East County. Exit at Pine Valley. Turn left, going north and proceed to the end of the road. If you do not possess a **California Wilderness Pass**, you will need to buy one at the little country store in **Pine Valley**. Turn right and it is immediately on your left. If you do have a pass, turn left at the end of the road and drive for about a mile outside of town. Turn right at the end of the bridge on Pine Creek Road and follow the road for about a mile to the parking lot on the right.

Highlights: Long, steady, challenging climb on paved road. Beautiful views of East County backcountry and a wonderfully exhilarating descent.

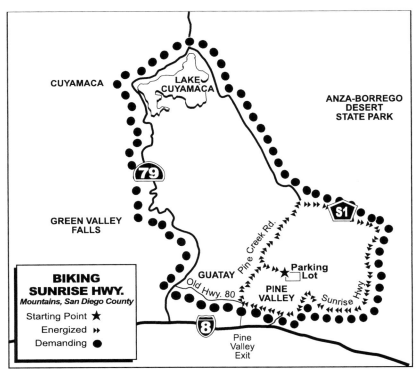

NOBLE CANYON/SUNRISE HIGHWAY TOUR - BIKING

Biking - Mountains & Backcountry

Noble Canyon - Bike Tour #28
Energized...Pine Creek Road (26.3 miles)

From the parking lot, proceed back out to Pine Creek Road and turn right. This road will take you all the way up to **Sunrise Highway**. It is a beautiful climb as you progress through scrub brush and pine forests. This is a wilderness ride with no residences in view. Stop at one of the switchback turns and drink in the beauty of the vista. You will be rewarded for this is beautiful backcountry terrain.

At the top of the climb, the road runs into Sunrise Highway. Turn right and proceed along Sunrise Highway. It is a beautiful ride as you pedal through the forest. Stop at any of the numerous vistas off to the east and enjoy the view.

After passing several of the mountain communities, you will begin your descent back to **Pine Valley**. This is a well-earned treat after your climb. The road has a good bike lane, and the curves are generous, making for a lovely, exhilarating descent. As you approach Interstate 8, turn right on Old Highway 80. This will take you back through Pine Valley and to your car.

San Diego's backcountry roads.

SUNRISE HIGHWAY BIKE TOUR

Equipment: Road Bike

Directions: Take Interstate 8 east approximately 45 miles from San Diego. Exit Pine Valley and turn left at the Stop sign. Turn right when the road ends at **Pine Valley**. Park in the commercial area on the left side of the road.

Highlights: A beautiful, challenging ride through forests. Some steep climbs with exhilarating descents and fun corners. This is one of San Diego County's premier inland tours.

Sunrise Highway
Bike Tour #29
Demanding...Sunrise Tour (45 miles)

Begin your ride by turning left out of the strip mall and heading east. This will end at **Sunrise Highway**. Turn left on Sunrise Highway and you are on your way. The road climbs steadily up and up and up. Leave early in the day so you can avoid the heat and the cars. This is a popular route on weekends for sightseers and motorcycle tourers. Take time to stop at some of the overlooks on the east side of the road. They provide lovely vistas of the desert to the east. As you approach the top of your climb, you will be rewarded with a country store if you are interested in stopping for a rest or refreshments. Proceed along the Highway and it will end at Highway 79. Turn left and pedal past **Lake Cuyamaca**. If you didn't stop at the first country store, you have another opportunity at the lake. Just past the lake on the left side of the road, you will find another country store to supply you with energy food or drinks.

Once past the store, you will begin an exhilarating lengthy downhill with some steep grades and hairpin turns. Because the bike paths are narrow to non-existent in some sections, be very careful and watch your speed. At the bottom of the descent, turn left on Old Highway 80 and it will take you through the little town of **Guatay** and back into **Pine Valley** and your car.

JULIAN BIKE TOUR

Equipment: Road Bike

Directions: From Interstate 15, take Poway Road east until it ends at Highway 67. Turn left and take Highway 67 up through Ramona and then Julian. Park on any of the side streets.

Highlights: The Julian Tour is a beautiful mountain tour whether you take the shorter Energized ride to **Lake Cuyamaca** or the longer Demanding ride along **Sunrise Highway**. Regardless of the ride, a highlight is getting some famous Julian apple pie a'la mode after your ride in anyone of several restaurants in town.

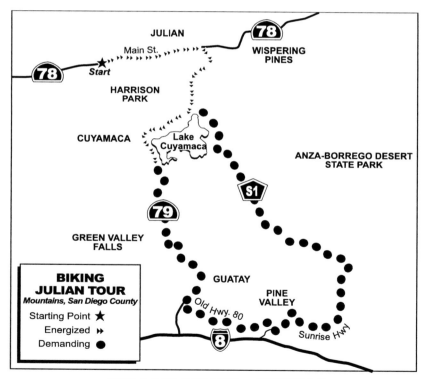

JULIAN TOUR - BIKING

Biking - Mountains & Backcountry

Julian
Bike Tour #30
Energized...Lake Cuyamaca (18 miles)

From your parking spot in town proceed to the main street of **Julian** and ride through the heart of this old gold rush town heading north. Founded in 1870, the citizens have done an outstanding job of maintaining the ambience of its heritage. Turn right on Highway 79 and proceed out into the country. The bike lane is narrow so be wary of cars. Approximately 9 miles from town, you will come to **Lake Cuyamaca**. Continue a bit further and you will come to a country store that will provide you with refreshments if you are inclined to stop. If you elect not to stop, this is your turnaround point to head back to Julian and some apple pie!

Julian
Bike Tour #31

Demanding...Lake Cuyamaca/Sunrise Tour
(57 miles)

For this beautiful and challenging ride, follow the directions for the Energized ride. Once you reach **Lake Cuyamaca** though, continue south on Highway 79. This is a beautiful and exhilarating ride as you descend through tree-lined sections of the highway and around hairpin turns. I would recommend that you ride this route early in the morning before traffic has had an opportunity to pick up. It will be safer and more enjoyable since you will be able to take the turns faster without competing for road space with automobiles. When you come to the end of Highway 79, turn left on Highway 80 which will take you through **Guatay** and **Pine Valley**. Proceed on through Pine Valley, where there are a couple of general stores at which you may want to stop. At the end of Highway 80, turn left on Sunrise Highway. This, too, is a beautiful section of the ride but one which will be more work than the rapid descent you took down Highway 79.

Sunrise Highway is a good climb. It is not particularly steep but it is long and will definitely get your heart pumping! As you continue to climb, avail yourself of any of the overlooks along the road which will give you a nice panorama to the east. If you haven't yet stopped at a store for refreshments, there is one last chance on Sunrise Highway as you enter the community of **Mount Laguna**. Proceed to the end of Sunrise Highway which dead ends into Highway 79. Turn right and Julian will be just six miles down the road. And don't forget to stop for the apple pie. You've earned it!

Roadside vegetation...prickly pear cactus.

CHAPTER 11

CAMPING

What would the world be, once bereft
Of wet and of wilderness? Let them be left.
O let them be left, wildness and wet:
Long live the weeds and the wilderness yet.

Gerard Manley Hopkins

COASTAL REGION

URBAN SAN DIEGO

SAN DIEGO INLAND

MOUNTAINS & BACKCOUNTRY

DESERT AREAS

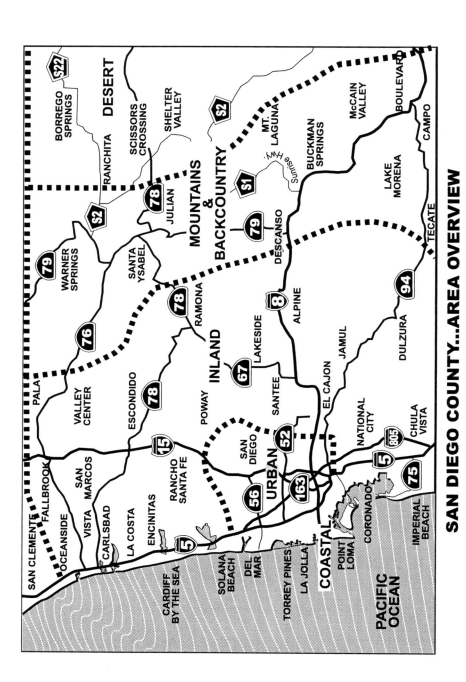

COASTAL REGION
CAMPING
Public Campgrounds

For state campground reservations, 800-444-7275 or
www.reserveamerica.com. For information: www.parks.ca/gov

CAMP PENDLETON...
Active and retired military can use three campgrounds:
Lake O'Neill, Del Mar Beach and San Onofre.
800-MWR-1314 or www.mwr.camppendleton.com.

CORONADO...
Silver Strand State Beach. Self-contained vehicles only. Camp right at beach
on asphalt parking lot. First come-first served here. Tight spaces. Across bridge
to Orange, left, through town out to Coronado Cays area.

CARDIFF...
San Elijo State Beach. 171 campsites for tents and RVs adjoining Cardiff
State Beach. Showers, no hookups. I-5 north to Birmingham, west to Pacific
Coast Highway south.

CARLSBAD...
South Carlsbad State Beach. 266 campsites plus day use areas. Showers, no
hookups, dump station. I-5 north to Poinsettia Lane, west into campground.

OCEANSIDE...
Oceanside City Campground. First come, first served. Restrooms, no hookups, 5 day maximum. This is right at the harbor inlet and beach. Information:
760-435-4000.

SAN ONOFRE...
San Onofre State Beach Bluffs Campground. This is the series of open
camping areas to the west of I-5 along old Highway 101 and south of the
nuclear power plant. 176 spaces unshaded, no hookups. Access over to beach
via trails. I-5 to Basilone Road west, then south past power plant.

SAN ONOFRE STATE BEACH...
San Mateo Campground. Inland 1.5 miles from beach. 157 spaces for tents
and RVs. Some electric hookups + dump station. Just north of the landmark
nuclear energy facility and south of San Clemente. I-5 to Christianitos and east.

Private Campgrounds - Coastal

SAN YSIDRO...
La Pacifica RV Resort. 619-428-4411.

IMPERIAL BEACH...
Bernardo Shores RV Park. 619-429-9000.

CHULA VISTA...
Chula Vista RV Resort & Marina in the city park. Top rated.
800-770-2878, local 619-422-0111 www.chulavistarv.com
KOA. 800-762-5267.

SAN DIEGO ...
De Anza Harbor Resort, on a quiet beach on Mission Bay.
800-924-7529
Campland on the Bay, on Mission Bay. 800-422-9386.
www.campland.com
Santa Fe Trailer & RV Park, just north of Mission Bay. 800-959-3787.

DEL MAR...
Surf & Turf RV Park, by race track. 858-481-9347.

ENCINITAS...
Trailer Rancho. 760-753-2741.

OCEANSIDE...
Oceanside RV Park. 760-722-4404.
Paradise by the Sea RV Park. 760-439-1376.

URBAN SAN DIEGO
CAMPING
Public Campgrounds

MISSION TRAILS REGIONAL PARK...
Kumeyaay Lake Campground. For tent campers and RVers, level camp-sites, excellent restrooms and showers, and camp hosts ready to help you get located and clue you in to the ways to sample more of the park's wares. Evening campfire programs. From here it's an easy walk to trails and the old dam. No hookups, but a dump station. Reserve at 619-668-2748 (M-F), www.sdparks.org or on space available basis.

SAN DIEGO INLAND
CAMPING
Public Campgrounds

For descriptions of many campgrounds see previous listings. For San Diego County Park reservations, call 858 (or 877)-565-3600 (M-F)   *, www.co.san-diego.ca.us/parks

BONITA...
Sweetwater Regional County Park. 60 campsites with water and electricity, overlooking Sweetwater Lake. Equestrian Staging Area. Open land with rolling hills.

EL CAJON...
Lake Jennings County Park. Wooded area with 100 sites overlooking the lake. Some partial hookups.

ESCONDIDO...
Dixon Lake Recreational Area. 45 sites, 4 for groups. Some with full hookups. Reservations at 760-741-33228 M-F, or on arrival if space available.

RAMONA...
Dos Picos County Park Wooded, rolling hills. Partial hookups. Short hop up through Ramona to Dudley's Bakery.
Mt. Gower. A little-known walk-in campground for tenters, with a dozen spaces separated by thick bushes. On-site host can give you hiking ideas. Drinking fountain and quality restrooms.

SANTEE...
Santee Lakes Recreational Preserve. 150+ full hookup campsites, well-spaced along several lakes and 190 acres. Take your fishing pole or just unwind. 619-596-3141.

VISTA...
Guajome County Park. Top-quality campground. Partial hookups. Fish, hike, visit San Luis Rey Mission, Guajome Rancho Adobe and Farm Equipment Museum.

Private Campgrounds - Inland

ALPINE...
Alpine Spring RV Park. Near Viejas Casino. 619-445-3162.
Viejas Indian Reservation, Ma-tar-awa RV Park. 619-445-3275.

EL CAJON...
Circle RV Ranch. 800-422-1835.
Oak Creek RV Resort. 800-365-1274.
Sunland Country Creek RV Resort. 800-365-1274.
Vacationeer RV Park. 619-442-0904.

ESCONDIDO...
Champagne Lakes RV Resort. 760-749-7572.
Sunland Escondido RV Resort. 800-331-355.
All Seasons RV Park & Campground. 760-749-2982.

JAMUL...
Diamond Jack's RV Ranch. 619-669-0099.
Thousand Trails Pio Pico RV Campground (membership). 800-560-8833.

LA MESA...
Sunland San Diego RV Resort. Off I-8. 877-787-6386.

LAKESIDE...
Rancho Los Coches RV Park. 800-630-0448.
LAKE WOHLFORD...
Oakvale Park Campground. 760-749-2895.

PAUMA VALLEY...
Rancho Corrido RV Resort. Special concerts as well as camping.
760-742-3755. www.ranchocorrido.com

RAMONA...
Ramona RV Resort. 800-931-1105. www.westernhorizons.com

SAN YSIDRO/SAN DIEGO...
La Pacifica RV Park, at the border. 619-428-4411.

MOUNTAINS
& BACKCOUNTRY
CAMPING
Public Campgrounds
For County Parks,
reserve at 858 (or 877)-565-3600 (M-F)
www.sdparks.org

LAKE MORENA...
Developed San Diego County Park. (100 sites) Trees, hills, lake, and Pacific
Crest Trail (PCT). Also ten cabins. 858-565-3600 or www.co.san-diego.ca.us/
parks. On the north side of the lake are primitive sites well-spaced among the
many oak groves. Here are fire rings and porta potties, with a first-come,
first- served policy.

BUCKMAN SPRINGS/KITCHEN CREEK...
Several USFS campgrounds. Just off I-8, **Boulder Oaks CG**, lightly-used,
yet right on PCT. **Kitchen Creek Road**, no-frills camping just off the road at
the creek, plus **Cibbetts Flat**, with falls and swimming hole. With a permit
(ask ranger office about these), you can also find you own spot within LMRA.

BOULEVARD/JACUMBA. MCCAIN VALLEY. HIGH DESERT...
Two BLM campgrounds with toilets, shade. First come first served except
for groups. Modest fee charged. Info at 760-337-4400 or www.ca.blm.gov.

CUYAMACA STATE PARK...
Right in beautiful large park - hiking, picnicking and riding. **Green Valley
Falls** or **Paso Picacho** campgrounds. Also cabins at Paso Pichacho.
800-444-7275 or www.reserveamerica.com.

PINE HILLS/JULIAN...
Wm. Heise County Park. Top-rated campground. (81 sites) Lots of oaks
and trails. Also two cabins. 858-565-3600.

LAGUNA MOUNTAIN RECREATIONAL AREA (USFS)...
Wooded Hill group campground; **Agua Dulce** hike-in CG; developed
campgrounds at **Burnt Rancheria** (closed in winter, PCT goes right through),
and **Laguna** (year round, near the lake). Terrific hiking and scenery. Some
reservations at 619-445-6235.

PALOMAR MOUNTAIN...
First-rate **Palomar Mountain State Park** campground with fishing at Doane
Pond. 800-444-7275. Also good are USFS **Observatory Campground** (just
reopened after major upgrade) and slightly further along, **Fry Creek** USFS
Campground (no trailers). Both are beautifully located amidst heavy forested
areas and are first come, first served.

POTRERO/CAMPO...
Potrero County Park. 49 sites, lots of shade here.

WARNER SPRINGS/PALOMAR NORTH SIDE HGHWAY 79...
USFS campgrounds: **Indian Flats** developed CG near creek (no reservations)
with two group campgrounds (reservations); **Dripping Springs** (34 sites)
and **Oak Grove Campgrounds** (81 spaces), first come first served; groups
can reserve. 760-788-0250.

Private Campgrounds - Mountains
CAMPO...
Outdoor World RV Park, 619-766-4480.

DESCANSCO...
Thousand Trails-Oakzanita Springs rustic resort, 619-445-3653.

JACUMBA...
De Anza Springs Nudist Resort. 619-766-4301.

LAKE CUYAMACA...
Lake Cuyamaca RV and tent camping at West and north sides.
Fishing, trails nearby, 760-765-0515. www.lakecuyamaca.org.

LAKE HENSHAW...
Lake Henshaw Resort. Across from the lake, fishing, store, spa, some
hookups, groups.760-782-3501. www.lakehenshawca.com.
POTRERO...
Twin Lakes Resort, 619-478-5505.

RAMONA...
Ramona Canyon RV Resort. East of Ramona on Highway.
Lots of shade, stream. 800-931-1105. www.westernhorizons.com

JULIAN...
Pinezanita Campground. Large, lots of trees. 760-765-0429.

PALOMAR AREA - BASE OF THE MOUNTAIN...
La Jolla Indian Reservation Campground. Along San Luis Rey River, with
water park. 760-742-1297.
Oak Knoll Campground, full hookups, RVs and tents, with pool.
760-742-3437 www.oaknoll.net

WARNER SPRINGS AREA...
Los Coyotes Indian Reservation. Well-shaded and spacious campground.
760-782-0711.

DESERT REGION
CAMPING
Public Campgrounds - Desert

For campers, Anza Borrego Desert State Park offers a wealth of possibilities,
from full-service campgrounds to find-your-own-spot-and-bush settings.

"Developed" come complete with toilets, maybe showers and RV hookups.

Reservations are strongly recommended for weekends:

State	800-444-7275
County	619-563-3600
Park Headquarters	760-767-5311
Reservations (ParkNet)	800-444-7275

"Primitive" have marked and level campsites, generally a toilet, and maybe fresh water. They're usually close to paved roads, making them easily accessible. Limited spaces, first come-first served.

"Bare sand" means you find your own place somewhere among the half-million acres. ALERT — many of the dirt or sandy roads are accessible with regular vehicles, but some can cause problems without four wheel drive, so believe the signs (maybe even take along your cellular phone). If in doubt, check with park rangers. Also observe the park rules of no ground fires (if you want a campfire, bring along a flat metal container). Also leave no trash, period.

Public Campgrounds - South Desert

DEVELOPED...

Agua Caliente County Campground, about halfway from I-8 and Scissors Crossing. Hookups. Big attraction is the hot soaking pool. 619-694-3049.

Four miles north, **Vallecito County Park**, site of old stage coach stop. RV and tent areas, water. Restrooms. No reservations.

Bow Willow. 16 miles north of I-8 on S2. Nestled back next to hills. Toilets, covered tables, fire rings, and a good getaway.

PRIMITIVE...

Mountain Palm Springs. Toilets but spaces unshaded.

BARE SAND...

Carrizo Badlands Overlook just off S2.

Dos Cabezas area near the railroad crossing, or back by the spring.

Palm Spring east from Canebrake.

Public Campgrounds - Central Desert

DEVELOPED...

Tamarisk Campground. Campsites are surrounded by tamarisk trees providing a good windbreak. You'll have the rare opportunity of spending the night in a former prison.

PRIMITIVE...

Blair Valley and **Little Blair** provide many camping spots near the mountains.

Yaqui Well, with sounds of many birds at the well and a nearby marked nature trail.

Yaqui Pass heading toward Borrego Springs.

Fish Creek in from Ocotillo Wells. Main attraction next to Split Mountain.

BARE SAND...

Any of the several washes to the north or south of Highway 78 and east of S3. These all offer good desert foliage, exploration and solitude. Try **Plum Canyon**, **Pinyon** or **Mine Washes** and beyond **Split Mountain**.

Public Campgrounds - North Desert

DEVELOPED...

Borrego Palm Canyon near Park Headquarters.

PRIMITIVE...

Culp Valley

Sheep Canyon in Coyote Canyon area.

Arroyo Salado toward Salton Sea.

BARE SAND...

Heading east on S-22 you can find many protected and pleasant camping spots.

Private Campgrounds - All Areas Desert

SHELTER VALLEY...south of Scissors Crossing.

Stagecoach Trails. Tents, RVs. Full hookups. Horse camping also. Store. 877-896-2267.

BORREGO SPRINGS...

Desert Sands, 760-767-5554.

At the base of
Palomar Mountain...
Oak Knoll Campground

La Jolla
Indian Reservation
Campground

Laguna Mountains

Camping

11 - 12

CHAPTER 12

SPECIAL OUTDOOR ADVENTURES

"Why are there trees I never walk under but large and melodious thoughts descend upon me?"

Walt Whitman

In this chapter we suggest outdoor places and activities to fit special interests relative to San Diego Outdoors. Many of these have appeared in the San Diego Magazine Online Outdoors Forum. For details, check descriptions within the specific region chapters.

- **Places for Those with Limited Mobility**
- **Enjoying Nature with the Kids**
- **Roaming with Rover**
- **Great Views at the Ready**
- **History in the Outdoors**

Places for Those with Limited Mobility
(Thanks to many who sent inputs)

For those whose ability to hike is limited, many places are available for them to get out into nature. The **Natural History Museum's Canyoneers** lead many nature walks appropriate for people with limited hiking capability and some trails are wheelchair accessible. Check listings at **www.sdnhm.org/canyoneers/index.html** for those with "W" for Wheelchair at end. Also for national parks, get the Golden Access Passport, at Cabrillo or check **www.nps.gov** and look for link. One needs ID and proof of permanent disability to be eligible. For full site descriptions and contact info see specific chapters.

Coastal Areas - Limited Mobility

1. Cabrillo National Monument. Parking lot has several spaces, with curb cuts for access over to visitor Center with auditorium, exhibits, gift shop. An accessible trail goes around to bay views. One car can now drive up to old lighthouse and whale view point, Check with ranger on arrival.

2. Chula Vista Nature Center. Call from the parking lot (619-409-5900), then follow the bus in. Once here, the center has a new tide pool and many exhibits inside and out. The trail is level and reasonably hard-packed around the bay, with markers and benches.

3. San Elijo Lagoon. Visitors Center on north side of lagoon west of I-5 on Manchester. Paved path out along the lagoon, with kiosks.

4. Silver Strand State Park. Three reserved parking spaces with 50 foot paved path onto beach, also picnic tables.

5. Tijuana Estuary. Informative visitor's center/museum. Paths around 5-acre garden, with descriptive markers.

6. Torrey Pines State Reserve and State Beach. Get a beach style wheelchair to cavort for free from the park north estuary entry off Carmel Valley Road or at the south beach entry off Torrey Pines Road. Call ahead to reserve (858-755-2063). Up the hill is a new trail around the Visitors Center, through the gardens, with canyon and park views to the west. Restrooms.

Urban San Diego - Limited Mobility

1. Chollas Park. San Diego City Park with paved path around lake.

2. Mission Valley San Diego River. Paved walkway from I-163 east to Qualcomm Way on both sides of the river. Good access from parking lot off

Mission Center Road.

3. San Clemente Canyon/Marian Bear Park. From Clairemont Mesa entrance, east side is level dirt path, west side some access.

4. Mission Trails Regional Park. (a) Paved pathway into the Visitor Center, with entry-way nature sounds, hands-on exhibits. (b) Padre Dam area, with kiosk and paved trail across the river. (c) Paved trail along lake by Kumeyaay Campground. (d) Lake Murray paved path around most of the lake.

5. Los Penasquitos County Park. Drive into the parking area north of the first lot (Mercy Road, north on Black Mountain Road, left at first light). Drive to handicapped parking lot at back. Picnic right there under the trees or take the paved path over to the restored Adobe Rancho for docents' informative guided tours and many special events.

Inland Areas - Limited Mobility

1. San Dieguito River Park. (a) Piedras Pintadas Trail, north side of Lake Hodges. As you enjoy an easy journey along the path, you'll see many informational kiosks. (b) Mule Hill Trail, east of Lake Hodges, is a paved, level pathway out to the hill, with kiosks describing nature and history.

2. Water Conservation Garden at Cuyamaca College. Several trails winding through the various habitats, displays and whimsical sculptures, plus a "sensory garden" for people with visual challenges. Connected is the Heritage of the Americas Museum.

3. Lake Miramar. Paved path around lake.

4. Lake Poway. Popular picnic area, plus paved trail around part of lake.

5. Blue Sky Ecological Preserve. Level trail into natural area.

6. Louis A. Stelzer County Park. This is a gift from Mr. Stelzer, dedicated to the children of San Diego for educational and recreational uses, and for all physical capabilities. Access from the parking lot across Wildcat Canyon Creek is along a wide path that is wheelchair usable, as are all the paths in this section. This part is a delightful picnic and play area, with wide-spreading oaks and sycamores providing lots of welcome shade.

7. Silverwood Wildlife Sanctuary. After registering at entry parking lot, call and then you can drive or get a ride up to the observation area. Or check out the reasonably accessible pathway.

8. Bataquitos Lagoon. Paved path on north side.

9. Rancho Guajome County Park. On weekends, visit the Rancho Adobe for a guided tour of this early ranch house.

Mountains & Backcountry - Limited Mobility

1. Rancho Cuyamaca State Park . At Park Headquarters is the interesting museum, with the Cold Stream Trail leading a short way north along the river. It's dirt but well graded with exhibits and informative kiosks.

(Heavily burnt in October 2003 fire - waiting for recovery.)

2. Inaja Memorial Picnic Area. Four sites are wheelchair-accesible.

3. Laguna Mountains Recreational Area. Desert View Picnic Area has accessible picnic sites and toilets; new is Storm Canyon Vista overlook off Sunrise Highway across from Shrine Camp. New facilities in campground in budgets ahead.

4. Palomar Mountain State Park. Silver Crest Picnic Area, restrooms. Campground, 3 spaces, plus restrooms. Cedar Grove Group Campground has one access space and restroom. Doane Pond, from parking lot dirt trail part way, to bridge.

Desert - Limited Mobility

1. Park Visitors' Center Trail - Pick this short trail right outside the door to the Center for a paved path through a cactus garden, with plants identified and described.

2. Full-Access Trail - This 0.25 mile trail is wheelchair accessible, with a gentle grade and a series of pull-out view points. Pick it up at the Visitors' Center entrance or from the parking lot at the "Campground Trail" marker.

Special Outdoor Adventures

Enjoying Nature with the Kids

Kids and parents don't necessarily have the same agenda and philosophy when it comes to hitting the trails. From my own experience, I found out a key was inviting a buddy along, or even better making it a group activity. Trying to get a kid to hike up Stonewall solo can be right up there with "How about a trip to the dentist?" Throw in a couple of chums and the kids charge up Stonewall, often ahead of the grown-ups.

Many parks have special events for kids; look for those in newsletters, papers and online. Here are some places you might find a favorable reception. These are all in the modest trek, high experiential category.

1. Cabrillo National Monument. Multi-sensory experience here, with high-interest films, great views, climbing up the lighthouse, peer out toward the passing whales, mess around at the tide pools below. Wow!

2. Tijuana Estuary. Hands-on exhibits add to the enthusiasm (and they're learning something besides).

3. Chula Vista Nature Center. With its many exhibits inside and out, plus a marked trail along the bay, kids can have a rich experience here.

4. Torrey Pines State Reserve and State Beach. Head out from the visitors center and watch the kids clamber up the wildly shaped hills, then on down to the beach via that tricky narrow walkway. (Yes, they'll gripe coming back up, so maybe have them walk north along the beach and pick them up at the entry there.)

5. Chollas Park, College Grove area. Special kids programs, plus fishing, lots of geese (to chase the kids) and a fun, paved path around lake.

6. Tecolote Canyon. Many kids events focused on the park visitors center, with easy hikes into the canyon or over to Fiesta Island.

7. Mission Beach. The jetty at South Mission is a favorite with kids.

8. Mission Trails Regional Park. Start with the sounds and sights outside and inside the Visitors Center, then head down to the Padre Dam area, a favorite kids poke around area. Take in the evening programs around the fire at the campground, whether camping or not.

9. San Dieguito River Park. Many guided walks tailored for kids, such as along the Highland Valley Trail. Kids have been extensively involved in the park, building bridges and kiosks for scout projects.

10. San Pasqual Battlefield State Historical Park. Look for the historical enactments when the two forces in full regalia dash at each other, plus festivities, exhibits and a short trail up from the center.

11. Blue Sky Ecological Preserve. Frequent evening walks and talks with campfires, with s'mores.

12. Louis A. Stelzer County Park, Wildcat Canyon Road. Special events throughout the year, from Easter egg hunts to Santa visits to family campouts.

13. Los Penasquitos Canyon. Get them to the falls and watch them clamber around.

14. Guajome Regional Park. Fishing in the northern part, combined with a visit to the Farm Equipment Museum, especially if they're harvesting.

15. Lake Morena. Camp, fish, hike out along the lake and possibly beyond (that's the Pacific Crest Trail).

16. Heise County Park. Super camping area, with many opportunities for exploring. Weekend campfire programs.

17. Rancho Cuyamaca State Park. Cold Stream Trail, from Park HQ heading north along the river. It's dirt but well graded with exhibits and informative kiosks. Picnic or camp at Green Valley Falls and head for the falls. And yes, Stonewall, from Paso Picacho Campground.

18. Los Coyotes Indian Reservation. Enjoy camping or lots of splashing in their water park.

19. Palomar Mountain. Try fishing, camping or wandering in the Doane Pond area. Then head up to the observatory for a memorable look-see and picnic.

20. Anza Borrego Desert State Park. So many options. The obvious start out is at the visitors center with incredible displays and films. Then the hike along Borrego Palm Canyon. Drive through Split Mountain and stop often. Park or camp somewhere and explore.

Roaming with Rover
(Walks in the outdoors with your four-legged pals)

(NOTE: This section is based on input from dog pals Squirt, Roscoe, Cassie, Jazz, Leroy, Sadie and Christa....with interpretations from canine-eze by human companions, Leslie, Michele, Craig, Sondra, Jean, Penny and three Toms.)

San Diego has a number of designated "leash-free" areas. The most famous area in San Diego as it relates to canine inhabitants is **Dog Beach**...providing ocean fun for the brave and, for the less adventuresome, channel wading and paddling about. The beach is huge and there are always dozens of canine companions....of all shapes and sizes. And, you never have to worry about sharing the beach with folks who are not so dog crazy! North end of **Ocean Beach**.

Here is a summary of dog places for the various regions:

In general dogs on leash can access many beaches in early morning and late afternoon. Specific times are different in summer vs. winter. Check the signs to not get a ticket. More leash-free areas include:

  • Imperial Beach, north of jetty

  • Coronado, north end Ocean Boulevard

  • Del Mar, on beach, west of the racetrack. Parking fee required.

Most city parks allow dogs on leashes; some county and all state parks do not, unless in campgrounds.

The leash-free area in **Balboa Park** on the south side of the Laurel Street Bridge is a wonderful place to warm up. With dog on leash, walk any direction in the park and there are terrific events, vegetation and opportunities for relaxation that would appeal to any dog with a human in tow. If there's time, there is a section in the **Sculpture Garden** at the **Museum of Art** where dogs can sit politely at their masters' feet and share delectable goodies.

The trail around **Mission Bay Park**, just off I-5 is great for dog walking before 9 a.m. or after 6 p.m. The hours between 9 a.m. and 6 p.m. can be filled in with a stroll around **Fiesta Island** plus another leash free zone (with swimming included if you're so inclined).

San Diego City's Tri Canyons – Tecolote, San Clemente and Rose – allow dogs on leash, as do many of the other canyons throughout the urban areas. Still close to the city is **Mission Trails Regional Park** where dogs are welcome on most trails and in the new campground. The park's **Cowles Mountain** is a favorite trek for humans and doggies who are fit enough for a long uphill climb. The view at the top is worth the effort, but early morning or evening hours are recommended since the heat can become oppressive here.

Another location for enjoyable human/canine interaction is Chula Vista **Marina's Bayside Park**. There's a delightful paved trail along the bay, pretty flowers and green grass, shade and cool breezes. **The Galley**, an informal and good restaurant, has a dog friendly patio.

If your time is limited, then you and your dog can explore neighborhoods. **La Jolla, Pacific Beach, Mission Hills, Normal Heights, North Park,** all have interesting homes and coffee shops with outdoor tables where you can stop when you need to rest. Many of these neighborhoods are bordered by canyons which have hiking trails and shade trees and allow a break from the city streets. Don't forget your poop sacks, however!

The **Golden Hill** area, on the east side of Balboa Park, offers fun dog walking experiences. The **park on 26th Street,** just north of A Street has a quarter-mile road that encircles a grassy area with beautiful trees. Many trials lead up and down the hillsides and spectacular sunsets can be viewed from here. Also on this side of Balboa Park is **Grape Street leash-free area** and **Morley Field** (behind the tennis courts) with a huge gathering of dog and people regulars every day, especially in late afternoon.

Lake Murray in La Mesa has a wide trail 3/4 of the way around it, but park your car somewhere in the middle (north side of the lake) just in case you and/or your dog tires along the way. For other lake trails, try **Santee, Lindo (Lakeside), Miramar and Poway.**

Many other cities have leash-free areas and several parks have hikes specifically for dog owners and their pets. A lovely one is Vista's **Buena Vista Park**.

The **Laguna Mountains** in the far eastern region of San Diego County are part of the National Forest program, so dogs are allowed on all the trails. The **Sunset Trail** is readily accessed off Sunrise Highway. There are dense tree-filled forests and large meadows where one can spot deer and other critters. Dog pals will love overnight camping in the Lagunas. (In general most campgrounds will allow pets, though some not on trails. Ask before making a reservation.)

Great Views at the Ready

Consider an outing up to some of our many view points, where a scenic panorama spread below you may rejuvenate body and spirit. Here are some of
the best. Easy ones to drive to are **Cabrillo National Monument** (Point Loma),
Kate Sessions Park (Pacific Beach), **Mt. Soledad** (La Jolla). Here are some
other dandies - some easy, others taking a little (or a lot) of work.

1. Torrey Pines Reserve and Extension

These are both perched right above the Pacific Ocean. Many are regular
visitors to the main reserve, adjoining the golf course. A stroll along any of
the paths will lead you to the cliffs high above the ocean with views out to
Hawaii. Not nearly so many make it a bit north to the **Reserve Extension
area**. Walk in along the West Ridge Trail, through the pines to the Daughters
of the American Revolution dedicated area; this offers the best view of the
ocean and lagoon.

2. Mission Trails Park — Fortuna and Cowles Mountains

From Fortuna take in most of the San Diego urban area, as well as the Cuyamaca
range to the east. Over at Cowles you can find a quick reward after only a 20
minute hike, with a good view of Lake Murray. Keep on trekking to the top
(about 90 minutes) and you get the whole view package.

3. Black Mountain (Penasquitos)

Hiking trails lead up to a potpourri of views: far off the ocean and mountain
ranges; nearby the five-mile long **Los Penasquitos Canyon**; immediately
before the hang gliders which soar back and forth a few hundred feet from
your vantage point.

4. San Dieguito River Park (Escondido/San Pasqual Valley)

Bernardo Mountain, north side of Lake Hodges. San Pasqual Valley (Raptor
Ridge plus north and south trails),

5. Elfin Forest Recreational Reserve/ Mt. Israel (Escondido)

In Escondido is this substantial natural preserve. The suitably named **Way Up
Trail** emerges onto a series of vantage points, offering the usual 360-degree
views of the territory. One of the several trails leads to an overlook of Lake
Hodges and San Dieguito River Park.

6. Oakoasis and El Capitan (Wildcat Canyon)

From the **Oakoasis** parking lot, a trail leads down to the shaded oaks section,
out to a ridge overlooking Lake San Vicente and surrounding rolling hills.
For a real workout, park across the road and take on **El Capitan**. This is not

exactly a fun hike, but with expansive views, starting about a half hour up and continue to the ridge or 2 hours more out to the tip.

7. Iron Mountain and Mount Woodson

The trail up **Iron Mountain** has become one of our most popular weekend locales, and appropriately so as it provides a pleasant 2-hour hike along initially level and then gradually uphill terrain. Impressive views all around. For **Woodson**, keep driving a few miles further along to the signs marking the trails.

8. More Inland options

McGinty (Jamul), **Oakridge** (Crest), **Silverwood** (Wildcat Canyon), **Mt. Gower**, **Dos Picos County Park**, **Hellhole Canyon** (Valley Center), **Twin Peaks** (San Marcos).

9. Some Mountain Candidates

Lagunas: The trail down from Kitchen Creek, Sunset Trail, Desert View Picnic Area, Garnet Peak and Noble Canyon Trail.

Cuyamacas: Oakzanita Peak, Harvey Moore Trail, Cuyamaca Peak, Stonewall, Kelly Ditch Trail.

Julian" Inaja Picnic Area, Heise Glen's View, Volcan Mountain.

Warner Springs: Hot Springs Mountain.

Palomar: Observatory Trail and Boucher Lookout.

10. And for the Desert

Carrizo Badlands Overlook, **Moonlight Trail** (Agua Caliente County Park), **Ghost Mountain** (Blair Valley), **Whale Peak**, **Bill Kenyon Trail**, **California Riding & Hiking Trail** (above and below Culp Valley), **Font's Point**.

History in the Outdoors

We are blessed with many places where we can enjoy nature and outdoors activities while also absorbing history.

1. Balboa Park. Lots of historical adventures here. Start with a visit to the History Museum, right on the Prado up near the fountain. Usually several special exhibitions, plus book store and gift shop. Visit the **National History Museum** for current and historical exhibits.

2. Presidio Park. The **Junipero Serra Museum** is home of the SD Historical Society, with displays and book shop. Near by are ongoing archeological digs and the memorial to the earliest American to arrive in California. At the flag pole see kiosks marking the site of Fort Stockton and a memorial to the Mormon Battalion, which arrived here in 1846.

3. Old Town State Park. From the **Visitors Center**, docents lead walks every day at 11a.m. and 2p.m. At the plaza, stroll around and into many early buildings such as Casa de Estudillo and Casa de Bandini. See the carriages at Seeley Stables. Walk over to nearby **Heritage Park** with many early buildings and Morman Museum.

4. Mission San Diego de Alcala. This was established here in 1774 in San Diego by Junipero Serra and fellow padres. Open to visitors, plus religious services, special events and concerts keep this a working mission.

5. Mission Trails Regional Park. Outstanding **Visitors Center**, with entryway nature sounds, hands-on exhibits, and several trails right from the center. Walk down the road to the **Padre Dam**, built in 1813 over the San Diego River. Informative kiosks at the parking lot near the dam, plus several along the trails.

6. San Pasqual Battlefield (State Historical Park). On Highway 78 east of the Wild Animal Park is the spot where Kit Carson and the U.S. troops led by General Kearney met the Californios, who came out the victors. The museum here tells the full story. Then every December, come and watch the **re-enactment** of that battle, as mounted troops engage each other in the field across the highway.

The historic adobe at Los Penasquitos Canyon Preserve.

7. San Dieguito River Park. On the south side of **Lake Hodges** is the Piedras Pintadas Trail with kiosks about Native American culture and natural involvement. East of Lake Hodges and I-15 is the new Mule Hill Trail with kiosks relating the historical happenings.

8. Los Penasquitos County Park. The restored **Adobe Rancho** is the city's oldest residence, built in 1823 on San Diego's first land grant. Excellent introductory talks with costumed docents each weekend.

9. Rancho Guajome County Park. The **Rancho Adobe** structures have been nicely restored, and docents provide lots of tidbits of history every weekend. Also special events such as the annual meeting of Generals Grant & Lee, plus Christmas music and costumes. Nearby is the **Antique Farm Equipment Museum**, and **San Luis Rey Mission**.

10. Leo Carillo Historic Park. Old rancho now Carlsbad City Park. Home of Cisco Kid's sidekick, Sancho, and family, plus getaways for Hollywood types such sa honeymooners Clark Gable and Carol Lombard. Weekend guided tours of hacienda and rancho buildings, plush foliage and 60 strutting peacocks. 760-434-2924.

11. Otay Lakes County Park. Here's the place where the dam broke in 1916, when Hatfield the Rainmaker, may have had more success than he was contracted for. Unfortunately lots of people lost homes and lives when the waters flooded the area downstream from the dam. (More at **Lake Morena Campground**)

12. Laguna Mountains Recreational Area. For a fun way for kids of all ages to learn about our predecessors, take in the Living History Weekend put on in the fall each year by the re-enactors from the Laguna Mountain Volunteer Association. Stop in at the **Pioneer Mail Picnic Area** and read about Jackass Mail delivery.

13. Campo. Back around 1885 some bandidos came across the border and got into a shootout here. The Gaskill Brothers replaced their wood store with the stone one, now a museum with memorabilia from that era. Visit the **Train Museum** still running excursions in historical cars. Also **Camp Lockett** where WWII cavalry units trained and German and Italian POW's were housed.

14. Anza Borrego Desert State Park. Excellent background at the **Park Visitor Center** in Borrego Springs. For more, stop off at **Blair Valley, Box Canyon** (very tight squeeze where Mormon Battalion came through 150 years ago), **Vallecitos County Park** or at **Palm Spring**.

CHAPTER 13

TIPS TO ENHANCE YOUR OUTDOOR EXPERIENCE

TIPS FOR ENJOYABLE AND SAFE HIKING

BIKING - TECHNICAL ADVICE

CAMPING GUIDELINES

TIPS & TECHNICAL ADVICE

In this section we pass on tips for enjoying our outdoors world, while doing it safely and beneficially.

Keeping Our Outdoor World in Good Shape

It's difficult to comprehend why people will seek out a scenic place, then leave a mess when they move on. Who hasn't seen the empty cans on the beach or trash on a trail and shuddered at the inconsiderate behavior? When visiting any place, leave it as lovely as it was or better. Here are some simple and obvious strong recommendations:

• Find out and follow the rules for any park or preserve.
• Disturb as little as possible.
• Don't litter or let drop those aluminum foil gum wrappers, cigarette butts or empty beer bottles.
• Carry out your trash. Take along a plastic bag and carry out others' trash.
• Stay on trails; don't take shortcuts that look fun but can damage foliage and lead to serious erosion.
• Observe trail courtesy and be aware of others using the same trails. Right-of-way priorities will often be posted, typically horses, then walkers, then bicyclists.
• Know the rules for taking along dogs and pick up after yours. Observe the leash rules.

Alert/Aviso

San Diego has two residents that explorers away from the sidewalks should know about. Poison oak is likely to be found along the streams and wooded areas. Learning to recognize poison oak can prevent discomfort later. A simple guideline is "leaves of three, let it be" and if it has a reddish tint, that's probably it. However in winter, both those clues are often missing, as the leaves are gone.

The other party to avoid is the rattlesnake, found in canyons, rocky hillsides, the desert, backyards. They'll get out of your way if they're not surprised. Wear a good pair of boots, keep your eyes open, and move with care in rattlesnake territory.

TIPS FOR ENJOYABLE & SAFE HIKING

For modest hikes around city parks or well-visited areas, you don't have to be particularly concerned about safety precautions. However when you venture out along trails into the backcountry, mountains, and deserts, you want to definitely know about essentials for a good hike. Here are some of those **essentials**:

• Sun protection, especially a good hat, sun glasses and sunscreen
• Comfortable shoes (blisters you don't want on a hike)
• Ample water
• Food suitable for the time you'll be out
• Good hiking shoes, and for rough trails, lug soled boots are a must
• Trail map and pamphlets to help identify flora, fauna and natural features as inclined.

For **longer hikes or in more rugged country don't hike alone.** Also take:

• Walking stick, which has saved many hikers from a fall, especially helpful in rough terrain or heading downhill
• Trail map for sure
• Toilet needs, such as digger and toilet paper or carryout sack (Do not set toilet paper on fire.)
• Flashlight, with extra batteries
• Compass (even better if you know how to use it) and whistle
• Extra supplies, food and water
• An extra layer of clothing, in case conditions change
• First aid kit, with blister-prevention tape
• Cell phone, charged (though it may not be much good if outside range)

Always notify someone of where you are planning to go hiking and when your estimate return time.

BIKING
TECHNICAL ADVICE

"When I see an adult on a bicycle,
I do not despair for the future of the human race."

H.G. Wells

Bicyling Safety

Because you will be sharing the roadway with automobiles, practicing good safety techniques is extremely important. The following tips can help you prevent accidents and can help prevent serious injury if involved in a fall.

1. Always wear a helmet.

2. Keep your bicycle in good working order (see section on maintenance).

3. Don't wear a sound system.

4. Understand the rules of the road and obey them. Don't run stop signs and traffic lights!

5. Watch for railroad tracks and sewer gratings, they can catch a tire and throw you down.

6. Yield to pedestrians.

7. Use standard hand signals when turning so that automobiles know what you are doing.

8. Use a rear view mirror.

9. Use a light if riding at night.

10. Ride off the sidewalk on the right side of the road unless on a specified bike lane.

11. Watch out for the wild and crazy drivers; they won't be watching out for you.

12. Know your route to ensure that it is bicycle friendly, especially for your particular cycling abilities.

Bike Selection

If you do not own a bicycle, or the bicycle that you own is a rusted antique that only your sentimental memories of good times past have spared from a trip to the dump, then you most likely will be looking for a new ride. The good news here is that new technology and advances in materials and designs have combined to give you multiple options to enhance your riding pleasure. We are also fortunate in San Diego to have an abundance of high quality, knowledgeable bike shops to assist you in your purchase.

Before even heading to a bike shop though, you need to determine the kind of riding that you plan to do. To get you thinking about this, described below are four different types of bicycles that are each suited for four different types of riding.

1. Road Bike
This bike is designed for highly efficient riding on paved roads. It is lightweight, aerodynamic, and quite fast (depending on the rider!) To reduce rolling resistance on the road, its tires are quite narrow and carry air pressures of over 100psi. The materials with which these bikes are made vary from steel, aluminum, carbon fiber, and even titanium. A good rule of thumb is the lighter the bike, the more expensive it is.

In addition to the frame selection, you also want to talk with the bike salesman about the components on the bike because you will have a choice in this area as well. Components consist of the derailleurs, brakes, crank shafts, and gear shifters. Regardless of the brand of bike that you buy, the components will most likely be either Japanese, primarily Shimano, or Italian, Campagnolo. Both companies manufacture excellent components and your knowledgeable salesman can assist you with identifying the pros and cons of each brand as well as the quality level within each brand. This is not an area to skimp on cost, however. Again, as a general rule of thumb, the better quality components will equal an easier and more enjoyable ride.

The advantages of a road bike are that it is very light, highly efficient and fast. The disadvantages are that its narrow, high-pressure tires are more prone to punctures, the ride is a bit harder on your bottom, and it is only suited for paved roads or pathways.

2. Mountain Bike
The mountain bike is designed for off-road or trail riding, as well as more comfortable cruising on paved surfaces. Its tires are considerably larger than a Road Bike's, thus designed to navigate dirt, sand, rock, gravel and water. Today's technology has delivered its frames in the same materials as road

bikes. Consequently, you can purchase a frame in steel, aluminum, carbon fiber or titanium. You will find that the Japanese manufacturers own the components market for mountain bikes, again with Shimano being the predominant brand. Because mountain bikes operate over more difficult terrain than road bikes, you will find that they come equipped with a third chainring on the crankset which makes it much easier pedaling up hills or on difficult surfaces. Whereas most of the road bikes have two chainrings on the crankset, mountain bikes have a third, to provide an additional six to nine lower gears. These lower gears will enable you to climb hills easier and are much easier on your knees. (It should be noted that it is also possible to add a third smaller chainring to a road bike but it is most often optional, not coming as stock equipment)

The advantages of a mountain bike are that its wider wheels with thick knobby tires are less prone to punctures, they are the only way to explore off-road trails safely, and the lower gears are easy on your knees. The disadvantages are that the low to medium cost bikes are heavier than a comparable road bike and the knobby tires provide a rough ride on paved roads. It should be noted though that many people like the stability of the mountain bike and lower gearing for road riding, so they purchase the mountain bike but install smoother treaded tires instead of the knobbies to obtain a comfortable ride on pavements. This works well but then compromises the bikes efficiency in adverse off-road conditions. The key here is to decide the type of riding that you think you will most often be doing.

3. Hybrid Bike

The hybrid bike is simply a cross between a road bike and a mountain bike. It tries to take the best features of both bikes and make a more comfortable riding bike primarily for road use. Its tires are wider than a road bike's but smoother than knobby tires which provides more puncture resistance, good stability and a comfortable ride. Many have an upright set of handlebars that are easier on your back because you are not bending over as you are on a road bike. Many also have a triple crankset to provide you with lower gears to enable you to climb that pesky hill on your route a bit easier without getting sore knees.

The advantages of a hybrid are a smoother more comfortable ride on paved roadways, more puncture resistant tires, more stability and it can be ridden both on pavement and smooth trails. The disadvantages are that they are typically a bit heavier than a road bike, not as fast or efficient, and not functional in adverse off-road conditions.

4. Recumbent Bike

The recumbent bike is for road riding only and is the answer to those cyclists who have back problems. The frame's geometry allows the rider to sit in an upright position without any undue strain put on the lower back. There are two basic recumbent designs. One design allows you to sit on the bike with the handlebars positioned just below the seat, and your legs extended out in front of you. The other design allows you to sit on the bike with your legs extended out in front of you but the handlebars positioned in front of you at chest height. Both designs afford the rider a comfortable ride but the under seat handlebar design may be more radical for the novice recumbent rider and therefore more difficult with which to become comfortable and ride safely.

If the more conventional recumbent (handlebars out in front) is of interest to you, then you still have two choices to consider. One choice is a long wheelbase model and the other is a short wheelbase. The long wheelbase positions the pedals behind the front wheel. This style is more stable, better balanced and consequently easier to ride. However, it does not have a very tight turning radius. The short wheelbase positions the pedals out in front of the front wheel. It has a tighter turning radius and has much quicker handling.

The advantages of a recumbent are primarily focused around comfort. The geometry allows the rider to sit in an upright position which eliminates having to bend over the handlebars thus putting undue strain on the lower back, hands, arms and shoulders. The recumbent also is easily fitted with a front fairing which significantly lowers wind resistance enabling the rider to move along quite swiftly on the flats. The disadvantages are that it is heavier and longer than a standard bike and therefore more difficult to transport, it cannot be used for off road cycling, and it is sluggish ascending hills.

Biking Equipment

Once you have purchased a bicycle, the nice part about the sport of cycling is that you do not need to purchase a significant amount of additional gear. But there are some things that you do need to seriously consider.

1. Helmet.
This is at the top of the list because it may save your life. Hopefully that got your attention. Invest in a good helmet that is comfortable on your head, has adequate cooling vents for good ventilation, and is lightweight. You want protection but also comfort to ensure that you will wear it

2. Lock
This is only important if you plan on leaving your bicycle unattended, but over time you will eventually leave it unattended for one reason or another. Because your bicycle is a substantial investment, the price of a lock is a very reasonable price to pay to protect your investment. There are a number of excellent locks available today whether in the U-bolt configuration or simply a plastic coated chain or cable with a keyed or combination lock.

3. Gloves
I recommend standard bicycling gloves for several reasons. Number one is safety. If you do take a spill from your bike, most often one of the first parts of your body to come in contact with the asphalt is your hand as you attempt to cushion your fall. Therefore, rather than have a layer of skin removed, it is preferable to simply lose some leather from the glove. Furthermore, gloves will provide your hands with a measure of cushion by dampening the bike's vibration generated to your hands. On a longer ride, that extra cushioning is much appreciated.

4. Water Bottles
It is very important to stay well hydrated on all of your rides. Dehydration will sap your strength, decrease the level of your enjoyment, and even be dangerous. Make sure that you have at least one water bottle on your bike and preferably two. I like to add a slice of lemon or lime to my bottle to keep it fresh and put just a touch of flavor into the water. You also may want to use any of a number of sports energy drinks on the market today. More and more riders today are sporting Camel Bak hydration systems because they contain significantly more water and provide easy access to the water through the water tube.

5. Patch Kit and Extra Tube

While bicycles rarely break down, one of the more reoccurring problems is the "puncture". One thing that you will notice as you spend more time on your bike, is the large quantity of glass on the roadways. While not affecting automobiles significantly, the glass shards are the nemesis of cyclists. Thus, you should carry with you at all times, an extra tube, as well as a patch kit and a set of small tire irons. All of this equipment can be carried in a small pack underneath your saddle.

When purchasing your bike, you may want to inquire into the "puncture proof" liners that can be put on your wheel to protect your tube from unwanted thorns, nails and glass. In any case, before venturing out onto a bikeway, be sure that you know how to change a flat. Practice in your garage before you have to fix a puncture on the side of the road.

6. Pump

You should also be sure that you carry an air pump with you to inflate the tube should you have a flat tire. You can choose from a frame mounted pump, a small one that will fit inside your jersey pocket or mount onto your water bottle cage, or you can even choose a CO_2 cylinder which is small and compact.

7. Cell Phone and/or Pocket Change

As aforementioned, aside from punctures, bicycles rarely break down, however a prudent cyclist prepares for emergencies. One of the best preparations is to carry your cell phone with you. In case of an accident or emergency, cell phones are invaluable. If you do not use a cell phone, then at least carry spare change in your under seat bag so that you will be able to contact someone if you need assistance.

8. Clothing

While cycling clothing is not essential for enjoyment of the sport, it is extremely functional and definitely worth considering. The wild jerseys that you see so many cyclists wear actually have a purpose. The brightness is for safety. When on a bicycle sharing the road with a two-ton automobile, you want to have the highest level of visibility that you can. The bright, multi-colored jerseys provide this. In addition, they have two or three large pockets on the back which are extremely convenient for carrying food, maps, air pumps, cell phones or whatever other small gear you choose to bring along for the ride. Also, the cool max or polypropylene materials help wick away moisture, dry quickly and keep you cool.

And don't overlook the value of a well fitting pair of cycling shorts. They are purely functional and add to the comfort of the ride. Because most of them are made of a lycra based material, they are form fitting which means that you will not have excess material flapping in the wind. In addition, they are seamless in the bottom area which means that they won't chafe any sensitive areas. And of course, if you are going to be cycling in colder temperatures, be sure to consider cycling tights or even leg warmers which can be removed as the weather warms.

Bike Maintenance

While major repairs should be done at a Bike Shop by a qualified bicycle mechanic, there are many things that you can do yourself to maintain your bike and prolong the necessity for major repairs.

1. Store your bike in a dry place. If you live by the ocean, be sure to cover it with plastic to prevent the salt air from attacking the metallic portions of the bike.

2. Pay particular attention to your drive train. Keep your chain clean. There are a number of good solvents available to clean the grease, oil and road grit off of the chain. Then use a light oil or even a paraffin lubricant to protect it.

3. Before starting off on a ride, check the quick release lever or the axle bolts on the front wheel. Many times that wheel is removed when transporting the bike and it subsequently does not always get reassembled properly.

4. Keep the tire pressure at the recommended level. Even without a flat tire, tires gradually deflate with time. A poorly inflated tire is dangerous, and it creates risk for damaging the wheel.

5. Pay attention to the sound of your bike. It should make none! If it does, then check for something that is rubbing, grinding or wearing. Attention to this could prevent more significant problems.

6. Have your bicycle serviced regularly, at least annually, to ensure smooth and safe operation.

CAMPING GUIDELINES

With a few decades of camping in various degrees of luxury from sleeping bag on ground to VW camper to small RV, here are a dozen suggestions for making your camping experience more enjoyable for you and your fellow campers.

1. Be considerate of others and of nature.

2. Leave no trash; in fact, make your campsite better than when you arrived.

3. Don't inflict your noise on others. Turn the stereo down or off. Hold down the hollering and raucous conversations. Minimize generator running.

4. Don't cut through other's campsites.

5. Follow the rules about pets. Keep dogs on leash, pick up after them, and stop incessant barking.

6. Don't leave engine running for a long time.

7. If rules say no fires, have none or carry an off-ground unit.

8. Be congenial with neighbors while respecting their privacy wants.

9. Take lots of quarters; showers may require them.

10. Find out about educational programs and take them in: displays, activities, guided walks, campfire programs, etc.

11. Enjoy the setting, the environment. Get outside the camper. Turn off the TV. Explore. Take a walk. Watch the sunset. Identify the constellations.

12. Assume you will never be here again, that this is your last ever opportunity here, experience it.

CHAPTER 14

RESOURCES

*"Something will have gone out of us as a people
if we ever let the remaining wilderness be destroyed."*
Wallace Stegner

PUBLIC AGENCIES...GENERAL

PRIVATE, NON-PROFIT
ORGANIZATIONS...GENERAL

SPECIFIC REGIONS...
PUBLIC AND PRIVATE

BOOKS, VIDEOS, WEBSITES

BICYCLING RESOURCES

These public agencies have responsibility for the areas under their jurisdiction. Included are the major ones; many others operate under jurisdiction of the other cities in the county. The many private organizations provide significant support to outdoors places and activities. They invite your participation to help with educational programs, center support, trail maintenance and financial support. Contact them for further information.

Public Agencies...General

- California Dept. of Fish & Game. www.dfg.ca.gov. 916-327-5961
- California State Parks. 916-653-6995. Camping 800-444-7275 or ww.reserveamerica.com
- SD City Park & Recreation Department. 619-525-8247.
     City Multiple Species Conservation Program (MSCP) at www.sannet.gov/mscp
- SD County Park & Recreation. 858-694-3049. www.SDParks.org
     County MSCP at www.mscp-sandiego.org
- SD County Trails Council. www.sdctc.com. 619-563-5025.
- San Dieguito River Park. 858-674-2270. www.sdrp.org
- U.S. Fish & Wildlife Service/San Diego National Wildlife Refuge.
     760-930-0168, www.sandiegorefuges.fws.gov

Private, Non-profit Organizations...General

- American Hiking Society. www.americanhiking.org
- California Native Plant Society. 619-685-7321
- California State Parks Foundation. 415-258-9975
- Grossmont Adult School's Adult Walking program. 619-670-4555
- People for Trees. 619-223-8733
- Project Wildlife. 619-692-9453, www.projectwildlife.org
- SD Audubon Society. Frequent bird-watching outings and counts. 619-275-0557
- SD County Archaeological Society. 858-538-0935. Lectures, fieldtrips
- SD County Parks Society. 619-267-7323
- SD County Rockhoppers. Regular hikes of specific distances. 760-758-5667
- SD Friends of Parks. Supporting San Diego City parks. 619-582-8212

- SD Founders' Trail, information about many early places. 619-297-3258
    SD Natural History Museum. 619-232-3821, x 203.
    Many kids activities. Canyoneer-led educational hikes
- SD River Park Foundation. 619-297-7380. www.sandiegoriver.org
- SD Sea to Sea Trail Foundation. Working in conjunction with public
    agencies to help develop a 140 mile trail system. 619-303-6975.
    www.seatoseatrail.org
- SD Tracking Team. 858-484-3219
- San Dieguito River Valley Conservancy. 858-755-6956.
    Friends of River Valley, P.O. 973, Del Mar 92014
- Sierra Club. Programs, outings, back packs and car camps.
    619-299-1744. www-sierraclub.org/chapters/sandiego
- Sisters in Fitness. Hikes nearly every weekend. 619-233-7207
- The Nature Conservancywww.nature.org. 619-209-5832
- Trans County Trails. 858-679-5417
- Trust for Public Land. www.tpl.org
- Walkabout has a plethora of hikes of various levels and locales, from
    urban to wilderness. 619-231-7463. www.walkabout-int.org

Specific Regions...Public and Private
Coastal

- Bataquitos Lagoon Foundation. 760-431-5640
- Buena Vista Audubon Society. 760-439-2473. www.bvaudubon.org
- Buena Vista Lagoon Foundation P.O. Box 4516, Carlsbad, CA 92018
- Cabrillo National Monument, 619-557-5450; Foundation 619-222-4747
- Chula Vista Nature Center. 619-409-5900
- Famosa Slough Preserve, Friends of. 619-224-4591
- SD Wildlife Refuges, Friends of. 619-429-7761
- Quail Botanical Gardens. 760-436-3036
- San Diego BayKeeper. 619-758-7743
- San Elijo Lagoon Conservancy. 760-436-3944
- Silver Strand State Beach. 619-435-5184
- Tijuana Estuary National Reserve. 619-575-3613
- Torrey Pines State Reserve. 858-755-2063
    Docent Society, P. O. 2414, Del Mar, CA 92014
    Association, P. O. 345, La Jolla, CA 92038
- UCSD Tours. 858-534-4414

Urban San Diego City

- Chollas Lake Park. 619-527-7683
- Los Penasquitos Regional Park. Friends of. 858-484-3219 or
  www.penasquitos.org
- Mission Trails Regional Park, Friends of. 619-668-3275 www.mtrp.org
- Mission Valley Preserve, Friends of. 619-236-7756
- Ruffin Canyon. http://groups.yahoo.com/group/friendsofruffincanyon/

- San Diego City Tri-Canyons. 619-581-9952. Friends of Tecolote & Rose,
  same number. Marian Bear Recreation Council. 858-581-9952
- USD Tours. 619-260-4659

Inland

- Back Country Land Trust. 619-445-3904
- Blue Sky Ecological Reserve. 858-679-5469; Community Foundation.
  858-202-7249
- Daley Ranch 760-839-6266; Friends of. 760-839-4680
- Dixon Lake, City of Escondido. 760-839-4680
- Elfin Forest. 760-632-4212
- Fallbrook Trails Council. 760-731-94441; Land Conservancy.
  www.sdicc.org/flc
- Goodan Ranch, Friends of. www.goodanranch.org
- Jamul Trails Council. www.jamultrailscouncil.org
- Live Oak Park Coalition. 760-723-8780
- Preserve Calavera. 760-724-3887
- Ramona Trails Association. P.O. 2136. Ramona, CA 92065
  www.ramonarec.com/rta_main.html
- San Diego Audubon Society Silverwood Wildlife Sanctuary
  619-443-2998
- San Marcos Parks and Trails, Friends of. 760-744-9000, ext. 3505
- Santa Margarita River, Friends of. P.O. 923, Fallbrook, CA 92088
- San Pasqual Battlefield State Historical Park. 760-737-2201
- Santee Lakes Regional Preserve (Padre Dam Municipal Water District).
  619-596-3141
- Water Conservation Garden at Cuyamaca College. 619-660-0614.
  www.thegarden.org

Mountains/Backcountry
• Cleveland National Forest, U.S. Forest Service. Descanso District
      619-445-6235; Palomar District 760-788-0250.
      Cleveland National Forest Foundation. 619-595-3693
• Cuyamaca Rancho State Park. Interpretive Association (CRISPIA).
      760-765-0755. Cuyamaca Rancho Foundation.
      619-445-8377, www.creekbed.com/crf
• Laguna Mountain Volunteers Association. www.lmva.org. 619-445-6235
• Pacific Crest Trail Association. 916-349-2109, www.pcta.org
• Palomar Mountain State Park. 760-742-3462

Desert
• Anza Borrego (AB) Desert State Park. 760-767-5311
• AB Natural History Association. 760-767-3052
• AB Foundation. 760-767-0446
• Bureau of Land Management, California Desert District. 909-697-5200
• SD County Parks (Agua Caliente and Vallecito). 858-694-3049

Books, Videos, Websites...General
• *Afoot & Afield in San Diego County.* Jerry Schad. Wilderness Press, 1998
• *Best of San Diego,* Introduction by Neil Morgan. Los Angeles: Rosebud
      Books, 1982. (Hard to find but a classic, with contributions from
      many of San Diego's leading writers, including a Tom Leech
      chapter on the outdoors)
• *Birds of San Diego.* Chris Fisher & Herbert Clarke. Renton, WA: Lone
      Pine, 1997
• *Campgrounds of San Diego County.* Jeff Tyler. San Diego: Sunbelt, 2001
• *Campgrounds and Recreation in San Diego County* (pamphlet),
      San Diego Parks Department
• *Cycling San Diego 3rd Edition.* Jerry Schad & Nelson Copp. El Cajon:
      Sunbelt Press, 2002
• *Dayoutings From San Diego On A Tank Of Gas.* Rebecca Sanders,
      Premier Publishing, 2004
• *Explore San Diego - Secret Sites of Historic Trivia.* Bill Carroll

- *San Diego: An Introduction to the Region.* Philip Pryde. Dubuque: Kendall/Hunt, 1976
- *San Diego County Place Names.* Lou Stein. San Diego: Tofua Press, 1975
- *San Diego Mountain Bike Guide.* Dan Greenstadt. Sunbelt Press, 1998
- *San Diego On Foot.* Carol Mendel. 1973
- *San Diego Magazine Outdoors Forum.* Tom Leech Editor. http://www.sandiegomag.com/forums/outdoors
- *San Diego's Mission Trails Regional Park (Official Guidebook).* Pamela Crooks. Ridgeway Park Publishing, 2003
- *Walking San Diego.* Lonnie Hewitt & Barbara Moore. Seattle: The Mountaineers, 1989

Books, Videos, Websites...Specific Regions

Coastal
- *Beach Walking in San Diego County.* Bill Carroll, Premier Publishing
Urban
- *Romance of Balboa Park,* 4th Edition. Florence Christman. San Diego Historical Society, 1985
Mountains
- *A Good Camp.* Leland Fetzer. Sunbelt, 2002
Desert
- *A Desert Wilderness: Anza-Borrego* (Video), from Anza Borrego Foundation
- *All the Wild & Lonely Places.* Larry Hogue. Shearwater Books, 2000
- *The Anza-Borrego Desert Region, 4th Ed.* Lowell & Diana Lindsay, Berkeley: Wilderness Press 1998
- *Anza-Borrego A to Z,* Diana Lindsay, San Diego: Sunbelt Press, 2001
- *Anza-Borrego Desert State Park.* Paul R. Johnson and others. ABDNHA. Large size, beautiful photos
- *Weekender's Guide: Points of Interest and Walks Along the Paved Roads of Anza-Borrego Desert State Park.* Paul Johnson: ABDNHA, 1992, Pamphlets from Park Visitor's Center, "Desert Introduction", "4-Wheel Drive Trips", "Hikers/Backpackers," "Wildflowers of Anza Borrego Desert State Park"

Bicycling Resources

*"Like dogs, bicycles are social catalysts that attract
a superior category of people."*

Chip Brown

Cycling Clubs
There is a large number of cycling clubs in the San Diego region that can
provide a wonderful resource of information for newcomers to bicycling or
even to veterans. Cycling Clubs can also provide an opportunity to meet a
variety of new people with similar interests as well as companionship on
your weekend rides. Listed below is information on several local clubs. You
will find that many of them have a particular emphasis for their members and
therefore it is important that you research them carefully to determine the
club that best suits your needs. Many of them have web sites which will
enable you to easily gather information about them.

Cyclo-Vets
This group was incorporated to preserve, develop and administer the sport of
amateur racing at the Masters age group. Cyclo-Vets is the nation's "Best
Masters Club" having won the UCSF's Team Challenge Trophy every year
since its inception. 619-670-0626 or log on www.cyclo-vets.org.

Easy Rider Recumbent Club
This group feature mostly social and dun day rides on Tuesdays, Thursdays,
and Saturdays often with coffee breaks and lunch stops. They also feature
longer tours for those interested. The Club's objective is to promote the use
of recumbent bicycles while enjoying the camaraderie of compatible friends.
619-235-0854 or log on www.home.earthlink.net/r2parks.

Knickerbikers
This club provides a regular program of bicycle touring experiences without
involving institutional encumbrances. The club is not organized; no rules,
no regulations, no officers. They provide several on and off road bikes each
week. www.znetwork.net/knickerbikers.

North County Cycle Club
This is a recreational club featuring rides for all types and level of riders.
Rides are held every Saturday and Sunday as well as some weekdays, starting
from various North County locations. 760-729-5250 or visit
www.northcountycycleclub.com.

Rainbow Cyclists

This bicycle club is for the Lesbian and Gay community. They hold non-competitive rides for ability levels and membership is not required to participate on any ride. www.rainbowcyclists.org.

Ranchos Bike Club

This inland north county racing and recreational cycling club supports road, track, mountain bike, triathlon races and rides. Saturday training rides leave the Bike Empire Bicycle Shop which is located at 12630 Poway Road at 7:30 a.m. Distances vary between 30-95 miles. 760-484-2684.

Recumbent Riders of San Diego

This group meets the last Saturday of every month at 9 a.m. in the north parking lot of the Mission Bay Visitor's Center located at the intersection of I-5 and Clairemont Drive.

San Diego Bicycle Club

This club is the oldest club in San Diego. It supports men and women of all age groups including highly competitive juniors. The club provides its members with coaching, training, racing, and social events. Training rides and development rides are held every Saturday leaving from Costa Verde Shopping Center parking lot (across from UTC) at 8:30 a.m.
619-495-2454 or log on at www.sdbc.org.

San Diego Tandem Club

This group holds social and faster paced rides and other events for tandem enthusiasts. Visit their web site at wwwcse.ucsd.edu/users/esimon/tandem/SDTC.html.

San Diego Wheelmen

This group was the first organized cycling club in San Diego County. It publishes a ride schedule two months in advance that includes weekend road rides and during the summer months weekly off-road rides. The club stresses recreational riders with social and moderate rides.
858-453-5739 or 858-571-6621.

CHAPTER 15

INDEX

INDEX

COASTAL REGION

URBAN SAN DIEGO

SAN DIEGO INLAND

MOUNTAINS & BACKCOUNTRY

DESERT AREA

NOTES

NOTES

More Explore Books Offered by Premier Publishing
Tel: 858.586.7692 • Fax: 858.586.7389
dayoutings@earthlink.net • www.dayoutings.com

Name: _____

Address: _____

City/State/Zip:_____

Phone: _____

Email: _____

Qty	Title	Unit	Price
_____	**Day Outings From SAN DIEGO**	$19.95	$_____
_____	**Day Outings From LOS ANGELES**	$16.95	$_____
_____	**Day Outings From PHOENIX**	$18.95	$_____
_____	**So. California Garden Getaways**	$18.95	$_____
_____	**San Diego: Home Base For Freedom**	$12.95	$_____
_____	**Outdoors San Diego:** **Hiking, Biking & Camping**	$19.95	$_____
_____	**Hidden History: Day Tours in San Diego**	$16.95	$_____
_____	**Beach Walking in San Diego County**	$10.00	$_____
_____	**Street Walking in San Diego County**	$10.00	$_____
	CA Sales Tax (.0775)		$_____
	Shipping & Handling		$_____ 5.00
	TOTAL:		$_____

Make check payable to: Premier Publishing
15721 Bernardo Heights Parkway • Suite B, Box 17 • San Diego, CA 92128